Use Case Maps for
Object-Oriented Systems

Use Case Maps for
Object-Oriented Systems

R. J. A. Buhr

Systems and Computer
  Engineering Department
Carleton University
Ottawa, Ontario, Canada

R. S. Casselman

Systems and Computer
  Engineering Department
Carleton Univeristy
Ottawa, Ontario, Canada

An Alan R. Apt Book

Prentice Hall, Upper Saddle River, New Jersey 07458

Library of Congress Cataloging-in-Publication Data

Buhr, R. J. A.
   Use case maps for object-oriented systems / R. J. A. Buhr, R. S.
Casselman.
     p.   cm.
   Includes bibliographical references and index.
   ISBN 0-13-456542-8
   1. Object-oriented programming (Computer Science) 2. Computer
-aided software engineering. I. Casselman, R. S. (Ron S.), 1962 — .
  II. Title.
QA76.64.B84   1996
005.1'2'028—dc20   95-31100
                       CIP

Acquisitions editor: **ALAN APT**
Production editor: **IRWIN ZUCKER**
Cover designer: **BRUCE KENSELAAR**
Buyer: **DONNA SULLIVAN**
Editorial assistant: **SHIRLEY MCGUIRE**

© 1996 by Prentice-Hall, Inc.
Simon & Schuster / A Viacom Company
Upper Saddle River, New Jersey 07458

Printed in the United States of America
10 9 8 7 6 5 4 3 2 1

ISBN 0-13-456542-8

Prentice-Hall International (UK) Limited, *London*
Prentice-Hall of Australia Pty. Limited, *Sydney*
Prentice-Hall Canada Inc., *Toronto*
Prentice-Hall Hispanoamericana, S.A., *Mexico*
Prentice-Hall of India Private Limited, *New Delhi*
Prentice-Hall of Japan, Inc., *Tokyo*
Simon & Schuster Asia Pte. Ltd., *Singapore*
Editora Prentice-Hall do Brasil, Ltda., *Rio de Janeiro*

To Sheila, Heather, Jon, Michael, and Nancy for putting up with me while I was physically in their space, but mentally in the different space of this book. I love you guys.
Ray Buhr

To my loving wife Diane for providing the stability and encouragement needed to get this job done. To Amanda and Rebecca, look kids your names are in a book.
Ron Casselman

Foreword

R ay Buhr is one of the few people who has been able to combine sound software engineering practices with new theories and approaches. Ray has a credo: There is nothing as practical as a good theory. Whenever Ray presents something new we have learned to pay close attention, because his contributions to our discipline have, over the years, been adopted not only by the academic community but most importantly by practitioners of software development.

Now Ray Buhr together with Ron Casselman have given us a new contribution: use case maps. The authors have noticed how excellent software engineers have been working for years and observed how they intuitively reasoned about the behavior of systems and systems components. They have identified the need for a semi-formal tool (not mathematical) to express use case behavior at different levels of abstraction. This tool captures the way these superb designers work and makes that available to the rest of us.

Use cases have been accepted by many practitioners of modern software development. Requirements are statically expressed in a use case model in terms of actor and use case objects. The behavior of this model is described either in prose or by using interaction diagrams and state transition diagrams. Then each use case is mapped onto an object model. An object model is a static model of the design of the system. The mapping is described again in terms of interaction diagrams and state transition diagrams. This is basically what the development process looks like for those methods that have adopted use case thinking.

Use case maps fill a very important need. They fill the gap between verbal descriptions and detailed descriptions in terms of interaction diagrams. Interaction diagrams focus on the interaction between components, let these be actors, subsystems, objects, or the like. The responsibilities of the components are verbal annotations to the interaction diagrams. Use case maps allow us to reason about the responsibilities of the components without going into details about the messaging between the components. Using use case maps frees the designers from having to hold their own mental models of the dynamic behavior when they do detailed design. Instead the designers can focus their thinking on other higher level issues, such as the alternative object structures to realize the use cases. Therefore use case maps will help us to iterate over the use case model and the object models until we have identified the most feasible system. We will be able to build more well-structured systems—more robust and reusable systems.

Use case maps are one of the most important contributions to our understanding of use cases. I highly recommend this book to people who already have learned the basics of use cases from my own books or papers and who want to take a step further. I also recommend this book to those people who have learned about basic object-orientation from, for instance, Grady Booch, Derek Coleman, Brian Henderson-Sellers, Steve Mellor, Jim Odell, Jim Rumbugh, and Rebecca Wirfs-Brock. This is a more advanced book and reading it will provide you with new insights in the very difficult discipline of developing software.

Ivar Jacobson

Contents

Preface

*O*ur justification for adding yet another book to an overcrowded field is that it offers something new: *use case maps*. In this preface we try to give you a quick glimpse of why you should be interested in them.

Use cases [18] are structured prose descriptions of interaction scenarios between a system to be designed and users of the system. Use cases explain preconditions, postconditions, and the scenario itself (or possibly a set of scenarios that are so closely related that they can be better described as a theme with variations). The presumption is that a well chosen set of critical scenarios is a good starting point for design and, ultimately, for testing the implementation. Use case maps provide a visual notation for use cases and also a means of extending them into high-level design. However, understanding use case maps does not depend on familiarity with use cases. They are a new abstraction in their own right. To understand the nature of this abstraction, why it is new and why we think it is useful, we need to fill in some background.

Ever increasing demands on software for more of everything—functionality, flexibility, reusability, extensibility, performance, robustness, distributed operation—seem to ensure that software complexity keeps pushing the limits of both tools and human intellect. Tools—new languages, compilers, operating systems, application packages, CASE tools—provide more productive capacity (or try to) but the problems always seem to outpace them. This historical problem with software is showing no signs of going away.

Systems—sets of collaborating components that jointly achieve some overall purpose—are at the heart of all modern applications of computers, as the following examples indicate. Object-oriented programs in execution, even considered purely in software terms, are systems (of collaborating objects). They are also components of larger systems: the application environments in which they run. Computer communication networks are systems that are part software, part physical. Applications distributed over such networks are systems that are also part software, part physical, for example, they contain collaborating processes, objects, clients, and servers, to name but a few of many possibilities. Computers embedded as components in automobiles, aircraft, nuclear power plants, and medical instruments are systems. Because, by definition, the operation of a system is decentralized among its collaborating components, the purposeful behaviour of a system as a whole is difficult to visualize. This is particularly true with software, for a number of reasons. Software is nonphysical, the code we see in its source files may express the components of the running system only in a somewhat indirect fashion, and the conceptual world of programming languages is typically weak on system concepts (for example, the same object oriented programs that we said above are systems, do not look like systems when you read the code, just sets of class definitions).

Use case maps provide a notation to aid humans in expressing and reasoning about large-grained behaviour patterns in systems.

One of the most difficult problems with systems is understanding and expressing the large-grained behaviour patterns that will be jointly achieved by the components of a system while the system is running. To understand this term, think of a stimulus like a mouse click or an interrupt from a communications device that triggers some chain of causally related responsibilities performed in software (or in a mix of software and intervening hardware in a distributed system). One way of looking at this is from outside the system, for example, a mouse click causes a file icon to open on a screen (the system as a whole has the responsibility of making this happen). Another way to view this is from inside, for example, the responsibilities of handling the click are decentralized in a set of objects in a running program and the click propagates through this set by means of a causally connected sequence of interobject collaborations. This causes objects along the way to perform responsibilities in relation to the click. This ultimately results in one of the objects causing the file icon to open on the screen. Either way, the chain of causally related responsibilities is a "large-grained behaviour pattern".

Use case maps provide notations for indicating intended coupling between large-grained behaviour patterns.

An important design issue with large-grained behaviour patterns is that several may be in progress through a system at the same time, and may be coupled to each other. Patterns that are independent may simply be interleaved, but this is not what we mean by "coupled". Coupling may be intended or not. An example of an intended coupling is the following: a pattern triggered by a mouse click requests data that will, in the normal course of events, come from a physically remote part of the system through some large-grained behaviour pattern initiated there; the original mouse-initiated pattern must wait part way through for the remotely initiated one. On the other hand, interpattern coupling may be unintended, and cause errors. In other words there may be conflicts between patterns.

Use case maps bridge a modeling gap between requirements and design.

Large-grained behaviour patterns seem to belong to *both* requirements and high-level design. Expressing them only with prose use cases at the requirements level leaves a big gap between requirements and design. Expressing them during design without use case maps requires making commitments to realization details. Use case maps fill a gap in the suite of design models by providing a way of representing large-grained behaviour patterns as first-class abstractions above the level of realization details. It is true that people design systems successfully without use case maps by holding the patterns in their minds, but the mental models are often lost afterwards. There is a chicken-and-egg problem: The patterns won't happen in the actual system until all the details are resolved, but designers need to think about the patterns in a high-level way to make high-level decisions about how to realize them, before the details are resolved.

Use case maps offer something new in relation to architecture. They provide a behavioural framework for making architectural decisions at a high level of design, and also for characterizing behaviour at the architectural level once the architecture is decided.

The high-level structural form of a system, above the level of the details of its components, is often called its architecture. Architecture is hard to define in the abstract, but companies that make products with software in them have a view of what it is. Architecture is defined by answers to high-level questions such as the following: How many components of what types should there be in the running system? How should components be clustered into large-grained units like layers or peer subsystems? What types of structures should connect components into collaborating teams to handle higher-level responsibilities, for example, structures like pipelines, rings, or networks? What additional structures are needed to monitor for failures and to recover from them? Should component structures be fixed or dynamic? How should responsibilities be allocated among the components of the structures? Which structures are likely to give the best performance along critical paths through them, or be the most robust in the presence of failures? Which structures are likely to give the best flexibility, reusability and extensibility? What structures are needed to build families of products that may use different mixes of components? And so forth. Such questions are at the same level of abstraction as large-grained behaviour patterns and need to be related to them. However, while we have had adequate means in the past for representing the structures of architecture, there has been a missing link up till now: a good way of expressing the large-grained behaviour patterns of architecture.

Use case maps provide a new technique for capturing large-grained behaviour patterns as concrete work products that may be saved, manipulated, extended, and reused to guide implementation, maintenance, and evolution.

People making high-level decisions need to think in a high-level way. People making detailed decisions to implement high-level ones need to understand the high-level thinking in order to get the details right. People making changes to details for maintenance or evolution purposes need to understand the high level-thinking in order not to make changes that inadvertently damage the big picture. Capturing the high-level thinking in concrete form helps with all of these things.

Use case maps bring real time and object-oriented issues together under a common conceptual umbrella.

Object-oriented programming is important as a technique for improving reusability and extensibility of software. As explained further in Chapter 1, properties of systems such as concurrency and robust operation in the presence of failure are often suggested by using the term *real time* as a modifier of the term *system*. The ever increasing demands on software for more of everything identified above are creating a need for a broader view of object oriented programs as systems in their own right and as components of real time systems. A problem is that this broader view is hard to see at the level of object-oriented programming languages. The combination of real time issues, object oriented issues, and more-of-everything issues creates interesting challenges that have motivated this book.

Use case maps add to the repertoire of patterns available to the designer.

Patterns are currently the focus of much interest in the object oriented community. Use case maps provide a new kind of pattern that adds to the repertoire of patterns available for both object-oriented and real time applications.

CONTENT OF THE BOOK

This book stands alone as a comprehensive text on use case maps and their applications to high-level design of systems. It also shows how to use the maps in a coordinated way with other standard requirements/design models for object-oriented and real time systems (for example, prose use cases, class relationship diagrams, collaboration graphs, interaction sequence diagrams, and so on). However, readers should not look to this book to provide a comprehensive, step-by-step, life-cycle method that covers all aspects of design and development, or to provide a tutorial on basic object-oriented and real time concepts.

ASSUMED PREREQUISITES

Prescribing prerequisites for this book is difficult because it covers so much ground at a high level of abstraction.

A blanket set of prerequisites for reading it end to end and proceeding directly to applying it across the range of object-oriented and real time implementation techniques would be the following: general knowledge of the basic issues and principles of object-oriented programming (with classes and objects) and real time programming (with interrupts and concurrent processes), with some implementation experience in both areas. This preparation is necessary because this is—deliberately—a relatively short book and it would take a very long one to tell readers without this background how to fill in all the details for the wide range of implementation technologies that might be used for these kinds of systems.

However, the principles of the book are accessible to people with less background than this. Much of the book is new material introduced from first principles in a tutorial fashion. As such, much of it can be read and understood at an overview level by relative novices (for example, second or third year undergraduate university students in computer science or engineering). At the end of this preface is a guided tour of the book for readers with different backgrounds. Readers with only object-oriented background or only real time systems background can both read a large fraction of the book without additional preparation.

Although implementation experience would be required to translate this book's ideas into practice, and some programming examples are presented in the form of fragments of code in C++ and Smalltalk for those who want a sense of the path to implementation, the bulk of the book is not in any way dependent on knowledge of the specifics of particular implementation technologies for software.

The material in this book is intended for a wide audience, including, for example, real-time programmers, distributed-system programmers, object-oriented programmers, computer scientists, software engineers, electrical engineers with some software specialization, software designers, and software architects.

This book does not aim to provide a tutorial on basic principle of object-orientation or real time systems. We refer the reader to other books such as Jacobson [18], Selic [27], Coleman [13], to name a few, for background. We particularly recommend Jacobson for treatment of the basics of object orientation and the use case approach (as distinct from the *use case map* approach) and Selic for a system perspective that combines object-oriented and real time concerns.

METHODS THAT THESE TECHNIQUES SUPPLEMENT

The techniques of this book supplement a number of other object-oriented and real time design methods, as follows (in the discussion below we refer to the approach of this book as UCM, standing for use case maps):

- OOSE, by Jacobson et al [18]: UCM is philosophically compatible with OOSE in the sense that both focus on system design rather than programming. UCM is complementary to OOSE in the sense that it provides a high-level-design bridge across the rather large gap between OOSE's use cases and its detailed design approach with interaction sequence diagrams.

- ROOM, by Selic, Ward, Gulekson [27]: UCM is philosophically compatible with and complementary with ROOM in the same sense as above. UCM provides a high-level-design front end that complements the cooperating-state-machines approach of ROOM.

- OMT, by Rumbaugh et. al. [26]: UCM provides a high-level design front end that complements OMT in much the same way as above. OMT is more focused on class than system design. A strong point is its clean, practical notation for representing class relationships. Otherwise, OMT contains many elements that are superficially similar to OOSE and ROOM, namely scenario diagrams and state machines, but is weaker than either from a system design and modelling perspective.

- OOD, by Booch [3]: Booch has become a de-facto standard on fundamentals. We agree with many of Booch's observations on the design process. However, we find his notations reflect programming issues more than system issues. UCM focuses on system issues first and brings in programming issues as details later. As such it can provide a high-level system-design front end to detailed design of object-oriented programs with Booch's approach.

- FUSION, by Coleman et al [13]: The Fusion method combines and extends the use case approach of OOSE with class-based design as in OMT and OOD. UCM can be used to supplement this approach by providing a transition from use case modeling to interaction-style diagrams.

- CRC or Responsibility Driven Design, by Wirfs-Brock, Wilkerson, Wiener [32]: This approach does not have a systems perspective but does use a front end modeling approach that is compatible with UCM.

- DP (Design Patterns), by Gamma, Helm, Johnson, Vlissides [14]: UCM adds a new type of high-level reusable pattern expressed with use case maps that complements DP patterns. UCM and DP patterns together cover a very wide range of problems and issues.

- SDWA (System Design With Ada [6]) and PVTSD (Practical Visual Techniques in System Design [7]), by R.J.A. Buhr: SDWA and PVTSD provide concepts, notations, and IPC patterns for real time systems, that have become standard in the Ada community. UCM provides techniques that supplement SDWA and PVTSD without invalidating their basic notions. UCM provides a better model of large-grained behaviour patterns than PVTSD's event scenarios. It also provides a more compact detailed-design notation than either of them.

RELATION TO SYSTEM MODELING TECHNIQUES

The UCM approach comes at system modeling from an entirely different angle than, for example, state machine models or Petri net models, to name just two of many types of executable or mathematical models of systems.

One use of techniques like state machines or Petri nets is to express behaviour requirements for systems in a precise and relatively complete way, viewing the system as a black box. Among other things, this enables complex requirements to be checked by automatic techniques, to help spot mistakes before they are built into implementations. The problem with such approaches from a design perspective is that they do not provide a progressive path to resolving the high level design issues raised above. They tend to build a wall between requirements and design. The wall is not important if implementations can be generated directly from models and maintained and evolved by changing the models, but this is still out of reach for the kinds of systems addressed by this book.

A different approach is to incorporate techniques like state machines or Petri nets into an executable system model, to specify the internal logic of the components. Such models exist and can even be used to generate implementation code, but they are at a detailed level of design, not the high level we are seeking in this book.

EXPERIENCE WITH THE APPROACH

The approach of this book came partly out of cooperative research and development projects with industry starting around 1990, partly out of experience teaching university undergraduate and graduate design classes starting around 1988, and partly from interactions with industry on the application of the techniques that resulted in refining them.

The approach has been thoroughly exercised in the classroom. It has been presented in approximately the form of this book to students in a series of undergraduate and graduate courses and several short courses to industry, during the period 1991 to 1995. A graduate course "Object-Oriented Design of Real Time and Distributed Systems" centering around this material has been offered several times, including to industry. A one-day training course on "Designing with Timethreads" (another way of saying "Designing with Use Case Maps") has been offered a number of times to industry. Some of the material on real-time systems has been used for several years in an undergraduate course on design and programming of real-time systems in a Computer System Engineering program and will appear in somewhat different form in another textbook that has evolved out of that course. This classroom experience smoothed the rough edges in the presentation of the ideas. However, it has also done more than that. Because the total audience has included a large number of experienced people from industry, the material has had a high level of "reality checking" that has resulted in a strong focus on practical applicability.

The ideas are relatively new and have not had time to have supporting tools developed or to have become established in widespread way in industry. So far, we can say that the techniques have met with enthusiastic response from many students, have acquired some champions in industry, and are being used on some practical projects, for example, during design reviews. The issue of tools is a chicken-and-egg one. Widespread use depends to some extent on tools, but the expense of developing tools is not justified until there is widespread use. If enough readers of this book judge the techniques are useful, experience suggests tools will follow.

OUTLINE OF THE BOOK

Chapter 1: Object Oriented and Real Time Come Together. This chapter sets the stage for the rest of the book. It starts from the premise that application push and design pull are driving object-oriented and real time issues together. Application push is the ever increasing demand on software for more of everything—functionality, flexibility, reusability, extensibility, performance, robustness, distributed operation. Design pull is the need for better design techniques to deal with the issues that this raises. This chapter associates the terms "object oriented" and "real time" with software implementation practices that are sufficiently different in detail that bringing the areas together is difficult with current design models. It identifies use case maps as a new kind of design model that helps to bring them together, and thus helps to satisfy both application push and design pull.

Chapter 2: The Behavioural Fabric of Systems. This chapter develops the idea of use case maps as concrete expressions of an abstract idea called the behavioural fabric. The behavioural fabric is the view we have in our minds of large-grained behaviour patterns of systems with which we are familiar. The notation is introduced and some examples presented taken from the physical and software worlds, including communicating fax machines and the model-view-controller paradigm of Smalltalk.

Chapter 3: Basic Use Case Map Model. This is a self-contained tutorial on the basics of the use case map model that explains the notation and provides rules and guidelines for creating legal maps, interpreting the maps in behaviour terms, binding the maps to components during design, and working with maps at different scales in a coordinated way. It defers issues of concurrent paths in maps to Chapter 7.

Chapter 4: A Context for Designing with Use Case Maps. This chapter describes a context in which design with use case maps may take place in a coordinated manner with other design models. The context positions design models in relation to four levels of design abstraction (requirements, high-level design, detailed design, implementation) and three basic domains of separable concerns within the levels (operation, manufacturing, assembly). The context includes notations for component types to cover the range of issues identified in Chapter 1.

Chapter 5: A Simple Example. A simple producer-consumer example is used to take a tour through the suite of models of Chapter 4. A very important feature of this chapter is that it shows in detail how to deal with the difficult problem of bringing dynamically changing software run-time structures into the high-level design picture. For concreteness, C++ code examples are provided.

Chapter 6: Case Study: A Conventional Object-Oriented Application from an Unconventional Perspective. Here the focus is on showing how to work with the use case maps to help with the design of a representative object-oriented application, a graphical user interface system called BGETool. A set of use case maps for this application is constructed using maps for the model-view-controller paradigm of Smalltalk as starting points. The case study uses all the design models in a coordinated way at all levels of design and implementation (some code is also provided).

Chapter 7: Advanced Use Case Map Model. This chapter extends the use case map model of Chapter 3 to include concurrent scenarios that may proceed at unpredictable rates relative to each other, may influence each other, may conflict with each other, and may fail before completion. It presents design at this level as an activity that positions components along paths to imply appropriate solution properties.

Chapter 8: Case Study: High-Level Design of a Real Time, Distributed System. This chapter focuses on issues in high-level design of a simple distributed application that is intended to be implemented using real time techniques, namely concurrent processes, timers, and interrupt service routines. It covers the following topics: discovering processes from maps, factoring maps to give smaller maps for subsystems, using maps as invariants for making design trade-offs, and working with maps at different scales in a coordinated manner. The example is a computer communications problem called the MTU (Message Transfer Utility) that, although superficially simple, exemplifies many of the characteristics that make designing real time systems difficult.

Chapter 9: Detailed Design Notation. This chapter provides a general collaboration graph notation that is both particularly simple and particularly widely applicable to a range of object-oriented and real time implementation techniques. It is positioned here to set the stage for detailed developments in the following two chapters. However, except for an overview section, the focus of the chapter is rather detailed and most of it is not needed to understand the essence of the following chapters.

Chapter 10: Case Study: Rounding Out the Real Time, Distributed System Example. This chapter rounds out the case study, not only in its own terms, but also in object-oriented terms. It shows how to make the transition from use case maps to collaboration graphs with processes in them. It shows how to examine a difficult detailed issue (dynamic buffering) in a high-level way using use case maps and how to bring the results back into the detailed domain. It shows how to bring in a class hierarchy that includes all the components in the maps and collaboration graphs, including processes, slots, teams, and fixed objects. It illustrates the idea of making use case maps a common denominator for evaluating trade-offs between real time and object-oriented issues.

Chapter 11: Patterns. This chapter draws together various patterns threads in this book and the literature. It does so by sketching some elements that might go into a patterns handbook that covers a wide range of concerns, including patterns in use case maps (called path patterns), IPC patterns, layering patterns, object interaction patterns, construction patterns for objects to fill slots, and construction patterns for processes and teams. The patterns are illustrated by examples drawn from the MTU and BGETool case studies.

Chapter 12: Supplementing Familiar Design Methods. This chapter recaps the design models and the context for design used in this book, summarizes the reasons for including use case maps in any suite of design models, and suggests how use case maps may be used to supplement existing design methods.

Appendix A: Notation Summary. Reference cards for the new notations are provided, as well as a summary of some standard notations that we have borrowed from elsewhere.

Appendix B: Some Coding Examples. Several code examples are given for pieces of the case studies presented in the body of the text. The examples are in the C++ programming language. We have chosen C++ because it is a popular language, not because the ideas of this text are in any way tied to a specific language. There is enough explanation of the code that non-C++ programmers should be able to read and understand it.

A TOUR OF THE BOOK WITH USE CASE MAPS

We provide a simple use case map below to suggest three selective patterns of reading this book. A path superimposed on a chapter box means *read the chapter*. It goes without saying that there is a fourth pattern that does not need a map—read the whole book from start to finish in the order in which it appears.

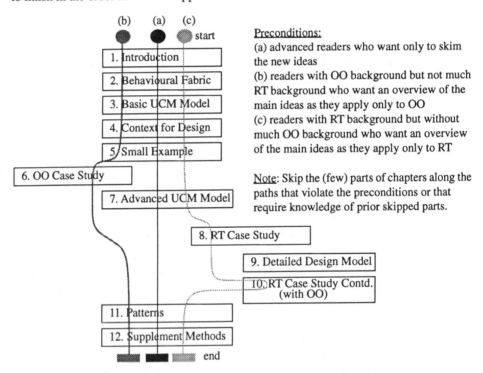

Preconditions:
(a) advanced readers who want only to skim the new ideas
(b) readers with OO background but not much RT background who want an overview of the main ideas as they apply only to OO
(c) readers with RT background but without much OO background who want an overview of the main ideas as they apply only to RT

Note: Skip the (few) parts of chapters along the paths that violate the preconditions or that require knowledge of prior skipped parts.

To give both a fuller sense of use case maps and some additional insight into other patterns for reading the book, we show a number of composite use case maps below as they would be actually drawn using the techniques of the book. On the left is the pattern above, redrawn to superimpose the shared parts of the paths. In the middle is a workable, out-of-order reading pattern for the whole book (this is not the only one). On the right is a concurrent study pattern that might be followed by a team of people who all read along the same path to begin with (1-5) and then follow different paths until (a) has finished 7, (b) has finished 6, and (c) has finished 8 and 10, whereupon they synchronize to pool their knowledge, and then desynchronize to continue independently through 11-12. This map looks like the one on the left, except for the synchronization and desynchronization bars. The difference is that the map on the left makes no assumptions about how many readers are following the different paths, whereas the one on the right assumes that at least one reader is following each path—otherwise no path could complete.

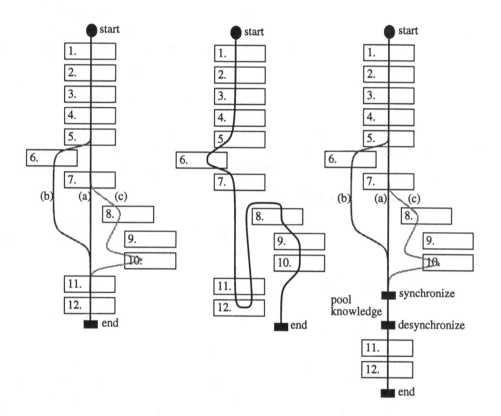

APPLICATIONS

There are two case studies in this book that were chosen to be representative of issues that are encountered at the two extremes of the range of implementation technologies for systems, namely *object oriented* and *real time*. One is a GUI program (Chapter 6) and the other is a small computer communications system (Chapter 8 and Chapter 10). To fit within the scope of a short book, they are relatively small-scale and self-contained problems that can be carried all the way through from high-level design to fragmentary implementation. We have tried to use the case studies as means to the end of illustrating different modes of application of use case maps, rather than as ends in their own right. The case studies should not be viewed as defining the scale and type of systems to which the techniques can be applied. We have tried to present the case studies in such a way that they will serve as both starting points and models for applying the approach to problems of different scales and types.

Listed below, to whet your interest, are some possible applications of use case maps:

- For straight-ahead, high-level design thinking and documentation for a new object-oriented or real time system project, or one that combines both aspects.
- To document large-grained behaviour patterns that should not be violated while evolving or re-engineering actual systems.
- To document behavioural aspects of object-oriented code frameworks to help new-comers understand them and to serve as a basis for re-engineering them.
- As elements in libraries of reusable design patterns.
- In visualization displays to help understanding (2D, 3D, hyperlinked).
- As starting points for design validation based on formalization of the maps and their relationship to detailed design models that are supported by tools.

ACKNOWLEDGMENTS

Research supported by the National Research Council of Canada, Bell Northern Research, and the Telecommunications Research Institute of Ontario contributed to the development of the material in this book. We also acknowledge helpful technical discussions, comments, support, and encouragement during the development of this material from (alphabetically): Daniel Amyot, Don Bailey, Francis Bordeleau, John Bryant, Don Cameron, Gary Driver, Bill Foster, Rick Holt, Curtis Hrishchuk, Ivar Jacobson, Gerald Karam, Doug Lea, Michel Locas, Luigi Logrippo, Trevor Pearce, Mike Petras, Francois Pomerleau, Bob Probert, Bran Selic, Mark Vigder, D'Arcy Walsh, Steve Watson, and Murray Woodside. We thank students in Carleton undergraduate course 94.333 and graduate course 94.586 who served as test subjects for this material over several years. Thanks go also to students from industry who tried the techniques at work, championed them among colleagues, and provided us with feedback. We thank Carleton's Department of Systems and Computer Engineering for stimulating the book by providing a stimulating environment in which to work, and for providing time for writing through sabbatical leave for one of us (Buhr).

1

Object Oriented and *Real Time* Come Together

*T*his chapter sets the stage for the rest of the book. It starts from the premise that application push and design pull are driving object-oriented and real time issues together. Application push is the ever increasing demand on software for more of everything—functionality, flexibility, reusability, extensibility, performance, robustness, distributed operation. Design pull is the need for better design techniques to deal with the issues that this raises. This chapter associates the terms "object oriented" and "real time" with software implementation practices that are sufficiently different in detail that bringing the areas together is difficult with current design models. It identifies *use case maps* as a new kind of design model that helps to bring them together, and thus helps to satisfy both application push and design pull.

The terms "real time" and "object oriented" conjure up different images in the mind but are very difficult to define in an abstract way that makes clear precisely what is different. All real time systems can be seen to be composed of "objects" of some kind, whether or not they are implemented with object-oriented programming techniques. All object-oriented programs can be seen to have "real time" characteristics when viewed as parts of systems that include physical computer hardware and input/output software. This difficulty of defining distinguishing features at a high level of abstraction is a clue that suggests concerns at this level are not fundamentally different. We call this level the *system* level. Later on we call designing at this level *high-level design*.

On the other hand, object-oriented programming and real time programming can be distinguished by differences in the basic tools of the trade (ignoring CASE tools that aim to raise the working level of abstraction) as follows:

- The *distinguishing* basic tools of object-oriented programmers are class hierarchies, supported directly in programming languages, and libraries of reusable class hierarchies. These tools have enabled object-oriented programming to achieve reusability and extensibility in such high measure that almost everyone seems to have either jumped on the object-oriented bandwagon, or to be thinking of jumping on it.
- The *distinguishing* basic tools of real time programmers include concurrent processes, interrupt service routines, real time clocks, and physical input/output devices. Concurrent processes run asynchronously under the control of a "real time" executive or operating system that is implicitly assumed to be part of the tool set. There is also a school of "hard real time" programming that does not use processes, but uses synchronous techniques instead, meaning the scheduling is fixed and deterministic before a program runs. However, the more flexible asynchronous techniques are usually used in the areas where real time and object-oriented programming are coming together. The distinguishing tools of this kind of real time programming are needed because, for example, applications may run on multiple processors, may be physically distributed, and may have to operate continuously and robustly in the presence of failures of parts of them.

All programs must be "fast" enough to meet the requirements of their users. The tools of the real time programming trade do not *guarantee* "fast" (except possibly the hard real time ones). In particular, the use of processes does not guarantee "fast". Processes are used for many reasons in real time programming. They help with "fast" by enabling performance to be tuned by changing process priorities or migrating processes to additional processors, but they also help deal with system issues at the programming level in a flexible way.

At the highest level of abstraction, we should be able to view either object-oriented programs or real time programs as systems in a common way. However, differences in programming detail get in the way. We need to rise above these differences to get a system view, which will provide benefits even in cases where the programming worlds are not pushed together.

Circumstances are increasingly pushing these two programming worlds together. On one hand, almost everyone is moving toward object-oriented programming, or thinking of moving toward it, for the reasons identified above. On the other hand, the ability to deal with real time issues at the programming level is increasingly being required in object-oriented programs. As an example of the push to bring the worlds together, Grady Booch predicts in an article titled "Coming of age in an object-oriented world" [4] that increasing connectivity and consumer demands will power an unprecedented growth in software's volume and complexity, then explains why the flexibility of an object-oriented approach can best meet these future challenges.

Figure 1.1 provides a perspective that drives the rest of this book. Key issues addressed by the book—expressed in terms of Figure 1.1—are how to model the system characteristics at the apex for design purposes; how to move downward from the apex in an orderly way towards the base (and vice versa); and where along the way to bring in design models that are closer to the base. The above characterizations of object-oriented programming and real time programming are positioned at the ends of the base. Some combination of programming techniques (complementary or unified) would be positioned along the middle.

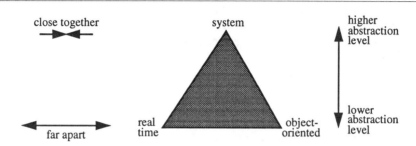

Figure 1.1 "Real time" and "object-oriented" issues at high and low levels.

Now we need to consider tensions at the base in a little more detail in order to lay the groundwork for understanding the new approach of this book.

1.1 TENSIONS AT THE BASE

1.1.1 The Real Time End of the Base

At the real time end of the base we have:

- Large grained, prioritized concurrent processes that reflect system issues into the program.
- Interrupt services routines (ISRs) that handle physical stimuli arriving in the form of prioritized interrupts from hardware.
- Real time clocks that are used to trigger process switching and to adjust process queues.
- Complex issues associated with processes and physical distribution, for example, scheduling, priority, interprocess communication (IPC), process-ISR communication, error detection and recovery, process destruction and cleanup, protection of shared resources, and so on.

These matters strongly affect how designers think about the software during the design process. They must somehow keep large-grained behaviour patterns in mind, to make sure that performance and robustness issues are properly addressed in a whole-system context. This can be complex because a process that is working on something following some stimulus (announced via an interrupt) may be preempted by a higher-priority process that must start working on something else that is more urgent, following a later stimulus. The consequence is that bursts of stimuli may propagate through a set of processes concurrently. This creates the potential for interference along the way that might adversely affect both performance and robustness. To minimize the possibility of getting things wrong, designers and implementors tend to make processes relatively large grained, numbers of processes relatively small, and process structures relatively static (apart from initialization, recovery from failure, and changes of major operating modes). This makes the run-time structure and the (static) code structure sufficiently congruent that run-time issues are reflected relatively directly in the code. The term "relatively" above means relative to the other (object-oriented) end of the base.

1.1.2 The Object-Oriented End of the Base

At the object-oriented end of the base we have:

- Code structured as inheritance hierarchies of classes. This provides reusability and extensibility in a measure that has not been matched by other programming technologies.
- A run-time structure consisting of sets of objects created dynamically from the classes that communicate with each other through dynamically bound procedure calls (called *messages* in some contexts). Dynamic binding enhances extensibility and reusability by avoiding too much commitment to fixed structures in code. It also supports polymorphism, a powerful technique that further enhances reusability and extensibility; polymorphism enables standard interfaces to be prescribed that do not have to be changed as extensions are made to the code.

There is no free lunch. The programming practices used to achieve reusability and extensibility drive implementations toward many fine-grained classes (because small things are more reusable) with much dynamic binding between run time instances of them (objects). The result is that, instead of a relatively small number of large-grained processes to think about, as at the other (real time) end of the base, there tends to be a relatively large number of fine-grained objects. Thus the dynamic run-time structure is not congruent with the static code structure of class hierarchies, making it difficult to reason about behaviour by reading code. Furthermore the relatively high level of run-time "structural dynamics" makes large-grained behaviour patterns difficult to see.

Although there may be no free lunch, lunch is often judged to be worth the price. Reusability and extensibility of code are achieved to an extent that has proved to be difficult with other programming techniques. The no-free-lunch issues tend to fade into the background when reusing and extending an existing set of class hierarchies, because the large-grained behaviour patterns are already built in and are presumably judged to be acceptable, or at least good enough that some relatively minor adjustments will make them acceptable. The power of object-oriented implementation technology is that, once a reusable set of class hierarchies has been established for an application area (often called a framework), variations that fall within the same general application area may be added quickly. Direct concern with the overall behaviour patterns tends to surface only when the built-in patterns break down (for example, are too slow, or don't cover intended new applications) or new ones have to be designed into new frameworks.

1.1.3 Bringing the Ends to the Middle

Bringing the ends of the base to the middle means bringing fine-grained sequential objects organized in time-varying structures together with coarse-grained concurrent processes organized in relatively static structures. Many conceptual and practical questions come to mind. Are processes an inherently different abstraction from objects, introduced for a different purpose? Are objects inherently finer grained than processes and therefore inappropriate candidates to become processes? Do the inheritance and polymorphism features of object-oriented programming make programs inherently slow, or does slowness—in cases where it is observed—result from pursuing specific objectives (extensibility and reusability) to the exclusion of others? What are the trade-offs between granularity, structural dynamics, concurrency, robustness and performance? The major issue in relation to this book is the difficulty in finding a common denominator in current design methods for answering these questions. This difficulty exists because the issues tend to be embedded in different conceptual frameworks imposed by different implementation techniques. Answering these questions in current practice tends to require a build-it-and-see approach.

1.2   THE BIG PICTURE

Let us now return to the big picture of Figure 1.1. We have emphasized the need to bring issues together at the apex, whether or not programming techniques are also brought together at the base. We have also highlighted an issue that pervades systems in general, namely the importance of large-grained behaviour patterns. These patterns are where performance and robustness problems show up in real time programming and they are implicitly reused in object oriented programming when reusing class hierarchies. However, the difficulty of seeing them in code, particularly for object-oriented programs, but also for real time programs, makes designing new systems or redesigning existing ones difficult.

Figure 1.2 highlights some questions that must be answered to get a system view and to manipulate that system view into a real time and/or object-oriented implementation.

1.2.1   At the High Level

As we move toward the apex of the triangle, the distinctions at the base begin to recede. We need to be concerned with large-grained patterns of behaviour that span whole systems. We need to think more in terms of larger-grained components (than processes or objects), and structural relationships between them. We need to think in terms of reusable generalizations of specific large-grained behaviour patterns and large-grained component structures.

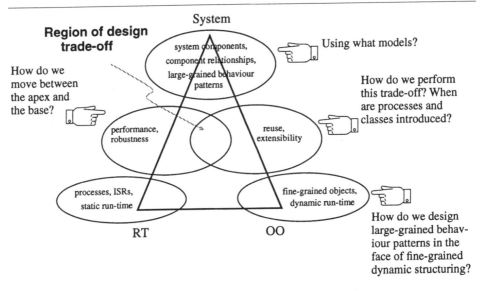

Figure 1.2 Issues in getting a common system view.

Large-Grained Behaviour Patterns We need a model to represent large-grained behaviour patterns of systems in a concrete way, above the level of interprocess and interobject communication mechanisms and sequences. Such a model is needed for the following reasons:

- The gap between behaviour requirements expressed in prose (for example, in use cases [18]) and details at the level of interprocess and interobject communication mechanisms is too large, requiring humans to perform design magic. This point will be expanded throughout the book.
- One of the big issues on the real time side is where processes should be brought into the design picture between the system and implementation levels. There are arguments for bringing them in near the top and arguments for waiting until near the bottom. The lack of good models for large-grained behaviour patterns tends to force the issue by encouraging designers to leave processes until near the bottom, because bringing them in at a higher level requires also bringing in all the baggage they carry with them (for example, a wide range of different IPC mechanisms). Too much commitment to detail seems to be required to make it worthwhile. We need a model that

enables processes to be introduced at a high level if desired without this baggage, so that trade-offs can be evaluated at a high level between different organizations of processes and the large-grained behaviour patterns they generate.

- Because of the fine-grained and dynamic nature of the objects in many object-oriented programs at the implementation level, getting a view of large-grained behaviour patterns in terms of interobject calls or messages may be difficult. This can encourage designers to focus attention on the organization of the class hierarchy and to leave overall behaviour patterns to be resolved by trial-and-error experiments with different class organizations. Ultimately, the behaviour patterns become decentralized properties of the class hierarchies that are implicitly reused when hierarchies are extended to handle different applications of the same general kind. However, their lack of visibility makes developing new frameworks or modifying old ones in a major way difficult.

Large-Grained Component Structures To get a high-level perspective on system behaviour, we need to think in terms of large-grained system components above the level of processes, objects and interrupt service routines.

As far as the components themselves are concerned, there is an "everything is an object" school of thought that would suggest identifying large-grained system components as "objects". However, differences at the lower level make this usage potentially confusing. It seems that to reason at the high level in a way that can be related easily to implementation concerns, we need to distinguish objects as they appear in object-oriented programs from object-like components, namely processes, that appear in real time implementations; we also need to distinguish both objects and processes from large-grained components that provide system abstractions. At the low level, processes address operational concerns (for example, concurrency, run-time performance tuning) and objects address code-extensibility concerns. Both concerns are important and, in our opinion, should be kept distinct. This does not mean that processes cannot benefit from the reusability and extensibility advantages of classes. However, the issue of having classes for processes is distinct from the issue of calling them objects.

There are many useful models for structural relationships between components that can be helpful for understanding large-grained component structures, for example, *operational containment* relationships, *uses* (or *visibility*) relationships and *is a* relationships. However, dynamic structuring is a difficult issue with all of them. Dynamic structuring is not just a property of fine grained objects in object-oriented programs. It may also occur with large grained components. For example, a real time system may have to reconfigure itself to provide continued operation in a different mode after a failure. The reconfiguration may involve replacing entire subsystems.

The dynamic structuring issue is difficult to deal with at any level of granularity in terms of actual interactions between components. The problem is that the creation, changing visibility, and destruction of components is handled through the same interfaces that enable the components to interact. Therefore, the only way of showing structural dynamics is to show sequences of snapshots of different configurations of components. The transition between the snapshots is left as a detail. The trouble is, it is not a detail, *it is a large-grained pattern in the behaviour of the system as a whole*. Diagrams like *uses diagrams* or *visibility graphs* may be used to show condensed pictures of different configurations at different times, but this still does not help with expressing how to make the transition between snapshots. The worst case is when configuration changes are occurring continuously, as they often are at a fine-grained level in object-oriented programs. We seem to need continuous moving pictures, which is far too cumbersome to be useful for high-level design. We need a better representation.

1.2.2 At the Intermediate Level

Midway down the triangle of Figure 1.2 we have highlighted a region where real time and object-oriented concerns must be addressed jointly, not just in high-level terms but also with an eye to low-level implications. On one hand, there is a need for performance and robustness in relation to the large-grained behaviour patterns. On the other hand, there is a need to build systems that are reusable and extensible. In the terms of the object-oriented community, we need to capture the required large-grained behaviour patterns of a system in a framework of classes such that these patterns may be implicitly reused in other design efforts. Needed are models or sets of models that allow us to express and reason about these matters in a high-level way.

1.3 FOCUS OF THE BOOK

The missing ingredient in existing design methods is a good model of large-grained behaviour patterns. The model we seek must cover not only statically structured systems but also dynamically structured ones. The consequences of not having such a model can be serious:

- Trial and error at the detailed level to get large-grained behaviour patterns correct lengthens development cycles.
- Detailed changes in completed systems that unintentionally violate implicit models of large-grained behaviour patterns cause errors that become visible too late, thus lengthening change cycles.
- Knowledge of large-grained behaviour patterns is held in an informal manner in the minds of a few experts (likely the ones who designed the system in the first place), and is not otherwise generally available or accessible. This makes it difficult to impart this knowledge to new or transferred employees, thus slowing the rate at which they can become productive. It also makes long-lived products too sensitive to the continuing presence of the experts.
- Lack of concrete high-level models of large-grained behaviour patterns makes adapting to new requirements slow and error-prone.

The central purpose of this book is to introduce a new model for large-grained behaviour patterns that covers both statically and dynamically structured systems. The model is called *Use Case Maps*. The book aims to show how to use this model for design in a coordinated way with more familiar design models at all levels of abstraction. Use case maps are so called because they are strongly related to the "use case" approach of Jacobson et al [18]. The maps can be viewed as a concrete means of moving use cases into the domain of high-level design. Use case maps can also be viewed as concrete expressions of the scenarios of the responsibility-driven design process [18] in which so-called CRC cards (C, class; R, responsibility; C, collaboration) are manipulated by humans to understand design issues in the context of large-grained behaviour patterns. We mention these relationships only to point out their existence to readers who may be familiar with these techniques, not to suggest that all readers must be familiar with them. The use case map model is presented from first principles in its own terms. Its relationship to these techniques in their terms is made specific in Chapter 12.

1.4 SUMMARY

In this chapter we have:

- Identified the terms "object oriented" and "real time" as associated both with different concerns at a low level of abstraction and common concerns at a high level.
- Argued that the different concerns at the low level are exemplified by the differences between processes (and associated interrupt service routines) on the "real time" side, and objects in conventional object-oriented programming languages on the "object-oriented" side, and that these differences address different real concerns that will continue to be different.
- Proposed that the high level requires a shift of perspective to a "system" view in which low-level differences recede into the background and there is a common concern for large-grained behaviour patterns in relation to large-grained components.
- Emphasized that we need to be able to move smoothly from requirements to high-level abstractions to base-level ones and vice versa.
- Identified the existence of a major missing piece in the suite of available high-level models that this book aims to fill with a model called *Use Case Maps* that will be introduced from first principles in the next chapter.
- Raised many issues without necessarily resolving them, to set the stage for the rest of the book.

CHAPTER 2

The Behavioural Fabric
of Systems

*T*his chapter develops the idea of use case maps as concrete expressions of an abstract idea called the behavioural fabric. The behavioural fabric of a system is the view we have in our minds of its large-grained behaviour patterns. The notation is introduced and some examples presented, taken from the physical and software worlds, including communicating fax machines and the model-view-controller paradigm used for programming graphical user interfaces (GUIs) in Smalltalk.

The purpose of this chapter is to introduce the new notations and associated concepts in an informal way; it is not to give a complete description of them or to bring everything into sharp focus immediately. We are trying in this chapter only to establish a mindset and introduce a notation that expresses it. Don't worry if some aspects still seem fuzzy even at the end of the chapter. We recommend forging ahead and waiting for the book to sharpen the focus as it proceeds.

2.1 THE IDEA OF A BEHAVIOURAL FABRIC

One way of approaching the problem of trying to understand a system is to look at its components. Figure 2.1 shows an example of a type of diagram that may be used for this purpose, called a *component context diagram*. The system is a familiar one from everyday life, a pair of fax stations that may interact through a telephone network (a fax station is a fax machine plus, when necessary, a human operator). A component context diagram is an arrangement of boxes representing system components, without any paths or links of any kind drawn between the boxes (these are added in different kinds of diagrams that will be explained shortly). The relative positioning of boxes in such diagrams is not arbitrary. We choose structural patterns that are helpful for understanding how the components will work together and then stick to them. Thus we give meaning to the structural patterns by convention. The meaning will be rounded out in other diagrams by adding paths or connections, but these are not part of component context diagrams (although having them in mind when drawing the diagrams helps).

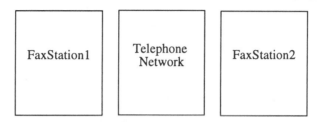

Figure 2.1   An example of a component context diagram of a system.

Component context diagrams indicate how we think about the configuration of a running system. For this reason we often call such diagrams and the components in them *operational*. In general, we may freely intermix hardware and software operational components in component context diagrams.

Now we are going to try to establish the plausibility of the *behavioural fabric* as something that at least exists in the mind when we think about systems.

When we think about the behaviour of a fax system like the one suggested by Figure 2.1, we can think about it in a detailed way, or in a high-level way. The detailed way would be in terms of sequences of actual interactions between the fax stations and the telephone network that produce all the squeals and beeps that you hear when you listen in. We would think in terms of sequences of such signals that ultimately result in a document being sent and successfully received. With this approach, however, it is easy to get lost in the detail.

The high-level way of thinking would be more like saying to ourselves "the fax stations synchronize themselves to make a temporary commitment that one will act as a sender and the other as a receiver, then a document is sent and received, and finally the temporary commitment is undone so that either fax station can act as a sender or receiver next time." Written down in prose in a structured way as part of requirements documentation, this would be called a use case [18]. However, we do not necessarily think about such things in prose. We are more likely to have a mental image of causally connected sequences of responsibilities performed by components, at a higher level of abstraction than sequences of interactions between them. We might think in terms of responsibilities like "FaxStation1 sets itself up as a sender", "FaxStation2 agrees to set itself up as a receiver", "FaxStation1 sends page", and so on. The mental image would be of causally connected sequences of these responsibilities traced through the components of the system. In other words, the image would be of paths superimposed on a component context diagram, not of prose sentences. This mental image is the "behavioural fabric" we have in mind. Even if we have not yet explained what the behavioural fabric *is*, we have identified what it is not: It is *not* a set of use cases expressed in sentences and it is *not* a detailed description of interaction sequences.

The ideas we have discussed up to now are summarized in Figure 2.2: (a) points to an amorphous shape spanning the whole system that *symbolizes* the existence of the behavioural fabric; (b) points out that this fabric is at a higher level than details of interactions and internal logic.

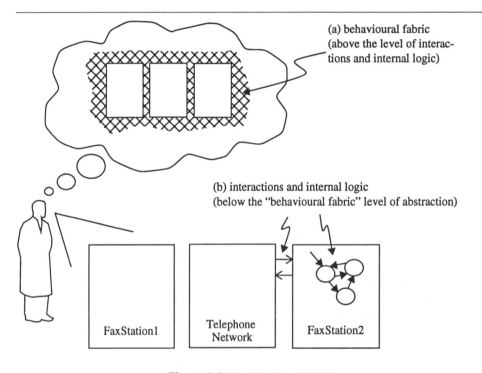

Figure 2.2 The behavioural fabric.

A mental image of this kind goes well beyond the idea of a prose use case at the requirements level, because we can just as easily visualize behaviour patterns as they propagate through the internal components of systems, not just through components that users see. In other words we can think in a seamless way about large-grained behaviour patterns across the requirements/design boundary.

We are aiming for a diagramming notation for humans to express such patterns in a way that mirrors how they appear in the mind before they are formed into sentences. If we think that humans can hold such patterns in mind, then there should be a way of putting them into concrete diagrams. It is this possibility that gives rise to the term "fabric". Fabric suggests two things: the weaving together of components in a way that is analogous to the weaving of cloth fabrics; and the possibility of a concrete existence, like real fabric.

2.2 PATTERNS IN THE BEHAVIOURAL FABRIC

Now we are ready to discuss how to represent the behavioural fabric. The behavioural patterns of systems in which we are interested come about in response to *stimuli*. Stimuli may arrive from outside the system, but they may also be spontaneously generated by its components. At the level of abstraction of the behavioural fabric, we tend to be concerned with higher-level stimuli than interactions with components, to avoid losing the big picture in too many details. For example, we may imagine a single stimulus in the fax example to be "start a document transmission", although actually doing it requires many detailed interactions inside one fax station, such as placing a document in a fax machine and pushing a number of buttons on the machine.

Many systems that may be characterized as object oriented or real time display patterns that are essentially point to point. *Point to point* means that each stimulus—given suitable preconditions—triggers progressive action along a single path that touches the affected components of the system point by point, in sequence. The points along the path are places where internal components perform responsibilities; we call them *responsibility points*. The path chains responsibility points together in cause-effect sequence in relation to the stimulus and a set of preconditions. The original cause is the stimulus. The immediate effect is that the first responsibility along the path is performed. This in turn is a cause relative to the next point along the path after that, and so on as the *causes accumulate to result in each next effect*. The path ends where the ultimate effect is felt. The path is progressive in the sense that each point along it advances the path toward the end. The path may be viewed as representing a *transaction* that must be performed to completion by the system as a whole.

Note that just because there is a cause-effect relationship between two responsibilities of a component along *one* path does not mean that there will be a similar relationship between the same two responsibilities along other paths. The cause-effect relationship is a property of each path and the preconditions that cause it, not of the responsibilities themselves.

Figure 2.3 gives an example of a point-to-point path for normal operation of a fax system. We draw point-to-point paths as smooth curves with labels along them to identify responsibility points. This particular path expresses in diagram form the pattern given earlier in prose: *the fax stations synchronize themselves to make a temporary commitment that one will act as a sender and the other as a receiver, then a document is sent and received, and finally the temporary commitment is undone so that either fax station can act as a sender or receiver next time.*

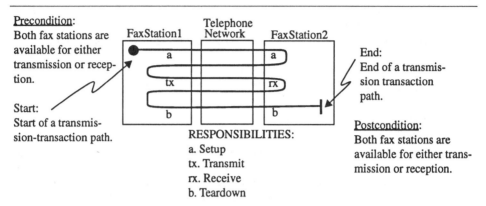

Figure 2.3 Example of a point-to-point behaviour pattern.

We call such a diagram a use case map. The paths in the maps are called use case paths. However, note that the notation is independent of prose descriptions of use cases and goes beyond the view of use cases as requirements level descriptions of external system behaviour. It aims to express what people have in their minds when they think of whole system behaviour patterns in a non-verbal way. The map notation will be introduced through examples in this chapter. Chapter 3 and Chapter 7 provide a detailed description of the notation, its meaning and rules for drawing diagrams with it. The notation has been written and talked about fairly widely as "timethreads" so if you have encountered timethreads before, note that the term "use case paths" identifies the same concept. If you have not encountered the notation before, all you need to know about it at the moment is the following:

- A filled circle identifies the start of a path, the path is a continuous curve that touches components at labelled responsibility points, the sequence along the path identifies the causal order in which the responsibilities are to be performed, and the end is a perpendicular bar terminating the curved body.
- The paths are not properties of the components along them, but of the system as a whole. Components just perform their responsibilities in the context of interactions with other components. The paths happen through the cumulative effects of many interactions. Details of the interactions are below the path level of description.
- Responsibility points are at a level of abstraction above interfaces and interactions. With respect to paths, responsibilities are labeled points that may be associated with components. With respect to components, responsibilities are things the component must do along paths. In other words, the responsibilities belong to both paths and components and provide the link between them. Paths and component context diagrams may be drawn independently and then linked through responsibility names.

Designers can draw paths with only responsibilities but no components, and then add the components. They can reallocate responsibilities along paths to accommodate different component configurations by distorting path segments or repositioning components in relation to the paths.

Notice that responsibilities like setup may be shared between components (in other words, they may have to interact to accomplish them). A similar observation applies to send-receive and teardown. We could indicate such cases explicitly by showing the path traversing back and forth, but this gets very messy and is beside the point, which is that we want to defer such details at this level. The way to interpret this diagram is that the setup responsibilities on *both* sides have to be completed before going on the transmit-receive ones, and they must be completed before going on the teardown ones. Chapter 3 provides a simple annotation convention for shared responsibilities that enables us to distinguish cases like this from ones that are explicitly *not* intended to be shared, if we have a need to do so.

Note that we rely on path context to resolve different meanings for responsibilities with the same names at different points along the paths. This is a form of polymorphism.

A fax station may or may not require a human operator to handle the setup responsibility (for example, by phoning another human operator directly to say that a document is about to be transmitted). Notice how such diagrams both defer commitments about internal details of components and provide a context for thinking about them.

Figure 2.4 shows that there are actually two mutually exclusive mirror-image patterns for the fax system.

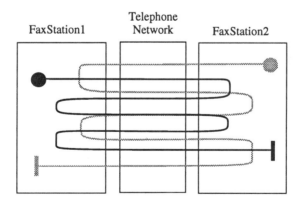

Figure 2.4 Mutually exclusive mirror-image paths (an unnecessary diagram from a documentation perspective).

The assumed precondition for each of the mirror-image paths in Figure 2.4 is that they do not overlap in time. Our convention in such cases is to draw the patterns separately. When the patterns are mirror images of each other, as in this case, drawing one of them is often sufficient, which is why we have identified this figure as unnecessary from a documentation perspective. However, it is useful as a mental model.

We hope the reader will now have a sense of what we mean by the behavioural fabric and how we represent it in a concrete way with use case maps for systems whose behaviour has a point-to-point character (Figure 2.5). If not, we recommend forging ahead anyway and waiting for the focus to sharpen as more examples are covered. The ultimate recourse is to read Chapter 3 and Chapter 7. We revisit the fax system in more detail in section 2.3.2 .

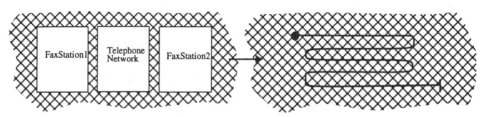

Figure 2.5 The behavioural fabric is composed of paths like this.

2.3 WORKING WITH THE BEHAVIOURAL FABRIC

Designers must do many things to get practical systems right, but one very important one is to get the behavioural fabric right. The elusiveness of this fabric when viewing a system in terms of interactions between components and the internal logic of components is one of the things that makes designing systems difficult.

We think that engineers working with systems typified by the fax example do their high-level design thinking about behaviour in terms of mental models of paths running through components like the one shown in Figure 2.3, in other words in terms of a mental model of the behavioural fabric. Engineers make trade-offs between design alternatives based on these mental models by evaluating system properties such as performance and robustness in a qualitative way in relation to the paths. They do so without concerning themselves with specific design details, by drawing on general domain knowledge about the intended implementation. When changing an existing system, they use the mental models as reference points to make sure they do not inadvertently violate the behavioural fabric by making inappropriate changes to details. However, we have observed that although this thinking goes on in the minds of designers, it is often lost to others.

The *results* of the thinking may be captured as work products in the form of detailed diagrams of components and interactions, but this is not the same as capturing the thinking itself. Capturing the details is generally the focus of CASE tools, for example [27]. Understanding the behavioural fabric in these terms requires mentally abstracting it from *interaction sequences* between the components. This makes the behavioural fabric a second-class abstraction, in the sense that it must be abstracted from details. In contrast, expressing the fabric with paths like the one in Figure 2.3 enables the fabric to be a first-class abstraction that can be expressed and reasoned about independently of details.

Use case maps provide diagrammatic representations of the behavioural fabric that can both be held in the mind and captured as concrete work products on whiteboards, paper, and so on. They are related to, but not the same as, prose descriptions of use cases. They provide a visual representation that is probably closer to how most engineers think about systems than the prose sentences of use cases. They have a larger purpose than use cases that includes actual high-level design.

We will now present a range of examples to consolidate these ideas, including a more complete working out of the fax example. Variations of some of the examples and their implications for detailed design will be worked out as we proceed through the book. We have tried to use examples that are likely to be familiar to all readers, or at least easily understood with little explanation, so we can focus on how to express the behavioural fabric.

We will stick to a neutral rectangular shape for the boxes in the component context diagrams of all examples in the remainder of this chapter for two reasons: This neutral shape is a suitable starting point for high-level design and using it avoids having to confront too many issues at once. Chapter 3 enlarges our view to include different component types.

2.3.1 Producer-Consumer

One of the most basic patterns in computing is the producer-consumer one shown in path form in Figure 2.6(a). For simplicity, the start of the path is shown inside the producer and the end inside the consumer, thus ignoring interactions with the environment. The salient feature of this pattern is that each component has a responsibility along only one path in one direction. Although this pattern is very simple when viewed like this, matters can become quite complicated when we get down to the details of components, their interfaces, and their collaboration sequences (Chapter 5). The essence of the pattern is better understood in path terms.

A more general pattern is the mutual produce-consume one of Figure 2.6(b) in which each component acts as both a producer and a consumer along different paths. The assumption of a diagram like this is that the paths can be concurrent (otherwise we would draw a separate diagram for each path, or draw only one diagram and place a comment on it saying that its mirror image is also possible, but not concurrently). An example is a system for transferring files in both directions at the same time between a pair of computers.

Patterns like these might be extended through many components in which the consumption responsibility in any component produces something for the next component along the path, forming a pipeline.

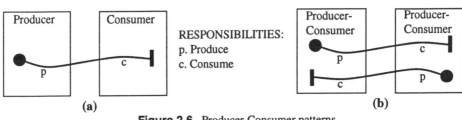

Figure 2.6 Producer-Consumer patterns.

Feuding Producer-Consumer Components An interesting in-between situation emerges when we allow components to fill both producer and consumer roles, but only one at a time, and we require them to resolve the issue among themselves (this is the situation with fax stations).

The requirement is for self-imposed mutual exclusion, but the issue is not just simple component-centered mutual exclusion (Figure 2.7(a)). The double-outline here is our notation for indicating that a component is required to impose mutual exclusion on the performance of its responsibilities. This kind of mutual exclusion is important and relatively easy to impose at the interaction level (for example, using mutex semaphores, interrupt disabling, hardware test-and-set, and so on.), but is not sufficient for our purposes here. It would allow PC1 and PC2 to be producers at the same time as long as the p and c responsibilities of each are not performed at the same time, which is not what we require. Component-centered mutual exclusion takes no account of the path context of responsibilities.

We require that (1) as soon as either PC1 or PC2 starts down a production path, the other is prevented from following a similar path itself, but can only participate as a consumer along the production path that starts from the other end, and (2) as soon as a production-path-in-progress is completed end to end, either PC1 or PC2 have the opportunity again to become producers. Figure 2.7(b) suggests the *idea* of such path-centered mutual exclusion by drawing a closed curve with a double outline around the affected paths. However, path-centered mutual exclusion is not as straightforward to impose as the component-centered variety, because the components must jointly impose it, taking account of the path context. To do this, new responsibilities must be added to the paths (Figure 2.7(c)). Completion of the setup responsibilities along one path excludes the path in the other direction. Completion of the teardown responsibilities along the same path removes the mutual exclusion condition. The pattern shown is for successful establishment of mutual exclusion by one of the paths; it does not show what happens when a race to establish mutual exclusion occurs. This is essentially the pattern shown earlier for the fax system example (Figure 2.3).

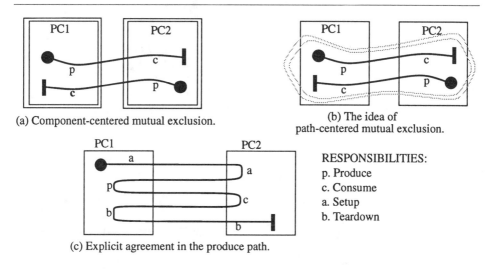

(a) Component-centered mutual exclusion.

(b) The idea of
path-centered mutual exclusion.

(c) Explicit agreement in the produce path.

RESPONSIBILITIES:
p. Produce
c. Consume
a. Setup
b. Teardown

Figure 2.7 Setting up temporary produce-consume agreements.

Race Conditions Situations where the relative order of events along concurrent
paths may be different at different times, with different system-wide effects, are called
races. Races are endemic to concurrent systems. To be avoided are critical races, defined
as ones that cause errors. In Figure 2.7 remembering that a mirror-image pattern starting
from the other end is also possible, we can see that there may be races when the system
tries to move down both this path and its mirror image at the same time.

Figure 2.8 takes account of the possibility of races by adding paths to the earlier
map that loop back from attempts to perform setup responsibilities that must fail because a
mirror-image path got there first. Here we adopt the convention of identifying path segments with italicized names, such as *succeed, fail*. We rely on context to resolve ambiguity; for example, the *fail* path in PC1 means "fail locally"; the one in PC2 means "fail
remotely". Because these paths are alternatives to the earlier one, we can superimpose
them to give a composite map, as we have done here. In general, when doing this, paths
may be distorted to align responsibilities as we have done here. The forks and joins in the
paths of the composite pattern are called OR forks and OR joins because they represent
alternative paths. However, they are only artifacts of path superposition, *not* points where
we attach OR logic to the maps. Which path should be followed out of an OR fork
depends on the particular end-to-end path that is being followed. There are many ways of
identifying end-to-end paths (we do it in Figure 2.8 by different shading, supplemented
for explanation purposes by segment labels like *succeed* and *fail*).

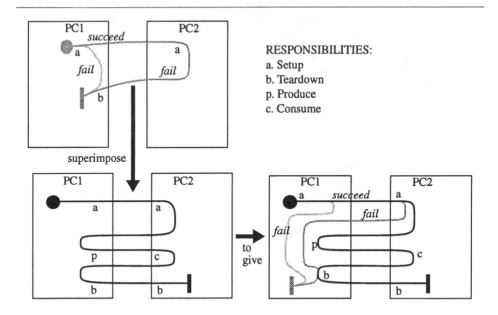

Figure 2.8 Taking account of race conditions.

Understanding the Map The end-to-end path starting in PC1 identified by the sequence a-*succeed*-a-*fail*-b is one that succeeds in performing a local setup in PC1 but not in PC2. In this context, this means that a mirror-image path starting in PC2 has already performed a local setup by the time PC1's path gets there (both paths will fail symmetrically as a result). It ends by passing through b because the local setup at a in PC1 has to be undone (the other failure path does not require this because it fails locally and there is nothing to undo).

Understanding these kinds of relationships is helped by diagrams like Figure 2.9, which shows the map and its mirror image with compatible combinations of paths highlighted. This figure in effect states that, when there is competition, one of two things happens: (a) one end has to give up its attempt to establish itself as a producer, leaving it available only to act as a consumer in relation to a pattern initiated from the other end; (b) both have to give up and try again. A critical race in this example would be for PC1 and PC2 both to decide they could produce at the same time. The map we have developed defines a high-level strategy for avoiding such a critical race. Details of how to implement the strategy using interactions among components are at a lower level of abstraction.

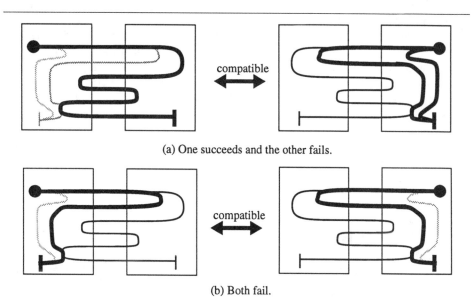

(a) One succeeds and the other fails.

(b) Both fail.

Note: Imagine the patterns on the left and the mirror-image ones on the right as superimposed.

Figure 2.9 Understanding the map.

Discovering Components in Maps It may be well to pause at this stage and reiterate that the responsibilities along the paths in the foregoing maps do not identify internal *components* of the boxes shown, they only identify *responsibilities* that internal components must be capable of performing when we eventually decide what the components should be. The meaning of the term "component" is critical here. We mean ones like processes or objects (or teams of them) that may be viewed as self-contained, operational units with internal state and interfaces that enable them to interact with other components in a variety of ways. Although at this level of design we are not directly concerned with interfaces or interactions, we keep in mind the fact that they will exist. "Components" here are *not basic* programming units like methods, procedures, or functions. We think of such basic units as elements in the interfaces and interactions that we have pushed down to a lower level of detail, not as components.

With this in mind, responsibilities are viewed as actions the eventual internal components will perform along paths as a result of underlying collaborations that are assumed to take place at a lower level of detail. In this particular example so far, we have compo-

nents PC1 and PC2, but no internal components of them. We might decide that responsibilities a and b should be performed by one type of internal component (for example, a
controller) and responsibilities p and c by another (for example, a data transfer agent).
However, we have made no commitments yet. It is significant that maps that traverse
black boxes do not require the presence of components along the paths to be meaningful,
even if the paths have interesting shapes as they traverse the boxes.

Figure 2.10 gives an example of discovering components by grouping responsibilities in relation to maps. This is one of many ways of discovering components. Other ways
include object-oriented problem analysis and experience with similar problems. Sometimes requirements statements may even identify the need for them explicitly. In this figure, the control responsibilities are grouped into a component C and the data transfer
responsibilities are grouped into a component DT.

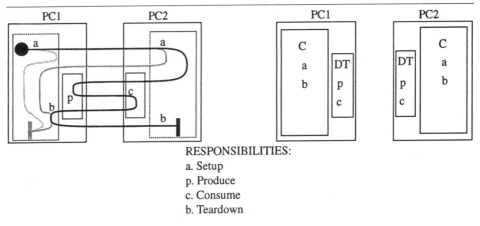

RESPONSIBILITIES:
a. Setup
p. Produce
c. Consume
b. Teardown

Figure 2.10 Discovering components by grouping responsibilities.

Remembering that this picture shows the pattern only in one direction and that the
complete pattern is actually one of compatible, competing paths in opposite directions that
are superimposed, we can interpret the figure to mean that coupling between competing
paths occurs *indirectly* through the C component (for example, Figure 2.11). A precondition for this scenario is that the black path gets to responsibility a first. This implicitly
commits the left-hand system to being a producer. The responsibility a along the grey path
fails to set up the left-hand system as a consumer. The assumption is that some internal
state of the C component registered a commitment through responsibility a along the black
path that was sensed by responsibility a along the grey path by means not shown. This is
the one form of interpath coupling. Other forms of coupling are also possible (Chapter 3,
Chapter 7).

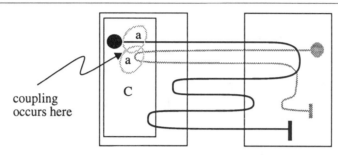

Figure 2.11 Indirect path coupling through a shared component.

2.3.2 Feuding Faxes

A pair of communicating fax stations forms a producer-consumer system like the one explored Figure 2.7 through Figure 2.11, with an extra component in between that acts as an intermediary (the telephone network). One way of resolving competition between fax stations that wish to send documents to each other at the same time is by a prior phone call between human operators in which one agrees to be receiver. In other words, the C components of Figure 2.10 will be human operators, and the fax machines will be the DT components. Another way is for the fax machines themselves to resolve the issue, in which case both the C and DT components must be part of the fax machines themselves. In this case, the fax machines must have knowledge built into them about how to use telephony signals to coordinate their affairs. Exploring this would take us too deep into the nature of telephone networks and fax machines for our purposes here, so we shall restrict our discussion of this example to the case where the control is performed by human operators. Note that nothing we have done so far commits to one way or the other and that the patterns we have developed define a high-level strategy for either. Only the interaction details between components would be different.

First let us complete the fax pattern in relation to the telephone network. A new property (Figure 2.12) is that there may be a failure to set up a producer-consumer relationship because the line is busy.

At first glance it appears that the busy condition resolves the path-mutual-exclusion problem in a simple way by preventing communication from being established if both ends are trying at the same time. However, every reader has probably experienced the confusing situation of lifting a telephone handset to call someone and finding the person is already on the line because a call was placed in the other direction at exactly the right time. People can resolve this confusion by talking and listening simultaneously, but fax machines would send data to each other simultaneously, which would not work.

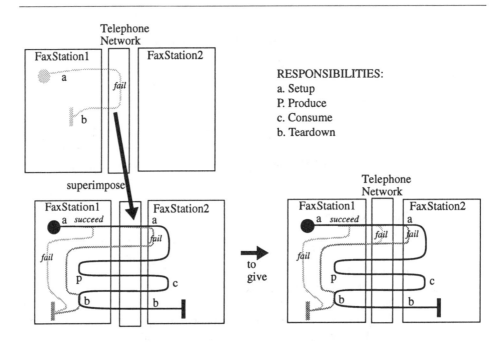

Figure 2.12 Fax stations communicating via a telephone network.

Contrast with Interaction Sequences The strength of use case maps is the way they capture whole-system behaviour patterns in one diagram, helping us to focus on big issues. Contrast this view of the behavioural fabric with one that relies on the interactions between components like the ones in Figure 2.13. The diagram shown here is called a *collaboration graph* and the arrows in it are called *connections*. The connections provide the paths over which interactions may take place. This is a very detailed view, with many detailed commitments required before things can be pieced together to get a high-level view of large-grained behaviour patterns (even though it is detailed, it leaves out nuances of telephony interactions). The only way of building up an understanding of the behavioural fabric from such details is to piece together sequences of interactions that use the connections. Notice in particular that to understand behaviour at this level of detail we have no choice but to make a commitment up front to how human operators enter the picture in a detailed way, something we were able to defer at the map level. In general, maps let us express and reason about the big picture while deferring such commitments.

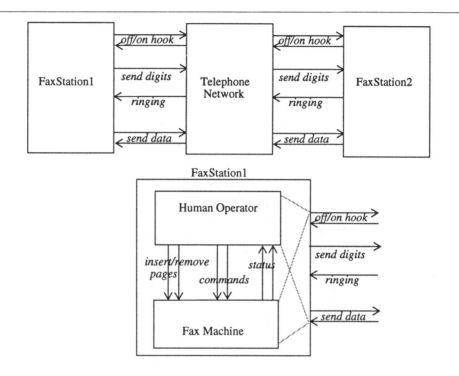

Figure 2.13 Collaboration graphs at the detailed level.

Behavioural patterns at the level of collaboration graphs may be quite intricate, as illustrated by Figure 2.14 (we assume here that human operators communicate via an ordinary telephone *separate* from the fax machines). We could develop different interaction sequences for different solutions to this problem—for example, using an internal phone in the fax machine to send data over the same call that performs the setup between human operators, or having the fax machines themselves perform the setup—but the point is they would be *different*. Being different means that changing from one solution to the other invalidates interaction sequence diagrams. In contrast, the patterns shown in use case maps, one level of abstraction higher, can remain the same over quite a wide variation of changes in details.

The point is that viewing things independently from different levels of abstraction can be useful. Use the higher level to get the sweep of patterns across the whole system right. Use the lower level to get details right.

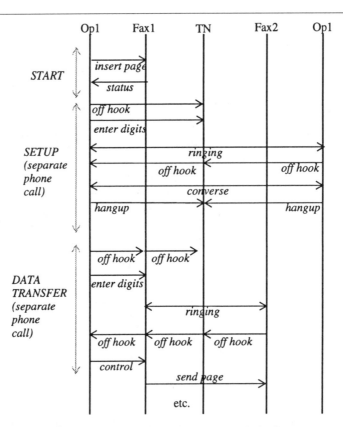

Figure 2.14 Interaction sequences may be intricate.

2.3.3 Model-View-Controller

Figure 2.15 provides the starting point for a completely different kind of example, taken from object-oriented programming. The idea here is that a model-view-controller (MVC) [22] triad of components manages an area of the screen in a GUI (Graphical User Interface) system. The triad is called the MVC team. In general, there may be different areas on the screen managed by different MVC teams; for example, in a simple GUI application there might be a tool palette area, a menu bar area, and a drawing area, each managed by a different team.

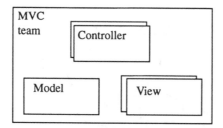

Figure 2.15 A component context diagram for part of a GUI system.

The purpose of the MVC organization is to promote reuse in systems with interactive displays. Its does so by separating the handling of application data, user input, and user output. Model components maintain the semantic data of an application, in other words the part of the data that is independent of how it is displayed. View components display the Model's data on display devices. Controller components interact with users through input devices. In general, a Model's data may be displayed in different ways, therefore, a Model may be associated with several Views (this is the reason for the replication of the View components in the figure). Views and Controllers come in pairs, because a Controller is responsible for user input in a View's output display area (this is the reason for the corresponding replication of the Controller components).

A typical use case against an MVC application is the following:

Direct Interaction: The user of the application interacts with the application through an input device, for example a mouse or keyboard. The application receives the user's input, changes its internal data if needed and updates the display of its internal data.

The use case path in Figure 2.16 traces the Direct Interaction use case through an MVC organization. The Controller handles the user request, the Model changes the data and the Views update their displays. The branch in the path that looks like a fork with its tines projecting from a crossbar is known as an AND fork. Each branch leading from it has don't-care ordering of responsibilities in relation to the other branches (in principle, the branches could be concurrent). This models the fact that all Views must be updated, but we don't care in which order. The end of the use case paths in this example signify that the Model's data has changed and that the new data is displayed on the screen in each of the views. By showing the path superimposed on one controller branching to many views, we convey that any controller may cause all views to be updated.

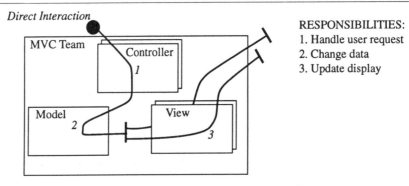

Figure 2.16 The Model-View-Controller team.

Other MVC Patterns We hasten to point out that this pattern is not the only MVC one. There may be different styles of use of the MVC organization in practice, such as updating the model from the views. This pattern represents one style. The issue is not which style is right, but that the patterns of any style can be expressed at a high level of abstraction in an understandable fashion with use case maps. Other patterns following the same general style as the one in Figure 2.16 are described below.

It is common that a user must interact several times with an MVC team during a single use case. For example, a user may interact twice, once to request a menu and a second time to choose an item from it; or three times, if a menu selection pops up a dialogue box for the user to fill in. Figure 2.17 introduces two new use cases to the direct interaction use case; namely, *interaction with feedback*, which has two interactions with a user, and *dialogue box*, which has three.

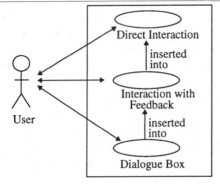

Interaction with feedback is inserted into *Direct interaction* after the users initial request. The application displays a menu of options for the user to interact with.

Dialogue box is inserted into *Interaction with feedback* after the user selects a menu item. The application displays a dialogue box for the user to fill in.

Figure 2.17 New use cases for an mvc team (notation inspired by Jacobson)

The new use cases result in additional use case paths through the MVC map. The additional paths allow for multiple interactions between a user of an MVC application and the Controller of the corresponding MVC team. Figure 2.18 (a), (b) and (c) show the use case paths through the Controller of an MVC team to handle the three use cases of Figure 2.17. The in-and-out path of case (c) does not signify that multiple view updates will be needed, just that there is a sequence of interactions with the user involving a dialogue box that we want to capture in the map. This kind of back-and-forth pattern may be captured with a shared responsibility (Chapter 3). Figure 2.18 (d) combines the three use case paths into a *composite use case map*. The composite map has an OR fork after responsibility (1) and again after responsibility (3) where the scenarios follow different paths. All the paths rejoin at an OR join before responsibility (5). The scenarios then follow a common path. Not all responsibilities in the composite map are performed for each scenario, for example the single interaction use case hits responsibilities (1), (5), (6), and (7) only. Showing back-and-forth interactions like this in maps is not *necessary*, but it is a design choice; the other design choice is to hide them in the definitions of large-grained responsibilities.

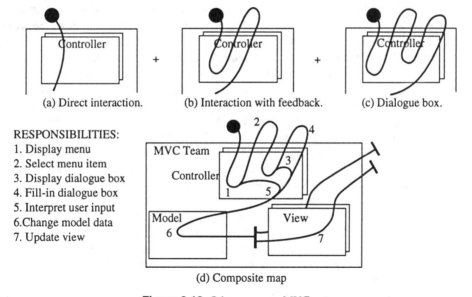

(a) Direct interaction.   (b) Interaction with feedback.   (c) Dialogue box.

RESPONSIBILITIES:
1. Display menu
2. Select menu item
3. Display dialogue box
4. Fill-in dialogue box
5. Interpret user input
6. Change model data
7. Update view

(d) Composite map

Figure 2.18 Other common MVC patterns.

2.3.4 A Model of Structural Dynamics

Chapter 1 pointed out that dynamic structuring occurs at all levels of granularity in systems, from fine grained objects in object-oriented programs to coarse-grained subsystems in real time systems. Dynamic structuring is equally difficult to express at any level of granularity with design diagrams of a conventional kind. The difficulty is that expressing it with conventional diagrams like collaboration graphs or uses diagrams (a.k.a. visibility graphs) requires showing sequences of snapshots of different structures at different times—in other words, moving pictures. The difficulty is particularly nasty when dynamic structuring is as fine-grained as it often is in object-oriented programs, because we can become lost in detail. However, the issue is the same at all levels of granularity: We need a better technique than moving pictures for representing dynamic structuring.

We obtain inspiration from human organizations, which also dynamically restructure themselves during normal operation. People are hired, quit, move between projects, are promoted, form ad hoc collaborating groups, and so forth, all while the organization is going about its normal business. We would need moving pictures to understand such organizations in terms of *identifiable individual people*. The trick with human organizations is to separate the concept of an organization from the concept of how it is populated by people. Descriptions of organizations often show named *slots* (for example, chief accountant, software designer) that may be filled by different people at different times, between which people may move, and that sometimes may be empty. Entire divisions of companies, or even whole companies, may be viewed as slots in larger organizations.

This inspires us to model structural dynamics in software with fixed slots (we could imagine a model in which slots themselves are dynamic, but fixed slots are sufficient for our purposes in this book). The changing visibility of dynamic components to each other is modeled by their movement in and out of fixed slots in fixed structures. The slots and dynamic components may be at any level of granularity from fine-grained objects to whole systems that are parts of still larger systems. The movement at any level of granularity is easily shown with fixed use case maps. We illustrate the idea using the MVC example, but remember that it is not restricted to the level of granularity of this example, in which the slots are for fine-grained objects.

Figure 2.19 conveys the essence of the idea. An MVC triad that controls a part of the screen in which different drawings may be created, saved, and edited may have its Model component identified as a slot (the notation does this simply by showing components in dashed outline), to allow for the possibility of different drawings being present in the Model position at different times. The changing visibility of drawings to the Controller and View components during the execution of a program is then modeled at this high level by their movement in and out of this slot.

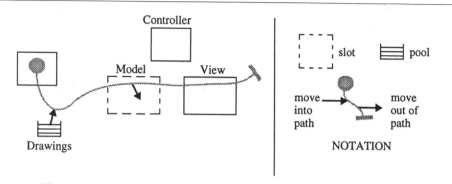

Figure 2.19 An example of structural dynamics expressed with a use case map.

Given this starting point, structural dynamics may be expressed in a lightweight and easy-to-understand fashion:

- An actual drawing (implied by the small arrows but not explicitly shown) is moved from a Drawings pool (represented by a queue-like symbol in this notation) into a use case path (how it gets into that pool in the first place is not shown here but can be shown by the full notation given in Chapter 3).
- It then moves along the path (implicitly), and into the Model slot, making the slot into a full-fledged operational component. While a slot is empty it is still viewed as a fixed part of the organization structure, but one that can only be activated by moving in an occupant.

The notational elements are as follows (there is more to the structural dynamics notation—see Chapter 3 and Chapter 7—but this gives the general idea):

- The small arrows into and out of the path indicate responsibilities to move components in and out of the path. They could be identified as ordinary named responsibility points, but the responsibilities are standard and the arrows help visualization.
- Pools are places where candidates to fill slots sit in readiness to be moved into slots. Pools may have many occupants. The model is that pools themselves are not places from which components can perform any responsibilities. Components have to be active elsewhere in maps to do that.
- Slots are places where one dynamic component at a time may fill an operational role defined by the slot context.

Getting a good high-level view of structural dynamics is very important in a practical sense. The fraction of code devoted to managing structural dynamics in practical programs may be large. The code that does the required pointer management to achieve
changing visibility may be decentralized among many places in code and be interdepen-
dent across these places (for example, gaining visibility in one place may require losing it
in another to avoid inadvertent aliasing). Pointer management is notoriously error prone
(due, among other things, to the possibility of inadvertent aliasing). The potential for error
is high. Structural dynamics must *not* be glossed over as secondary scaffolding. However,
thinking about it is very difficult at a low level of abstraction. The model suggested here
offers a way of expressing the essence of structural dynamics in a high-level way.

2.4 POINT-TO-POINT VS. RIPPLE PATTERNS

To provide a context for understanding the types of systems to which use case maps apply,
we categorize behaviour patterns displayed by systems in response to stimuli by positioning them in relation to a spectrum of behaviour that ranges from *point to point* to *ripple*
(Figure 2.20). Ripple means the effects of stimuli spread in a many directions at once (in
principle) like the ripple pattern on the surface of the pond when a stone is dropped into to
it. This book is about systems that are close enough to the point-to-point end of the spectrum that their behaviour can be usefully described in terms of paths.

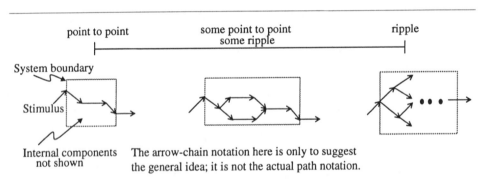

Figure 2.20 Spectrum of behaviour patterns in response to stimuli.

The fax example is at the point-to-point end. The MVC example is positioned somewhere along the line, although closer to the point-to-point end than to the ripple end. It has
some ripple because the stimulus propagates in several directions at once (in principle).
However it is also point to point because the ripple is clearly expressible as a set of concurrent point-to-point paths. We think that patterns like these characterize many practical
systems. The techniques of this book are specifically intended for these kinds of systems.

We are not speaking here of the way code executes. The progress of the program counter from one line of code to another in any program (even a "concurrent" one) executing on a single processor is "point to point" at that level, no matter what higher-level model we have in mind.

Ripple patterns, in contrast, are not expressible with paths in a useful way. This might be because there would be so many concurrent paths that diagrams would be black with them. Or it might be because the paths—and interaction between them—depend on incidental local detail so strongly that they are not predictable from the nature of the stimulus and a few simple preconditions. We mention this end of the spectrum here only to exclude it from the scope of this book, not to characterize it clearly. Data flow models may be particularly useful for this end of the spectrum because they explicitly do not commit to end-to-end paths. We have long held the opinion that data flow models are of limited usefulness for system design, and we speculate that this may be because many practical systems are not at the end of the behaviour spectrum where they would be most useful.

2.5 SUMMARY

In this chapter we have:

- Introduced the concept of the *behavioural fabric* of a system as something people have in mind when they think about large-grained behaviour patterns in a nonverbal way.
- Introduced *use case maps* as a means of expressing patterns in the behavioural fabric that are at or close to the point-to-point end of a behaviour spectrum.
- Showed that *use case maps* are *first-class design abstractions* at a level above details of component interfaces and interactions.
- Provided *examples* of maps for familiar problems from both the physical and the software worlds.
- Showed how use case maps can be used to model *dynamic structuring* at any level of granularity without resorting to moving pictures of changing structures.
- Did not completely explain the map model, but only tried to give its general nature to set the stage for studying it and its relationships to other design models, and for applying it.

Basic *Use Case Map* Model

*T*his is a self-contained tutorial on the basics of the use case map model that explains the notation and provides rules and guidelines for creating legal maps, interpreting the maps in behaviour terms, binding the maps to components during design, and working with maps at different scales in a coordinated way. It defers issues of concurrent paths in maps to Chapter 7.

The use case map model is a high-level design model to help humans express and reason about a system's large-grained behaviour patterns. The name comes from the fact that maps are a visual notation for use cases [18] and an extension of them into high-level design. However, the model does not depend on knowing what a "use case" is first. The model provides its own definition in its own terms.

There is a trap for the unwary in the parts of the model that relate to *interpreting maps in behaviour terms*. The trap is in looking for more than is intended to be there. There is no intent that use case maps provide complete behaviour specifications of systems. Because maps include some elements that provide cues to behaviour, it is easy to be misled into thinking they are for this purpose. From a behaviour-specification perspective, they are intended only as a framework for humans to use for reasoning and explanation purposes. Maps deliberately leave some decisions open that would have to be made to get a complete behaviour specification. We shall point out along the way specific places where this issue arises, but it is important to keep it in mind from the outset.

3.1 BASIC NOTATION AND INTERPRETATION

The basic symbols of the notation are as follows:

Path. A path may have any shape as long as it is continuous. A path may even cross itself, but this can create visual ambiguity related to other aspects of the notation, so the crossing must be distinguished by a small crossover arc or a break in one of the crossed lines.

Waiting place. A filled circle represents a start point in all the examples we have seen so far. In general, a start point is a waiting place for a stimulus to start the path. We use the same symbol for waiting places along paths, for example, to wait for events from other paths.

Timer. A timer is a generalized waiting place that expresses the idea that there is a time limit on waiting. It may be used anywhere a waiting place symbol is used.

Bar. A bar ends a path or marks a place where concurrent path segments begin or end.

Basic Path. The most basic, complete unit of a map is a path with a start marked by a waiting place and an end marked by a bar.

Direction (optional). Direction is indicated by the positioning of the start and end points but it is sometimes useful to show local direction in a complicated map or in an incomplete fragment of a larger map.

There are a few auxiliary symbols that will be introduced as we go along, but they are not fundamental to understanding the notation.

3.1.1 General Nature of Maps

Maps are composed of paths that may traverse components. They are intended to be used at the requirements level and for high-level design.

At the requirements level, a system is composed of one or more large-grained components that are viewed as black boxes (possibly only one, representing the entire system). At this level, the paths of maps traverse the black boxes but do not penetrate them (meaning we do not see internal components or the relationship of the paths to them). The paths are routes along which chains of causes and effects propagate through the system.

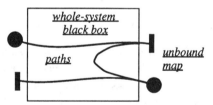

To design a system, we must open up the black box to expose its internal components. A black box with its internal components exposed is often called a white box (the

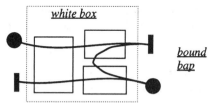

outline of the white box, shown dotted here, is often left out of such diagrams). One way
of characterizing use case maps is to say that they are a means of explicitly linking black-
box and white-box views of the large-grained behaviour patterns of systems.

In general, opening up a black box may add new paths that start in internal compo-

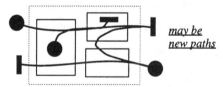

nents and either end internally, or follow one of the external path segments to its end.
However, this adds nothing new in principle to the meaning of the map model.

Observe that maps with system components visible along their paths are called
bound maps and ones without (not counting the whole-system box) are called *unbound
maps*. If we do not need to make the distinction, the term "map" by itself may refer to
either type.

Because components inside a white box may themselves be black boxes, the model
may be applied recursively. Later we show how to make a local map for an internal black
box from a white-box map that includes it by factoring the white-box map (Section 3.5).

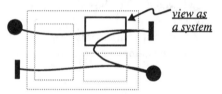

Levels of recursion of black-box and white-box maps are *not* the same as levels of abstraction in design (for example, high-level design, detailed design). Different levels of recursion may be at the same level of design, which would be high-level design as long as we stick with the map model. Detailed design begins when we shift to other models for black boxes at some level of the recursion, like collaboration graphs for interactions between them and state machines for their internal control logic (not covered in this book, but a standard technique).

Unbound maps provide a visual notation for use cases. They are useful for smoothing the transition from black boxes (requirements) to white boxes (design) by enabling a designer to begin with them and add binding and path refinements later as the need for system components is discovered. They can also be useful as reusable patterns that may apply to a range of bindings.

Bound maps are high-level design diagrams that show how a system's components contribute jointly to its large-grained behaviour patterns.

3.1.2 Responsibilities

There may be named responsibility points along any path. Whether or not they are visible

in a particular diagram, the existence of a least one is always implied. A *responsibility* is a named, short, prose description of some localized action a system must perform. By *localized* we mean that responsibilities are viewed as dimensionless *points* along paths. To keep maps as simple as possible, there is no extra notation to mark the points on the path itself; they are indicated only by responsibility names next to the path.

The path chains responsibility points together in cause-effect sequence in relation to the stimulus and a set of preconditions. The original cause is the stimulus. The immediate effect is that the first responsibility along the path is performed. This in turn is a cause relative to the next point along the path after that, and so on as the *causes accumulate to result in each next effect*. The path ends where the ultimate effect is felt. The path is progressive in the sense that each point along it advances the path toward the end. The path may be viewed as representing a *transaction* that must be performed to completion by the system as a whole. Note that just because there is a cause-effect relationship between two responsibilities along *one* path does not mean that there will be a similar relationship between the same two responsibilities along other paths. The cause-effect relationship is a property of each path and the preconditions that cause it, not of the responsibilities.

We say responsibilities are prose descriptions because that is what they are in this book. In principle, there is nothing to stop the notation from being formalized by requiring responsibilities to be expressed in some formal language that links them to changes in the state of the underlying system and, ultimately, to the transformation of preconditions into post conditions by chains of responsibilities. However, the notation is deliberately not formalized in this way in this book.

3.1.3 Scenarios and Use Cases

Maps are interpreted in behavioural terms as showing paths for scenarios. Imagine putting a map on a desktop and placing a pointer (symbolized here by —*not* part of the map notation) at the start of a path and then moving it along the path from point to point until the end is reached and the pointer is removed. The path traced is a scenario. We call it a

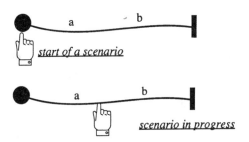

scenario whether we think of it as being traced by a person as above, or being made to happen by the collaborative action of the components of the system when it is running. In the former case it is a requirement stated by the map. In the latter case it is the observed achievement of the requirement.

The designer thinks about a scenario as showing operation of the system, but the map does not model the way responsibilities change the system state, cause information to flow, and ultimately convert preconditions into postconditions. Responsibilities are just named points on paths.

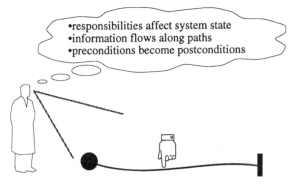

This interpretation of a path as visual representation of a scenario is the link to use cases. A use case is a prose description of a scenario or related set of them, with associated preconditions and postconditions, of a user's interactions with a system seen as a black box. An unbound map is a visual notation for a set of use cases.

To simplify descriptions, we often use *path* to mean *scenario*, relying on context to make the precise meaning clear. Otherwise, the effort to be more precise leads to wordiness. For example, we speak of a *path* being in progress when we mean a *scenario is in progress along a path*, or of *starting a path*, when we mean *starting a scenario down a path*.

3.1.4 Compound Maps

Maps like the ones we used to introduce this chapter are compound, that is they consist of

a number of different paths that may or may not be superimposed. The design model view of this is that the end-to-end paths are still distinct and that the points where paths seem to fork and join (called OR forks and joins) are *not* switching points, but only places where the individual paths enter or leave superimposed segments in a diagram. Not being switch-

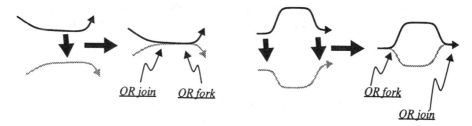

ing points, OR joins are unsynchronized and OR forks need no logic to determine which path to take; the path is implicit in the map to begin with. To identify the different end-to-end paths in diagrams in cases where it is not clear, we use shading , as in this book, or different colours, if drawing on, say, a whiteboard. Otherwise some other scheme must be employed, such as naming path segments and characterizing end-to-end paths by lists of segment names.

To single out for discussion individual paths identifying scenarios we highlight them with contrasting heavier lines.

3.1.5 Real Time Along Paths

Real time (meaning wall clock time here) is implicitly assumed to be required to move

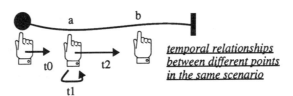

along the segments of the paths between responsibility points (for example, t0, t2), and
also to progress through each responsibility point (for example, t1). The progression along
the path takes time because of communication delays and possibly also because of
processing delays in components of an underlying layer that enables progress to take place
along the paths. The responsibilities take processing resources and therefore time.

However, this does not necessarily imply that the times are additive, because
responsibilities could overlap in time, as follows: Because the intent of use case maps is
that responsibilities are large-grained relative to the details of eventual implementations,
the possibility exists that responsibilities will be implemented by many fine-grained, concrete actions. Because the intent is that causal linkages along the path segments joining
responsibilities are similarly large-grained, the possibility exists that causal linkages may
be implemented by many fine-grained, concrete interactions between different components performing different responsibilities. The possibility of many fine-grained, concrete
actions and interactions suggests the further possibility that they may be interleaved over
time, causing the responsibilities at the use case map level to overlap in time. The only
constraints imposed by use case maps are on the relative times when responsibilities may
start and end. For example, in the path above, responsibility b cannot start before responsibility a and responsibility a cannot end after responsibility b.

Unbound maps tell us nothing about the sizes of responsibility times or inter-respon-
sibility times. They can only be resolved in bound maps in relation to components, and
then only qualitatively as far as the map model itself is concerned. For example, binding
responsibility a to a process in one hardware box and responsibility b to a process in
another would tell us that the ab path is realized by some interprocessor communication
hardware and software. This can give us some qualitative feel for the nature of the delay
along the path. If we know something about the speeds of the processors and the complexity of the responsibilities in relation to these speeds we would also get some qualitative
feel for the total real time along the path in the absence of other activity. The maps themselves are not intended to do more than this for purposes of reasoning about design issues

(although in principle they could provide a context for entering performance-related numbers into a performance model).

Real time may also enter maps explicitly. A timer may be used to mark a place where the propagation along a path is delayed by some time period. Because this is not a formally executable model, there is no provision for entering numbers into the map signifying actual timeout periods, and no means of doing anything with the numbers if there were, except displaying them to readers of the map for information. A timer indicates the *existence* of a time delay, not its details. Think of a timer as a special kind of responsibility along a path that takes up real time without taking up processing resources.

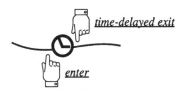

time-delayed exit

enter

3.1.6 Waiting Places

One of the most important requirements for use case maps is that they provide a means of explicitly showing coupling between scenarios. This is very difficult to do with prose use cases, which tend to bury coupling information in prose descriptions that have to be searched through to answer questions such as: Which other scenarios is this particular one coupled to, and where in the scenarios does the coupling take place? We defer the general issue to Chapter 7, and only explain the simplest form of coupling here. This is the positioning of a waiting place along a path to indicate that it must wait for events along another path. The concept is that the first path pauses until a trigger arrives along the second path.

A waiting place may be timed, in which case there may be a need to indicate an alternate timeout path.

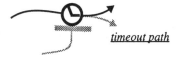

timeout path

3.1.7 Ripple

Explicit concurrency in the *same* scenario may be used to express patterns that are not pure point to point, but contain some ripple (recall Chapter 2). This is done by using AND forks. An AND fork is indicated by a bar that splits one entering path into several concurrent forks.

The effect is to split an entering scenario into multiple concurrent parts. The multiple parts progress concurrently in an unsynchronized fashion after the bar, but are still regarded as part of the same scenario. This concurrency may be interpreted to mean don't-care ordering in cases where concurrency is not possible or desired. When we speak of a *path in progress* relative to such cases, we mean the whole path, including the different parts after the AND forks.

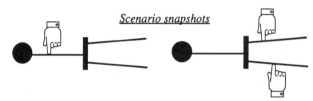

A following AND join may be used to end the concurrency. Just as above, the details of what happens when multiple scenarios may be in progress are deferred to components.

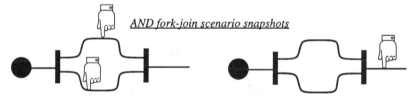

3.2 AN EXAMPLE: MOUSE DOUBLE CLICK

At this point it may be helpful to consider a simple example to consolidate these ideas.
Interesting patterns that may be described in a helpful way by use case maps exist at all scales in systems. When we say use case maps are for expressing large-grained patterns in systems, we mean that they are large grained on the scale of whatever system we use them for. However, we do not say what that scale is. Given the recursive black-box/white-

box view of systems expressed above, systems may exist at any scale. Here we consider a pattern that is very fine grained on the scale of the software of a system as a whole, but is large grained on a local scale.

A common pattern is to consolidate multiple related events into one event if they occur close enough together in time, and otherwise to treat them as distinct events. An example of such a pattern is double-clicking a mouse. Whether it is clicked once or twice, an object is selected on the screen, for example, a file folder icon over which the cursor has been positioned is highlighted. However, clicking twice quickly enough performs a second operation, such as opening a file represented by the icon. A single click that is not followed by another one quickly enough will only perform the selection. Such selection sets the stage for other operations, like dragging the selected object to a different place on the screen by moving the mouse.

Let us now specify the mouse double-clicking pattern with a use case map (Figure 3.1). The paths traverse the system box, but do not commit to internal components. The only commitment is that there must be a timer. Part (a) gives a double-click pattern but does not provide for the single-click timeout. Part (b) gives a single-click pattern with a timeout on waiting for the first click. Part (c) combines the two to give a composite map. This illustrates a general rule for composing maps: superimpose start points and initial path segments for stimuli that have the same source (the same goes for end points and destinations).

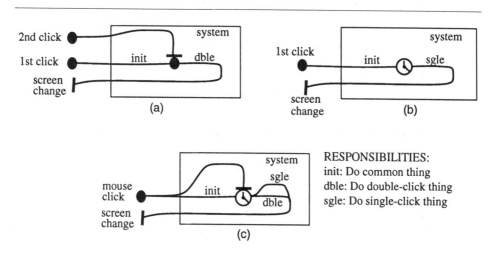

Figure 3.1 Mouse double-click example.

This map identifies the paths, but does not specify all the details of behaviour. For example, the map does not say what happens when clicks occur so fast that activity is still propagating along paths from previous clicks. The designer of the mouse click handler must take care of this. From that perspective this is a requirements map that helps the designer keep the big picture in mind while designing the details (see Chapter 7 for more on these issues).

We will return to this example in Section 3.5 in relation to issues of system scale.

3.3 BOUND MAPS (OPERATION DOMAIN)

We have explained the basics of the notation and illustrated it with some examples. However, the maps in this chapter so far have only had components that are large-grained black boxes at the requirements level. When we open up the black boxes to make them white, how do we bind internal black boxes to the maps? What do the bound maps mean? How far can we go at this level with resolving issues that unbound maps leave open? In other words, to what extent can we imply *design solutions* at this level? We answer these questions in a basic way in relation to operation domain maps (static structure, no slots) in this section and then to assembly domain ones (static structures with slots to represent underlying structural dynamics) in Section 3.4. A more advanced treatment is provided in Chapter 7.

3.3.1 Components (Operation Domain)

In Chapter 4 we shall present a suite of different types of operational components. However, the binding conventions illustrated below are relatively independent of these component types, and so are illustrated below with simple rectangular black boxes (called *teams* in the notation). These may be replaced with other components, subject only to satisfying a few simple restrictions that apply to some component types.

3.3.2 Conventions for Binding Components to Maps (Operation Domain)

Simple Binding Binding components to paths is simplicity itself when we are dealing with only one level of recursive decomposition. Paths traversing components imply binding. Paths are only bound to the components they traverse. The binding is made specific with labeled responsibility points that are both positioned along the paths and superimposed on the components, but traversal is sufficient to imply binding even without the labeled points.

Recursive Decomposition If we show several levels of recursive decomposition in the same map, then if the same binding convention as above is to work we must assume that the opened white boxes are just boundaries and the only "real" components with responsibilities are the black boxes at the bottom. With this convention the path below would be assumed to be bound only to three bottom level black boxes. This is the convention we have adopted for the examples of this book. We do not intend this convention to be a restrictive property of the notation, only a convenience for simplifying the examples.

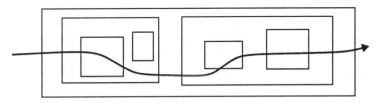

In general, white-box outlines may identify components with their own responsibilities and state. For such cases, diagrams without all responsibility points labeled are ambiguous. Below is a nonambiguous binding for such a case. Not only are three bottom-level black boxes bound to the path (through a, c, e) but so is a white box one level up (through b, d).

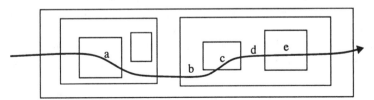

Shared Responsibilities Sometimes it is useful to simplify maps by making some responsibilities so large grained that they can only be *shared*. This is particularly useful in cases where interaction is required back and forth between components to accomplish the shared responsibility and we want to defer the details. We distinguish shared responsibilities from higher-level white-box responsibilities as follows:

shared responsibility
(alternate notations)

Applying this convention to the above example of recursive decomposition would enable us to identify, say, d, as a shared responsibility of the components on either side of it instead of a direct responsibility of the white box one level up.

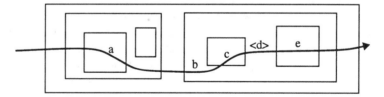

   We can now see that the fax example from Chapter 2 could be expressed with this convention.

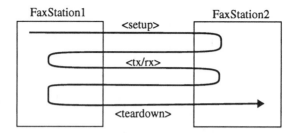

Indirect Coupling of Paths through Components A more subtle form of coupling than the direct interpath form we saw in Section 3.1.6 is indirect coupling through components. This occurs when we bind a component to a map in such a way that more than one path traverses the component and responsibilities on the different paths interact through the component. The need to show components to show this kind of cou-

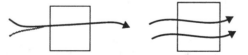

pling makes it a bit troublesome to express this in maps that are intended to show requirements in an abstract way, so we have a notation to express this without components that will be described in Chapter 7. The case where concurrent paths cause contention because of coupling through components is also deferred to Chapter 7.

   Indirect coupling through the responsibilities of a component occurs when different responsibilities of a component affect the system state in a related way. It may be indicated by showing paths passing through different responsibilities that are related by definition.

In this way one path may establish a precondition for another. The case where concurrent paths interact is deferred to Chapter 7.

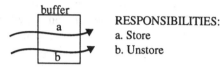

RESPONSIBILITIES:
a. Store
b. Unstore

Replication (Component Stacks) Replicating a bound component in a map means that there are multiple operationally identical, but distinct, components, all of which could perform responsibilities along this path, but only one of which is selected by path context. We call such a set a *stack*. An example is the stack of controller components in the model-view-controller paradigm; the path context that determines which controller is selected is set by the view that was selected on the screen. The superposition of the paths on top of the stack does not mean that the top component is selected, only that *one* of them is selected by each path. More than one may be selected along *different* paths at the same time.

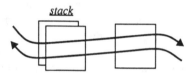

To indicate that *more than one* component of the stack is selected by the same path at the same time, an AND fork is required. To make the idea of *more than one at a time* visually distinct from the above case, the forks are routed through the stack, not just superimposed on top.

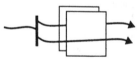

Stacks are different from pools or slots (Section 3.4). A slot is a single place where many *dynamic* components can operate, *one at a time*. Each different one has to be explicitly put there by separate system action. Many paths crossing the slot have nothing to select because only one component is there. Slots may be stacked as above if more than one slot is required at the same time. A pool is not an operational component, it is a place where dynamic components are held in readiness to occupy slots. They cannot perform responsibilities there. It would be incorrect to refer to a stack as a pool.

3.4 BOUND MAPS (ASSEMBLY DOMAIN)

Use case maps in the assembly domain model structural dynamics in a high-level way with only a few simple additions to the notation. Whether the structural dynamics is itself high level (for example, replacement of a macroscopic component like a communications server as part of a recovery operation) or the low-level kind that is pervasive with objects in object oriented programs is an orthogonal issue. The additions to the notation are two new component types (slots and pools) and some new notations for indicating responsibilities along paths in relation to them. We begin by characterizing the new component types.

3.4.1 Components (Assembly Domain)

We need some terminology first.

A *fixed component* is one that occupies the same organizational place during the lifetimes of the maps in which it appears. The lifetime of the map would normally be the lifetime of the system it models, unless the system somehow reconfigures itself so that different maps apply over different periods of time. The organizational places occupied by fixed components are not identified as slots. Identifying a component as fixed does not constrain how it is created and initially put in place (which may be at run time in code).

A *dynamic component* is one that may be created and destroyed at any time during the lifetimes of the maps that have slots for it, and that may move in and out of these slots at any time. Maps show only the slots, not the dynamic components themselves. This is a deliberate constraint of the notation, not an oversight, because not showing dynamic components leads to a simple, high-level model of structural dynamics based on fixed maps. While not occupying slots or moving between them, dynamic components are just data that has no operational place (in other words, is not represented by boxes in the map). Only while occupying slots (and in some case while moving along paths) are they actually operational components, and even then we do not see them directly in the maps.

 How dynamic components come into being while a system is running (that is, how they are "manufactured") is an orthogonal issue; for example, they may come from classes (as objects typically do) or from operating systems (as processes typically do).

The new notational elements are as follows:

A *slot* is an organizational place that may be transiently occupied by different dynamic components (one at a time), or be empty. Do not confuse the dashed-line notation with the light or dotted lines we sometimes use in diagrams to fade components into the background relative to some foreground map or connection scheme that we want to highlight. Slots are fixed components in maps, in the sense that they are assumed to have fixed positions and fixed responsibilities along paths that traverse them. Occupants of slots are assumed to be able to fulfil the required slot responsibilities.

▤   A *pool* is a place for holding dynamic components in readiness to move into slots. It is not the same as a stack of slots because it is not a place where the components are visible for operational purposes. Specifically, paths may not be drawn across pools to indicate components in them perform responsibilities along the paths. Pools do not have designer-determined responsibilities.

3.4.2 Conventions for Binding Components to Maps (Assembly Domain)

All the conventions and interpretations that apply to fixed components apply also to slots.

The slot model begs the questions: How do we identify where slots are needed in a design in the first place? If dynamic components can be moved around from place to place, are slots needed at every intermediate point? Are slots required where dynamic components are created and initialized? Guidelines are as follows:

- Slots are needed in maps wherever a dynamic component must be locally visible for a time, that is, visible to more than one path or to more than one traversal of the same path.
- Multiple slots enable the same component to be visible in different places at different times.
- With aliasing, the same component may be visible in different places at the same time.
- Components may be created and initialized at points along paths, or perform responsibilities at points along paths, without slots existing at those points, provided there is no need for the component's visibility to persist for longer than the time of a single traversal of the points.
- Slots are used to capture the idea of multiple, different operational roles for the same component in different places.

3.4.3 Movement of Dynamic Components in Maps (Assembly Domain)

The movement model includes the possibility of dynamic components being created and destroyed along paths and of them moving into, along, and out of paths. The sources and destinations of the movements into and out of paths are slots and pools. The notation to show movement uses small arrows (suitably annotated) with either their heads or their tails touching paths.

The full notation is described below.

→   **move:** Used for unaliased moves from a path to a slot, or vice versa (*unali-*

ased means the source forgets about the component).

⊢→ **move-stay:** Used for aliased moves (*aliased* means the source does not forget the component, but retains visibility of it).

⁺→ **create** and ⁻→ **destroy:** The component moved is created before the move, or destroyed after the move. Initialization is assumed to be part of the create responsibility.

⊢⁺→ **copy:** This is like move-stay, except that instead of moving the same component, a copy of it moves (so there is no aliasing).

One end of each arrow always touches a use case path. A path may be a source of dynamic components, in which case the *destination* is a slot or a storage pool (or the component is destroyed on the spot). Or a path may be a destination, in which case the *source* is a slot or a storage pool (or the component is created on the spot); then the component moves along the path to some other place.

In between the arrows, components move along use case paths as data; there is no special notation for such movement, because it is implicitly indicated by the relative positioning of the arrows. A moving component may momentarily "come alive" to enable some responsibility to be performed (for example, to extract some data from the component), provided that it is needed only for the duration of the responsibility.

The notation offers both unaliased and aliased moves. The unaliased move is the default (unlike programming, in which aliasing is the default). The aliased move (*move-leave*) ends up with the same component in more than one slot; think of the aliased component as playing different roles in different slots at the same time. This is possible in human organizations, so should not seem strange. It is very familiar in programming terms: it means that there are copies of a pointer to the same thing in different places in a program. Aliasing is different from *copy*, which ends up with different but identical components in more than one slot.

Below is an example where a single component created along the path ends up aliased in slots S1 and S2 and another component that was in the pool ends up in slot S3.

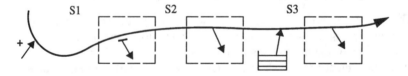

3.5 ISSUES OF SCALE

There may be many different scales of interest in practical problems. For example, in computer communications, scales of interest could be bit-level processing in hardware devices, character-level processing in interrupt service routines, packet-level communications between computers, and information exchanges between people over the Internet. In the MVC example, the scale of the mouse-click maps earlier in this chapter is different from the scale of MVC maps in Chapter 2. Considering structural dynamics, the scale of dynamic message buffering in computer communications is different from the scale of dynamic replacement of whole communication servers, say to service an alternative communication link after a failure.

We believe we have demonstrated by a number of examples that the maps themselves have no inherent scale. The issue of scale is, how can maps be used *in a coordinated way* across different but related scales? Maps too far apart in scale do not need to be related (such as ones at the scale of mouse clicks and Internet transactions). However maps at closely adjacent scales do need to be related. We present two map techniques below (*recursive decomposition by factoring* and *stubbing*) and show how to use one general system technique (layering) with maps.

3.5.1 Recursive Decomposition by Factoring

Here we show how to make a local map for an internal black box by factoring the larger map for the enclosing white box. This is a necessary stage if the smaller box is to be treated for design purposes as a system in its own right.

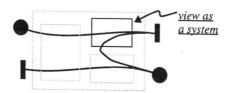

The factored maps are distinct maps that can help humans to reason about local design issues in local terms, while still maintaining the association with the larger map to provide context.

The essence of the procedure is to cut all the paths that traverse the black box of interest, outside the box, and then terminate the dangling ends properly.

The procedure for simple paths is shown below. The paths are factored by (1) cutting the path into two pieces, (2) forming the pieces into a pair of concatenated paths, and (3) separating the pieces. The original map is still assumed to exist to give global context.

A cross-reference must be maintained between the new end and start points of the pieces and the cut point in the original map.

Only one case is more complex than this. An AND fork may require cutting because one part remains in the black box and the other goes outside it. The procedure is a variation of the one above: (1) cut as above, (2) terminate and concatentate essentially as above, (3) form a main path with offshoots, and (4) separate the pieces. Again, a cross-ref-

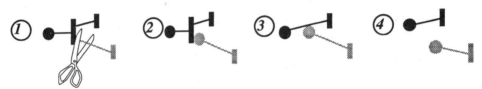

erence must be maintained between the end points of the pieces and the original map. Note that step (3) provides what is, in effect, a synonym for AND forks. AND forks are more fundamental because they do not distinguish main and offshoot paths, but this form can also be useful.

An AND join simply requires applying the single-path technique to each of its entering parts (or only one of them if only one comes from outside the black box). OR joins and forks do not require any special technique because they are just superimposed single paths.

Techniques for *composing* a larger map from smaller maps are exactly the reverse of those for factoring.

3.5.2 Stubbing

Stubbing is a map-drawing technique that pushes fine-grained detail off a main diagram into separate stub-expansion diagrams keyed to the main one.

The stub notation is shown in the figure below. The stub symbol is a superimposed start and end point, symbolizing a map with a single start point and a single end point that has been collapsed into a point. The map that has been stubbed may be as complex as you like between the start and end points. It may also include start and end points of paths that are not shown in the main map because they are regarded as detail relative to it. The top case in the figure shows a stub superimposed on a path, indicating that if it were expanded on the spot it would simply form a part of the larger map, with no identifiable start or end point. The cases below it show stubbing of concatenated parts of a factored map in which the stub is explicitly concatenated with a start or end point.

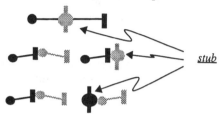

This simple notation is a useful one for unbound maps because it does not require stubs to be associated with components. We have no special notation for stubs with more than one start or end point. We must go to bound maps for this, representing the stubs as black-box components.

We will now illustrate the stub concept using the mouse double-click example. Figure 3.2(a) shows the mouse double-click map (Figure 3.1) as part of a larger map, perhaps for a GUI system (the existence of a map for it is hinted at by the wavy path). Figure 3.2(b) shows that we want to focus on the GUI system and treat the mouse click handler as pushed-down detail. Figure 3.2(c) shows the on-diagram stub notation, which is logically equivalent to (b), except it does not require showing it as a component when we do not want to. Figure 3.2(c) shows the off-diagram stub expansion.

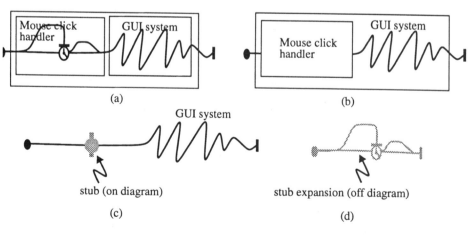

Figure 3.2 Stubbing.

3.5.3 Layering

Layering is a well-known component decomposition technique, *not* a special technique associated with use case maps. Layers are components that provide such widely used services that they may be regarded as implicit infrastructure (for example, real time executives that support concurrent processes). Decisions about layers are made at the level of component context diagrams of a whole system. However, relating layers to maps for explanation or reasoning purposes can be useful. This requires new notation, distinct from stubs.

A *layer boundary* in a component context diagram explicitly identifies one side as the layer and the other side as the set of components that uses the layer.

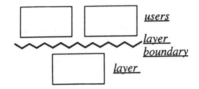

The layer is normally left out of maps (left-hand map below), even where it may be required to perform responsibilities along the paths (middle map below) or support path transitions between components (right-hand map below),

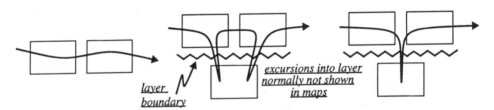

Identifying the *existence* of descents into layers along paths—without showing the layer itself—can sometimes useful (for example, to remind us of consequential performance hits). We do this with a *layer fold* symbol. The term comes from imagining that the layer boundary is folded such that the entire layer is collapsed into a point along the path.

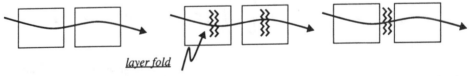

What is the difference between layer folds and stubs? There is no difference in the following respects in relation to use case maps: Both are superimposed on paths and both imply there is more complexity here than meets the eye. However, the design purpose is different. Stubs are used to simplify maps. Layers are used to organize the components of systems. The use of the layer-fold symbols in maps is for information purposes, not map decomposition.

Figure 3.3 illustrates how the mouse click handler example might be layered. Whether or not the handler is described in map terms is an orthogonal issue.

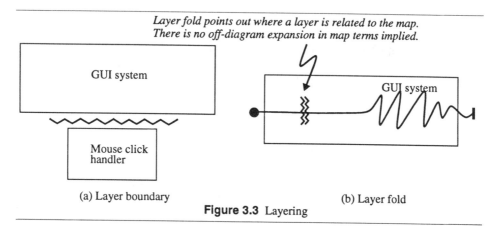

Layer fold points out where a layer is related to the map.
There is no off-diagram expansion in map terms implied.

GUI system

Mouse click handler

GUI system

(a) Layer boundary   (b) Layer fold

Figure 3.3 Layering

3.6 SUMMARY

In this chapter we have:

- Described the basic *use case map* model in some detail, including rules for forming legal maps, for interpreting maps in behaviour terms, for binding components to maps, and for using component binding to express design decisions.
- Explained that maps have meaning in behaviour terms as expressing the paths of scenarios, but cautioned against trying to create complete behaviour specifications with them.
- Showed how to express patterns with some ripple in them using AND forks and joins.
- Explained the simplest forms of path coupling, namely one path waiting for triggers from others, and multiple paths indirectly coupled through responsibilities of components.
- Explained stubbing and layering techniques for using maps in coordinated ways at different scales. Stubbing is specifically a map technique analogous to recursive decomposition of components. Layering is a system decomposition technique, independent of maps, that can be associated with maps where this may be useful.
- Deferred issues associated with concurrent scenarios, concurrent paths, and concurrent components to Chapter 7.

A Context for Designing with Use Case Maps

*T*his chapter describes a context in which design with use case maps may take place in a coordinated manner with other design models. The context positions design models in relation to four levels of design abstraction (requirements, high-level design, detailed design, and implementation) and three basic domains of separable concerns within the levels (operation, manufacturing, and assembly). A fourth domain, problem domain modeling, replaces the manufacturing and assembly domains at the requirements level. The context includes notations for component types to cover the range of issues identified in Chapter 1.

This context is needed to help us explain the relationship of our new models to more familiar ones. It is also intended to help the reader judge how models not mentioned in this book may or may not relate to ours. In this chapter we explain the *general nature* of the models of the suite and *identify* how they may be used both separately and together. We aim here only to establish a base of concepts and terminology to help readers understand explanations in later chapters. Chapter 5 gives more insight into the nature of the context by putting all of the models of the suite together for a very simple example, including showing the relationship to fragments of code that might be part of an implementation in one particular programming language. After that, chapters refer to the context without further explanation. Chapter 12 summarizes the unique features of this context in relation to other design methods.

Figure 4.1 emphasizes an important point about the suite of models that we are about to encounter. We want our models to give views that will help humans reason about how software under design will behave as a system when it eventually runs. This does not mean we want only behaviour models (the suite includes diagrams that express only structure). However, we want views that humans can integrate mentally to understand behaviour, no matter what else individual views are used for.

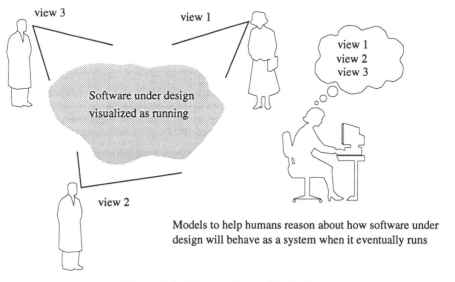

Models to help humans reason about how software under design will behave as a system when it eventually runs

Figure 4.1 Diagramming models for humans.

4.1 AN OVERVIEW OF THE CONTEXT

Figure 4.2 positions a suite of design models in relation to four levels of design abstraction (requirements, high-level design, detailed design and implementation) and three basic domains of separable concerns within the levels (operation, manufacturing, assembly). A fourth domain of separable concerns (problem domain modeling) applies only at the requirements level. The general purpose and nature of the levels should be apparent from their names and from previous chapters. Figure 4.2 does not suggest steps in a waterfall process. We expect practical designers to bounce up and down between the levels and across the domains in an opportunistic fashion.

Our focus in this book in on the second level down, namely *high-level design*, and specifically on use case maps both at that level and as a link between requirements one level up, and detailed design one level down. The detailed-design level is, naturally, where details are developed. Working with detailed design models is desirable and useful at stages in the design process where details are the focus of our concern. However, details tend to obscure the big picture at stages in the design process where the big picture is the focus of our concern. For this reason, there is a need for a level between requirements and detailed design. Although we position high-level design here as a distinct level, the line between requirements and high-level design is actually fuzzy, as the explanations below will indicate.

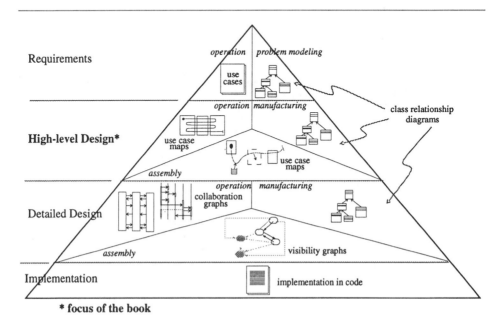

Figure 4.2 A suite of design models.

Figure 4.2 group models within each level into categories (called domains here) that address different issues. The requirements level is shown as having two domains, the *operation* domain, where use cases are positioned, and the *problem modeling* domain, where the object models of conventional object-oriented design are positioned. The models of high-level design and detailed design are shown as having three domains each, named *operation*, *assembly*, and *manufacturing*. The operation domain is concerned with all aspects of system operation except dynamic structuring. The assembly domain is specifically concerned with dynamic structuring. The name comes from imagining dynamic components being assembled into time-varying teams as the system is running. The manufacturing domain is concerned with how components come into existence at run time. These domains should be viewed from the perspective of Figure 4.1, namely that we want models to help humans reason about how software under design will behave as a system when it eventually runs. The names of the design domains relate to that objective, they do not refer to the process of producing actual code. Specifically, assembly does not refer to assembly language programming and manufacturing does not refer to writing source code or generating object code.

It may help to think of the combination of operation and assembly domains in terms of the following pseudo-equation:

Behaviour = Operation + Assembly

By this we mean that the combination of ordinary operation as expressed in use case maps without slots, and structural dynamics as expressed in use case maps with slots, expresses a higher form of behaviour that includes both. Relative to this view, the manufacturing domain records the existence of (and some information about) the infrastructure that enables the components that will jointly produce the behaviour to exist.

4.2 MODELS AT THE DIFFERENT LEVELS

We will not attempt to define the levels in prose here, but only to characterize them by the models that we have positioned in them, as follows.

4.2.1 Models at the Requirements Level

Operation Domain (Use Cases) In principle, prose use cases are the starting point for use case maps one level down. However, sometimes maps may come first; for example, some preliminary sketching of maps may be helpful to guide preparation of use cases. This can help to avoid spending too much time working out requirements details that will have to be changed later as a result of better understanding of what the system can actually be (yes, insight gained during design and implementation can affect requirements). This book is not about how to prepare use case descriptions (see Jacobson [18] for that). Nor is it really about how to produce use case maps from prose descriptions of use cases in standard form. This is because use case maps are a self-contained design model that generates its own approaches to creating them, only one of which is to start from prose use cases. Chapter 2 showed that use case maps could be drawn with relatively little commitment to component configurations, by expressing them mainly in terms of responsibility sequences. Doing this is a kind of advanced requirements analysis that segues seamlessly into high-level design as components are added and maps are refined to accommodate them. The relationship between such very-high-level use case maps and prose use cases is so close that we might think of them as alternative notations for each other at this level. Although we have left use case maps out of this level in Figure 4.2, for simplicity, they could be included.

Problem Modeling Domain (Class Relationship Diagrams) Classes are useful as an abstraction tool to model many things, not just class hierarchies in an object-oriented implementation, so at this level they may be quite distant from such an implementation. Classes may be discovered from problem analysis at this level complemented by reasoning with use case maps one level down (or even at this level). This lightens the load of creating object models (class relationship diagrams at this level are often called "object models").

4.2.2 Models at the High Level of Design

Operation and Assembly Domains (Use Case Maps) Maps are concrete work products of high-level design that link requirements in the form of use cases (perhaps drawn with maps also) to component organizations. They express large-grained behaviour patterns that can be saved, studied, and reused. The existence of the maps as concrete work products frees designers from having to hold personal mental models of the behavioural fabric while designing details, as we opined earlier that designers tend to do. This frees the mind to focus on other issues, such as trade-offs between alternative component configurations to realize the paths. It also ensures that the thinking is not lost after the details are decided and the designer turns to other projects. Maps provide a means of proceeding smoothly from use cases one level up to suitable component configurations. Exploration of alternatives is encouraged because the maps do not depend on knowing a lot of detail and can be relatively easily readjusted for different configurations.

Manufacturing Domain (Class Relationship Diagrams) During high-level design, classes are coordinated with the operational components of use case maps, without having to express behaviour by adding interfaces or bodies to classes. The presence of use case maps frees the designer from trying to explain behaviour with annotations on class relationship diagrams. Class relationship diagrams at this level are not used to describe behaviour, but only to identify classes of components in maps.

4.2.3 Models of the Detailed-Design Level

Operation Domain (Collaboration Graphs and Interaction Sequence Diagrams) Collaboration graphs follow in a relatively straightforward fashion from higher level use case maps. Interaction sequence diagrams may be used to show intricate sequences to supplement the combination of use case maps and collaboration graphs.

Assembly Domain (Visibility Graphs) The information in use case maps in the assembly domain, together with the collaboration graphs, may provide sufficient information to code structural dynamics directly. However other models, such as visibility graphs, may also be helpful in complicated cases.

Manufacturing Domain (Class Relationship Diagrams) At this level, class relationship diagrams are refined by adding interface elements (functions, methods) and some information about bodies following standard object-oriented design practices. They are close to code.

4.2.4 Implementation

The detailed class relationship diagrams from one level up provide the structure of the code that a programmer will write (if the implementation is to be object oriented) and the detailed operation and assembly models provide the information for programmers to fill in the code bodies. (This is not the only model for implementation. CASE tools may provide a different model.)

4.2.5 What About Tools to Support the Context?

CASE tools are available at the requirements level and at the detailed design level, but there is a shortage of tools in the intervening gap where we have positioned our models. Tools to support the use case map model on its own or within this suite of models would be helpful but do not exist yet. However the maps were designed as a diagramming technique for humans and as such can be used without tools in "back of the envelope" style. Furthermore, being at a high level of abstraction, they are relatively lightweight (meaning free of commitment to detail) and so do not present the same maintenance problems that more detailed diagrams do.

4.3 THE CONTEXT WITHOUT USE CASE MAPS

Without use case maps there is a large conceptual gap in the operation and assembly domains between requirements and detailed design that must be made up by models in the designer's mind and annotations on class relationship diagrams (or other diagrams not included in this suite) that may overload the design with behavioural detail. Here are the weaknesses of this approach:

- Use cases at the requirements level express specific behaviour patterns that are intended to occur. But they are not—expressed as they are in prose—high-level design models and do not give a sense of direction to the process of developing models at the detailed level. Design magic is required to make the leap to *discovering* detailed design models.
- "Object models" advocated in many object oriented design textbooks develop classes that appear through all levels of abstraction, from descriptions of the problem domain at the requirements level through to classes in the code of implementations. Therefore they provide useful connections between levels of abstraction that can be exploited for developing concepts at one level into details at the next lower one. Their biggest weakness from our point of view is the lack in them of first-class, high-level models of large-grained behaviour patterns. This lack can lead to too-early development of details of classes in order to get at behaviour that way.
- If you agree with our opinion that use case maps with components bound to them (or vice versa) provide a new way of looking at "architecture", then the lack of them

means we have a much weaker view of architecture that focuses only on large-grained components and structural relationships between them. (The term "architecture" is discussed in the Preface and in Section 4.5.2)

- Detailed assembly models have to take up the slack of the missing assembly domain maps. This can be very complex even for simple problems, as Chapter 5 will illustrate.

The problems these kind of omissions can cause, discussed in Chapter 1, motivated use case maps in the first place.

4.4 USE CASE MAPS IN DEVELOPMENT PROCESSES

An overview of steps in development processes helps to make clear *when* we see the use case map model being used (as opposed to *where* in a suite of models). The levels of abstraction identified earlier may appear in step-by-step processes in different ways (Figure 4.3), as described below. This diagram is not intended to be prescriptive about sequences of steps. We view the design process as an opportunistic jumping back and forth between different diagrams to piece together an understanding. The process of doing this should be distinguished from making the products of the process (diagrams) an official part of the project record, which is where prescribed steps come in.

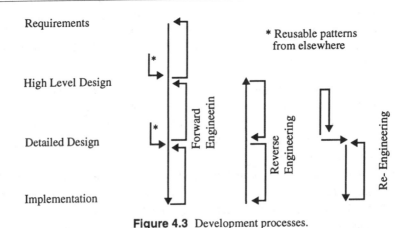

Figure 4.3 Development processes.

We have not tried to be comprehensive about development steps. For example we have not said anything about maintenance, which we might regard as including fixing code that does not reflect design intent and adding detailed functionality to code without modifying anything significant in the design. We are more concerned here with issues affecting design and re-design.

Forward Engineering In *forward engineering*, we proceed generally downward through the levels and associated models. We do not imply a linear sequence of steps from top to bottom, however. Actual progress tends to bounce up and down between levels in an opportunistic fashion, as insight at one level leads to changes at another higher or lower level.

We suggest using maps for high-level design thinking and documentation for any new project (whether object oriented or real time at the code/run-time level, or some combination). For example, in an object-oriented project, use maps in a coordinated way with high-level class relationship diagrams to get a broader perspective on how to design the classes. This enables design iteration to take place in a relatively lightweight fashion compared to the heavyweight method of iterating between detailed design and high-level design of class hierarchies in an attempt to get large-grained behaviour patterns right.

We suggest using maps to evaluate high-level design trade-offs. For example, in a real time system project, trade-offs could be made between different candidate configurations of processes in relation to a map that is invariant relative to them. This might be done to eliminate configurations that might have bad end-to-end performance along paths, for example due to interprocess communication overheads, the presence of in-line processes along paths that could be positioned out of line, or the presence of unnecessary processes that could be collapsed into procedures. Although done at the high level, such trade-offs would be based on knowledge about the implementation level. Even if the implementation does not exist yet, qualitative knowledge of the performance effects of different process configurations will exist from other implementations. Thus high-level design decisions may be based on low-level knowledge without having to design or implement the low level first.

The question raised in Chapter 1 of when concurrent processes should enter the design picture for real time systems is seen to be a nonissue when a high level design model can easily accommodate them, as this one can. The answer is they should be brought in when a designer needs to think about them. This may be in high-level design or detailed design. There is no need to be prescriptive about it.

We suggest maps might go into libraries of reusable, high-level patterns for future reference in relation to new forward engineering projects (this is where the reusable patterns in the figure would come from). Such libraries may also help new employees of a project get a high-level overview.

Because of their high level of abstraction, maps are less likely to become obsolete than other forms of description that are more committed to details, so they have a chance of being more useful as long-lived documentation. This is where tools to maintain maps would be particularly useful.

Reverse Engineering In *reverse engineering*, we try to extract detailed models from code, and high-level models from both code and detailed ones. The code may or may not have been produced by a forward engineering process. Reverse engineering may be used to document complete programs, but is probably more often used in industrial practice to understand programs that have to be modified.

We suggest using maps to capture a high-level view of large-grained behaviour patterns that can be used simply for documentation, or as a basis for re-engineering. We are skeptical about the prospects of fully automating such extraction because we have observed that extracting useful maps is still a problem for the human mind. However, housekeeping details may be automated.

Re-Engineering In *re-engineering*, we change the design and implementation, perhaps to satisfy new requirements, or perhaps to improve a system, say to respond to customer feedback about inadequate performance. If the original high-level design was well conceived, re-engineering may require only modifying the detailed level. Indeed, an objective of design at the higher level should be to try to make it as invariant as possible with respect to possible detailed changes. Otherwise, the higher level may have to be changed. Some combination of forward engineering and reverse engineering may be used to try to achieve a satisfactory re-engineering process.

We suggest using maps to express architecture that should not be violated while re-engineering actual systems at the detailed level. For example, use them to express operational aspects of object oriented-code frameworks that need to be preserved when modifying the frameworks.

4.5 SOME IMPORTANT ISSUES

4.5.1 Balanced Use of the Models

We have presented in this chapter a balanced view of how the models may be used together. However, the book as a whole does not give such a balanced view. It gives much more prominence to maps than to other models. It does not provide tutorials on the other models, because there are other books available that do that. It does not prescribe step-by-step design methods that include other models in a balanced way because being prescriptive about such matters is not our purpose. Readers should not conclude that we are promoting maps as the primary design model. We spend more time on them because they are new, not because they are more important. Readers must perform the necessary balancing themselves in relation to other methods, guided by Chapter 12.

4.5.2 "Design" and "Architecture"

"Architecture" is a term that is often used in industry to indicate a model of how whole systems and families of systems are organized at a high level of abstraction. Precise definitions of architecture are lacking but everyone knows it is important, and companies usually have some view of what it is in relation to their products.

We suggest that the suite of models we have placed in the high-level-design position in Figure 4.2 generates its own view of architecture that may be helpful wherever that term is used in industry. This view can be used for programming technologies that directly express none of the concepts in it, or only a subset. It is independent of details like interfaces of components, interaction sequences and internal control logic. We would not be uncomfortable with replacing the term "high-level design" with "architecture" everywhere it is used in this book to refer to diagrams (as opposed to the process of creating them).

This brings up the issue of possible confusion surrounding another widely used term, "design". We use the term as both a noun and a verb at two levels of abstraction, detailed design and high-level design. This may be at odds with some industrial usages of the term that associate the noun "design" with a specific level of abstraction. For example, some might replace what we have called "high-level design" with "architecture" and what we have called "detailed design" with just "design". Readers who come from backgrounds where this is done could find our use of "design" as a verb confusing. We use it to refer to the process of thinking about and deciding on the contents of a set of diagrams at either the high level or the detailed level, whatever those levels are called.

4.6 COMPONENT TYPES IN USE CASE MAPS

The rectangular boxes we have used so far in use case maps are useful as representations of large-grained components or of components of uncommitted types, but are insufficient to deal with all of the issues associated with components that were raised in Chapter 1. For object-oriented applications, we need objects and classes. For real time applications, we need processes, interrupt service routines, and possibly also classes for both. This section provides notations for these things and explains how they fit into the suite of models, including the relationship of slots and dynamic components to related concepts like objects and classes.

Fundamental, distinguishing features of the use case map model—relative to other design models like collaboration graphs and interaction sequence diagrams—are that maps display only three aspects of components, namely their presence, their responsibilities and their types, and do not display any representations of interfaces of components or connections between components. These features make the model a uniquely-high-level one because it defers messy details like: the existence of functions, procedures, methods, semaphores, mailboxes, messages, or entries (as in Ada); directions of calls; static versus dynamic binding of calls; unsynchronized, asynchronous, synchronous and timed-out interactions; different forms of data transfer during interactions, including parameter passing and direct sharing; and the changing of visibility relationships by passing pointers. The omission of such details and the provision of alternative, higher-level means for representing behaviour patterns without them makes the use case map model a uniquely high-level one.

The issue of component notations for use case maps is therefore very simple. All we need is a few shapes to distinguish different component types.

4.6.1 Six Component Types

Figure 4.4 provides a suite of six basic component types for use case maps (a seventh type, dynamic components, never appears directly in maps). This suite is sufficient for the purposes of this book. This figure is not intended to imply that all of these component types must be part of the map model, or that others are excluded. However, we have found these types to be useful across a wide range of system types, programming technologies and applications. *Teams*, *slots*, and *pools* are the *only* uniquely-high-level abstractions we shall need. Teams are used to represent large-grained components (in the sense of operational groupings) or components of uncommitted types. Pools are places to hold dynamic components in readiness to move into slots. Slots are places where dynamic components perform responsibilities. Teams may be fixed components or slots. Dynamic components never appear explicitly in maps because pools and slots are sufficient to express structural dynamics. We add *processes*, *objects* and *interrupt service routines* to round out the model, following the argument in Chapter 1 that we need representations for them that can be used to transition between high-level design and detailed design; these components can also be represented as fixed components or slots. All of these components except pools may be designed to have application-dependent responsibilities. Detailed characterizations of the components of the suite are given following Figure 4.4.

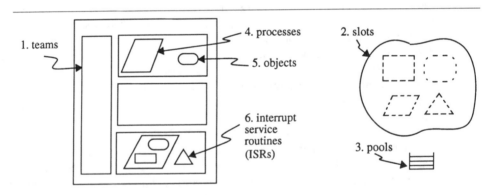

Figure 4.4 Six basic component types for use case maps.

Teams [ ]   Teams are lightweight abstractions for large-grained components at the level of use case maps. We can use them somewhat casually because no strong commitments are implied by this use. We may introduce them into maps to hide details without committing to whether or not they will actually exist as components with interfaces or will actually have members. Up till now we have used the team notation only to identify the *existence* of components that are operational black boxes, without making commitments to their nature, and we shall continue to use them this way. However, in general, a team is an operational grouping of components that, when opened up as white box, may include as members any or all of objects, processes, interrupt service routines or other teams. A team is said to be *passive* if it contains no processes or interrupt service routines (at any level of recursive decomposition of its members) and to be *active* otherwise.

When we speak of a team as a white box or a black box, or of recursive decomposition of a team, all we intend to imply is that its components and their components (and so on, recursively) are or are not visible in certain diagrams. Showing teams in use case maps implies nothing about implementing them as code-level containers. How they are to be implemented is a deferred detail.

In cases where a team symbol is used only to identify the *existence* of a component without committing to its *type*, the box does *not* necessarily have to be expanded later into more components. We may later reinterpret the team as a component of a specific type either by redrawing the map with the rectangle replaced by another shape, or by putting only one component of the required type in the white box view.

Objects   From the behavioural perspective of use case maps, an object is a component that supports a data or procedural abstraction through an interface. Although we *define* an object by saying it supports an abstraction through an interface, the *actual* interfaces of objects are below the level of abstraction of use case maps. The assumption is that the interface—when it is designed—will provide the means for other components to ask it to perform its responsibilities.

The model of behaviour is that objects perform their own responsibilities, but do not have ultimate control of *when* they perform them; the interfaces provide the means for other components to exercise control over "when". Ultimately, this control comes from processes, although it may come indirectly through other nonprocess components such as teams or other objects.

Objects are viewed in our design model as fine-grained components that do not have a team property. In other words they are not further decomposable into teams of still finer grained objects. If an abstraction is needed for a coarse-grained "object" that is decompos-

able into finer grained objects, we use a team.

In our design model there is no raw data, only objects that support data abstractions.

Whether or not a particular object is an instance of a class in an object-oriented class hierarchy is a separate issue.

Processes ⟋‾‾⟋   Processes are treated in depth in Chapter 7 in association with concurrent maps. Until then, the following will provide a sufficient characterization of them: A process is an autonomous, self-directed component that may operate concurrently with other processes. Its internal logic is sequential; in other words, there are no concurrent elements inside processes, the only concurrent elements are the processes themselves; multiply-concurrent components are modeled as active teams (teams with multiple processes in them).

Interrupt Service Routines (ISRs) △   Interrupt service routines (ISRs) provide the glue between physical stimuli and other components of the design model, particularly processes. They may often be omitted from high-level designs as lower-level detail. See Chapter 7 for more information.

4.6.2 Relationship to Other Models

All of these component types may appear with the same notation, but with details added, in detailed diagrams of the operation and assembly domains, such as collaboration graphs, visibility graphs and associated interaction sequence diagrams.

Collaboration Graphs and Visibility Graphs   Teams are lightweight components at the level of use case maps, but not so lightweight in collaboration graphs and visibility graphs. Commitments must be made about teams in these diagrams, as illustrated by Figure 4.5 and Figure 4.6. Figure 4.5 shows three ways (among others) of representing teams in visibility graphs, all of which imply different implementations: no implementation, a container, or a switchboard. Read the arrows from tail to head as *sees* or *has visibility of*. There is no commitment to actual interfaces, so this is a more lightweight way of representing intended implementation structure than collaboration graphs.

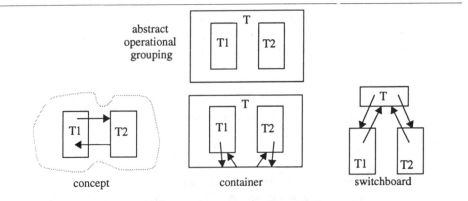

Figure 4.5 Teams expressed in visibility graphs.

Figure 4.6 shows three corresponding ways (among others) of representing teams in collaboration graphs. There is considerably more commitment here, because the arrows imply both interfaces and connections over which interactions may take place. We would normally make the effort of showing teams this way only if we expect them to be implemented as identifiable units in the implementation. Otherwise, why make the effort of defining interfaces that will never be explicitly implemented?

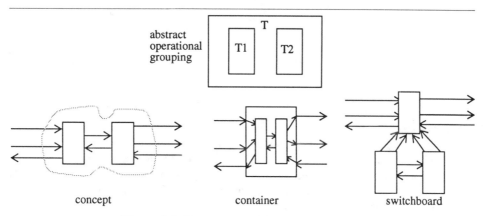

Figure 4.6 Teams expressed in collaboration graphs.

Figure 4.7 uses collaboration graphs and visibility graphs to illustrate, in a concrete way, the relationship between fixed components, slots, and dynamic components. Observe the appearance in the visibility graph of the invisible seventh component type mentioned earlier, namely dynamic components (represented by shaded boxes). They are invisible in all the diagrams in our suite of models except visibility graphs. The grey arrows in the visibility graphs represent dynamic visibility relationships and the black arrows represent fixed visibility relationships. By definition, visibility arrows directed at dynamic components must be dynamic, but dynamic components can have fixed visibility of static components. The intent of this diagram is to show that different dynamic components, such as C4 and C5, may be visible to a fixed component, such as C3, through a slot such as S2, at different times (and also that the fixed components may be visible to the dynamic ones). The visibility graph does not show the time sequences; we would need a sequence of snapshots of a changing visibility graph for that.

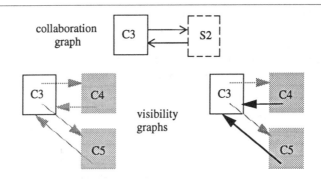

Figure 4.7 Relationship between fixed components, slots, and dynamic components

In relation to Figure 4.7, we say that the meaning of a slot being occupied is that all visibility relationships required to enable interactions to take place have been established between fixed components, such as C3, and dynamic components occupying slots such as S2. There may have to be exchange of information by means not shown in the collaboration graph to enable this visibility to be acquired. We do not show the means in collaboration graphs, not because we think it can be left as a detail, but because we have a better way of showing structural dynamics, namely with use case maps. Slots normally imply dynamic visibility, for example, as in the visibility graph on the left. However, if a slot is occupied at different times only by members of a set of dynamic components that themselves never occupy any other slots, the dynamic components may have static visibility of surrounding fixed components, as in the visibility graph on the right.

Classes Any of the component types may be implemented by classes in object-oriented programs, but none of them, not even the components we have called "objects", must be so implemented. However, when designing object-oriented programs, we need to understand clearly the relationships between these components and programming-language classes. Figure 4.8 gives an overview of the relationships assumed by this book. Subsequent chapters will fill in details. For simplicity, Figure 4.8 uses the team symbol to stand for any component that is an instance of a class (we could substitute objects, processes, or ISRs). The tree on the right is a class relationship diagram representing an inheritance hierarchy; the stylized boxes represent classes and the arrows represent *is a* relationships.

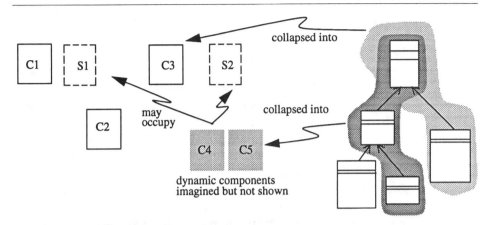

Figure 4.8 Relationships between classes, dynamic components, static components, and slots.

Figure 4.8 shows that fixed components are viewed as being instantiated from classes by collapsing the inheritance hierarchy into instances that becomes the fixed components, for example C3. Slots are viewed as being occupied by dynamic components that are instantiated from classes in a similar fashion, for example, C4 or C5 may occupy slots S1 or S2.

At the use case map level, classes may be viewed as defining the responsibilities of fixed components and slots; at the detailed-design level, they may be viewed as providing the required interfaces. How the class hierarchy is organized is a separable issue. For example, slots might not have any direct representation in the class hierarchy or they might be associated with abstract classes.

The imagined collapse of the inheritance hierarchy in Figure 4.8 pushes certain details in class hierarchies out of the operational picture represented by use case maps. For example, Smalltalk-style messages between subclasses and superclasses are assumed to be part of the internal functionality of instances that is not shown in our operational diagrams. This has the implication that responsibilities that are represented as points in use case maps may actually require traversal of an inheritance hierarchy in implementations. This is as it should be, considering that responsibilities in use case maps are intended to be large-grained quantities.

4.7 SUMMARY

In this chapter we have:

- Identified a context for designing with use case maps that consists of a suite of design models positioned in four levels of abstraction and four domains of separate concerns at each level. We have done this to help us to explain in subsequent chapters how to work in a coordinated way with use case maps and existing popular design models.

- Did not fully explain how to use the models together, only identified where they could be used together. The explanations follow in subsequent chapters that use this chapter to provide context.

- Explained that the focus of this book is on new models for *high-level design* in the *operation* and *assembly* domains. Explained how removing these models from this suite of models places a heavier load on other models, and results in a number of disadvantages.

- Gave some indication of where the new models fit into forward engineering, reverse engineering and re-engineering.

- Identified and characterized six *component types* that appear in the use case maps of this book (teams, slots, pools, processes, objects and interrupt service routines). Explained that a seventh component type, dynamic components, never appears explicitly in maps because of the unique way maps express structural dynamics.

- Related these component types to other models. Emphasized that use case maps provide a uniquely-high-level view of components because they identify only their presence, their responsibilities and their types.

CHAPTER 5

A Simple Example

A simple producer-consumer example is used to take a tour through the suite of models of Chapter 4. A very important feature of this chapter is that it shows in detail how to deal with the difficult problem of bringing dynamically changing software run-time structures into the high-level design picture. For readers who want to follow the ideas all the way to the code level, C++ code examples are provided at the end of the chapter; other readers may skip these examples without loss of continuity. The purpose of this chapter is to make the models and the relationships between them more concrete. Here is where we are going and why:

- The example is the simplest producer-consumer example from Figure 2.6(a) of Chapter 2. Although the example is simple, it is treated as if it were a whole system for purposes of exercising the design models. The split into high-level and detailed design is not determined by the complexity of the system but by the models used. Using the full range of models on a simple problem helps to make the models and their relationships clear.
- To illustrate the point made in Chapter 1 about the need for low-level components like processes to appear sometimes in high-level design diagrams, we bring processes into the highest-level models immediately. We do this to fix in the mind how processes can enter the high-level picture in a relatively lightweight fashion. In a more complex example, they would not be the first components to be introduced. The first ones would be teams, and processes might not appear until several decom-

73

positions of teams into more teams had occurred, with use case maps developed first in terms of the teams.

- We also use the example to present a detailed picture of structural dynamics in relation to all models at all levels, not just use case maps. This motivates the introduction of two detailed models in the Assembly domain: Code Snapshot Diagrams (useful for explaining code in a visual way, but less useful for design) and Visibility Graphs.

Figure 5.1 presents this chapter as a tour of models, with a use case map. The requirements level is omitted because this is not intended to be a design case study that shows how to move through the models from requirements to implementation in an orderly way. The named responsibilities along the path (ucm1, cg1, ...) are points of the tour that are identified in the headings of the sections that explain them, so that readers can quickly look up the context in this figure. The small diagrams along the path are icons representing models that will be explained in detail elsewhere, not diagrams to be understood from this figure. Some of them will look familiar, others that do not will be explained. As the chapter progresses the details will become clear; at the end the figure will provide a useful reference for remembering the models.

This application of use case maps is worth commenting on because it illustrates the generality of the concept. This map gives an overview of a large-grained pattern, embedded in the linear prose of this chapter, that can easily get lost in the details as we write it and you read it. The pattern is traced through concepts that have relationships that are orthogonal to the linear sequence of their presentation in prose. The map enables us to see these relationships while writing or reading the prose, to provide context. The map may be viewed as a design diagram for writing the chapter, a reference diagram for revising it, and a context diagram for reading and remembering it. The map says nothing about the details of the prose. There is a strong analogy with the way maps are employed in system design.

5.1 HIGH-LEVEL DESIGN, OPERATION (UCM1)

Figure 2.6(a) of Chapter 2 provides our starting point, recast in Figure 5.2. The different orientation of the map has no significance. Figure 5.2 shows a map that identifies a producer team, a consumer team, and a one-way producer-consumer pattern between them. In general, the producer and consumer teams might be complex systems in their own right (as in the fax example of Chapter 2). They might be decomposed into internal teams with associated map refinements. There might be more than one stage of such decomposition. If the original teams represent autonomous systems that must operate concurrently, then at some point in this decomposition we would introduce processes to model the concurrency explicitly. To keep this example simple, but still illustrate the point that processes are easily introduced into the highest level of design, we identify the earlier teams as processes. This illustrates once more that teams may be used to indicate uncommitted components in early stages of high-level design and then committed to being specific types of components in later stages.

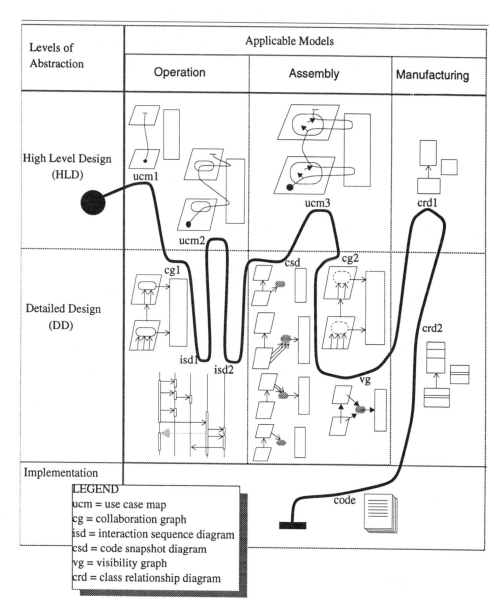

Figure 5.1 Tour of the models.

In Figure 5.2, we also make the problem a little more interesting by adding *printing* to the responsibilities, to indicate that the implementation is required to print a trace of the occurrence of production and consumption. In this and all subsequent figures of this chapter, necessary data flows are assumed to occur without showing them explicitly.

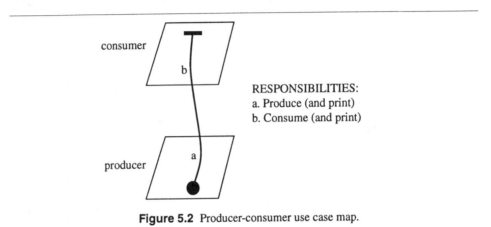

RESPONSIBILITIES:
a. Produce (and print)
b. Consume (and print)

Figure 5.2 Producer-consumer use case map.

5.2 DETAILED DESIGN, OPERATION (CG1, ISD1)

We jump straight to plausible collaboration graphs for implementing a system consisting of a producer process, a consumer process, two buffers to hold the items produced and consumed, and a printer (Figure 5.3). The figure shows two collaboration graphs that differ in one minor detail (the direction of the arrows between producer and consumer), to illustrate the issues that arise when simple changes are made to interaction details. Since we have not yet explained the detailed connection notation, we seem to be getting ahead of ourselves. However, collaboration graphs are so widely used and this figure is so simple that we don't think this should present a problem. The only point worth special attention is that the interprocess *get* and *give* connections represent synchronous IPC. The notation allows for other kinds of interactions between processes, but this will suffice for illustration here. The only strange-looking notation is the waiting place at the head of the *get* connection in (b) that identifies a send-blocked protocol, meaning the consumer is blocked until the producer has an item for it. Apart from that, the arrows imply ordinary call-return semantics. See Chapter 9 for more detailed explanations.

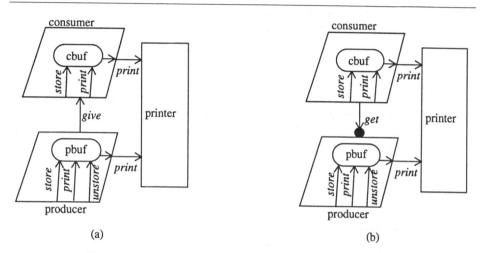

Figure 5.3 Collaboration graphs for a producer-consumer problem.

The interaction sequence for a produce-consume use case for the collaboration graph of Figure 5.3(a) is shown in two ways in Figure 5.4:

- One way of showing sequencing, shown in (a), is by associating indented sequence numbers with arrows on a copy of the collaboration graph (following Fusion [13]); for example, 2 is the second interaction that occurs and 2.1 follows from it before 3 occurs. There is a subtle point in relation to the sequence 4, 5, 6. It might seem like 5 and 6 should be 4.1 and 4.2 because they appear to follow from 4. However, because 4 is a rendezvous between two autonomous processes, both of which must agree to it, there is actually a hidden interaction not shown in the figure, namely consumer accepting the *send* interaction that producer initiated. There is no arrow for showing this acceptance, so there is nothing with which to associate a sequence number. Following the hidden interaction, interactions 5 and 6 are controlled by consumer. Numbering them 4.1 and 4.2 would suggest erroneously that they are controlled by producer. Observe that we cannot tell from this type of figure when the consumer completes the *send* interaction, thereby giving producer permission to continue.

- Another approach, shown in (b), is to draw a separate interaction-sequence diagram. The diagram shown in (b) is an example of what Jacobson calls "interaction diagrams" (we call them "interaction-*sequence* diagrams" to distinguish them clearly from collaboration graphs, which also might be viewed as interaction diagrams of a kind). The horizontal dotted arrow indicates that the consumer completes interaction 4 by issuing permission to continue to the producer after the *store* operation into cbuf is completed, enabling producer to resume operation at this point (the permission to continue is accomplished in programming by things like *end* or *reply* statements in the code of the consumer process). Recall that we cannot get this kind of information from (a).

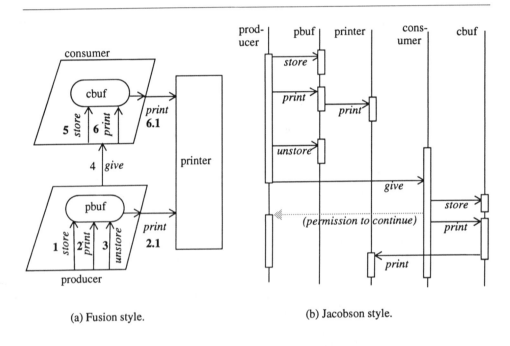

(a) Fusion style.   (b) Jacobson style.

Figure 5.4 Interaction sequence for a produce-consume use case.

Figure 5.5 shows what happens to the interaction-sequence diagrams as a consequence of the single changed arrow in Figure 5.3(b). In spite of the only change being the reversing of the direction of one arrow, many of the sequence numbers in the Fusion-style diagram are changed and the patterns of the Jacobson-style diagram are significantly changed. The point is that these diagrams represent a strong commitment to details and create a big maintenance headache when details are changed.

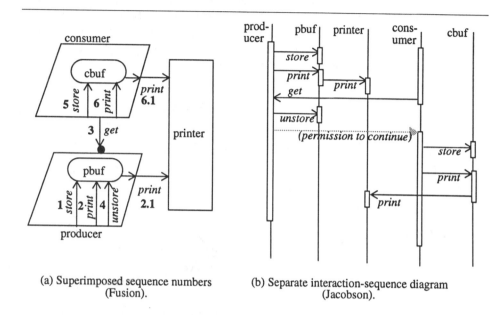

| (a) Superimposed sequence numbers (Fusion). | (b) Separate interaction-sequence diagram (Jacobson). |

Figure 5.5 Modified use case interaction sequences.

5.3 HIGH-LEVEL DESIGN, OPERATION (UCM2)

In spite of the many detailed differences between the different detailed design diagrams, nothing important is different when we stand back from the details to examine the desired behavioural fabric of the producer-consumer system as a whole. The essence of the desired behavioural fabric is: producer produces and causes consumer to consume. We can convey the desired behavioural fabric much more simply than any of the interaction-sequence diagrams do, without the need to make diagram changes when design details are changed, with a use case map. This does not mean diagrams of detailed sequences are never useful, but only that they should be used for what they are best at, namely showing the details, after we have committed to the them, in complex cases.

The map of Figure 5.2 conveys the essence but ignores the printer and the two buffers. Figure 5.6 includes them and thereby gives a little more detail. The map of Figure 5.6(b) raises two interesting points. First, unlike the collaboration sequences we have shown so far, the map does not require a return to pbuf to *unstore* its contents after leaving printer. The map would be satisfied if *unstore* was invoked before printing, so that a call could be made by producer to consumer immediately after returning from printing (a return to producer before calling consumer is required here only to complete a call-return control sequence, not to satisfy this map). Second, the map does *not* require the following control sequence: printer, after performing b2, calls consumer to force it to perform c1. This sequence would not make much sense, given that we would tend to view printer as a server component. In any case, the collaboration graphs we have drawn so far do not provide the connections for implementing it.

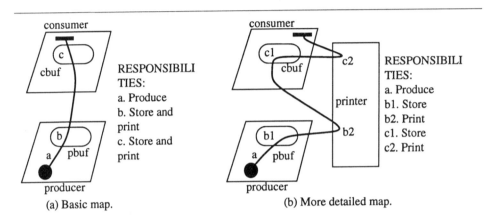

(a) Basic map.   (b) More detailed map.

Figure 5.6 Use case maps for the producer-consumer problem.

Thus maps convey the essence of the behavioural fabric while leaving all the details of interactions uncommitted. Such maps can be used as a starting point for detailed design of the interactions, leading to collaboration graphs like the ones in Figure 5.3. Interaction sequence diagrams like the ones in Figure 5.4 and Figure 5.5 only need to be drawn to make details clear, and then only after the details have solidified as a result of, first, exploring alternatives with maps and, second, capturing details with collaboration graphs.

5.4 DETAILED DESIGN, OPERATION (ISD2)

Maps and the collaboration graphs may be used together to *infer* interaction sequences (Figure 5.7), *without necessarily having to draw the actual interaction sequence diagrams*. For example, in Figure 5.7 the numbered points in the interaction sequence diagram may be inferred as follows:

1. Responsibility a in the map means the producer timeline must have an activity block started along it.

2. The only means of accomplishing responsibility b1 in the map is by means of the store connection pointing at pbuf.

3, 4. The only means of accomplishing responsibility b2 in the map is by means of the chain of print connections in the collaboration graph pointing at pbuf and then at printer.

5. The path between responsibilities b2 and c1 in the map does not specify the control sequence. However, it is clear from the collaboration graph that there is no way of doing it directly from the printer. Control must first return to producer.

6, 7. Now producer must cause responsibility c1 of the map to be performed. From the collaboration graph, the only way of setting this in motion is to give the data to the consumer. The unstore call precedes give on the twin assumptions that when producer is back in control it will no longer have the data in its possession, and that in any case it is desirable to clear out pbuf in preparation for the next *store*.

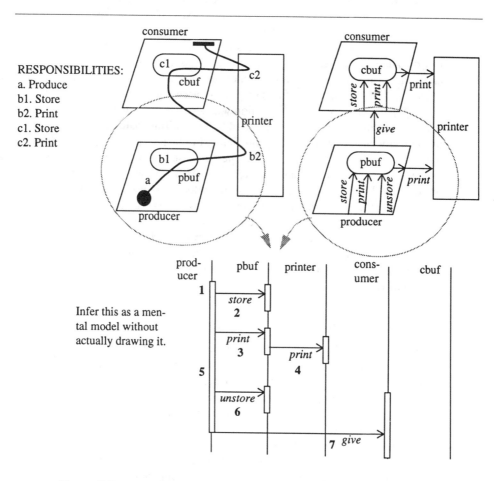

Figure 5.7 Inferring interaction sequences from a map and a collaboration graph.

We are not suggesting that diagrams showing explicit interaction sequences are not useful, but only pointing out that the big picture is better expressed in other ways, and that in cases where this enables the sequences to be inferred easily, actual interaction sequence diagrams are redundant.

5.5 DETAILED DESIGN, ASSEMBLY (CSD)

We will now add structural dynamics to the producer-consumer example starting from the lower level instead of from the abstract perspective of earlier chapters. Our objective in doing so is to give a clear picture of the complexity of approaches to structural dynamics that are built on lower-level concepts.

From a purely-programming perspective, the factors that make a program structurally dynamic may appear to be quite minor. *Necessary* conditions are that (1) dynamic creation and destruction of run-time components occurs in the program and (2) pointers (or other forms of dynamic identifiers) are used to access the components. However, these are not *sufficient* conditions. The distinction with structurally dynamic programs is that pointers (or other forms of identifiers) are used to form shifting patterns of connections between dynamically changing run-time components. In other words, it is how pointers (or other identifiers) are used, not the fact that they are used, that makes a program structurally dynamic. It may therefore take careful analysis of the text of a program to determine whether we should view a program as structurally static or structurally dynamic.

While the programming differences may appear minor, the effect of structural dynamics on design is profound. Suddenly, programs can no longer be understood at the run-time level in terms of fixed collaboration graphs. Must collaboration graphs be abandoned? Must we design in terms of low-level details of pointer manipulations? The answer to both questions is no. However a shift of perspective to a higher design level is required to see the big structural dynamics picture.

5.5.1 The Code Snapshot Model of Structural Dynamics

To see why a shift of perspective is required, let us revisit the structurally static producer-consumer example from a code snapshot perspective. Suppose that instead of the static arrangement in Figure 5.3, we require a more flexible arrangement in which a single buffer object is created when required and destroyed when no longer required. This changes the producer-consumer organization from the one of Figure 5.3, in which data transfer is accomplished by copying data from producer's fixed storage in pbuf to the consumer's in cbuf, to the one of Figure 5.8 (the arrows are identified by the sequence numbers of Figure 5.4 instead of by the names of Figure 5.3, for simplicity). In the new arrangement, data transfer is accomplished by passing visibility of a single, dynamically created buffer object buf from producer to consumer.

Figure 5.8 shows this new organization in terms of *actual components* that would appear at run time, shown in the places where they would exist at run time. For reasons that will become clear in a moment, we call a diagram like this a *code snapshot overlay*. It contains something new: a pair of arrows to indicate which process creates the shared, dynamic buffer object, and which destroys it. These are not conventional connection arrows, in the sense of showing interaction paths between connected components, but rather indications of interactions with a hidden layer that supports creation and destruction. The other arrows are operationally equivalent to the ones in Figure 5.3 (their actual implementation would be different in detail, because interactions would be indirect, through pointers, but this is programming detail that is easily inferred from context).

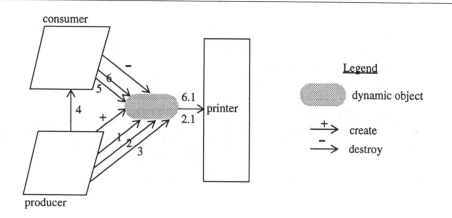

Figure 5.8 Code snapshot overlay of the structurally dynamic producer-consumer.

There are two problems with diagrams like this that show organizations in terms of actual dynamic components:

- They require showing connections from all places in the organization where a dynamic component is created, used, and destroyed to the single place where it exists. Even in the simple case shown in Figure 5.8, many arrows converge on the buffer component from different places in the organization. In practical situations where there may be many dynamic components, diagrams could become black with arrows and thus incomprehensible.
- They do not show the changing visibility of dynamic components over time from different places in the organization, that is part of the essence of structural dynamics. Although Figure 5.8 makes clear that producer creates buf and producer destroys it, and also who performs what operations in what sequence, it gives no indication of the changing visibility of buf to each during the course of the sequence. The sensible intent would be that buf is initially visible to producer but

not consumer, and later visible to consumer but not producer, but Figure 5.8 does not show this.

Figure 5.9 describes structural dynamics explicitly by means of a sequence of *snapshots* of the changing elements of Figure 5.8 as they come into being, are exercised, and then disappear; such a diagram is called a *code snapshot diagram*. These changing elements include not only the dynamic component buf itself, but also the connections to other components that make it visible to those components. Each snapshot shows a configuration that is active for a period of time while its elements are exercised and that then changes as a result of some operation performed while in that configuration. It also shows, by sequence numbers, how each configuration operates while it is active. The arrows here represent actual interactions between run-time components. The reason we called the earlier diagram a code snapshot overlay is now clear. It shows the result of overlaying all the snapshots one on top of the other.

For a small program, a sequence of code snapshots like this clearly describes structural dynamics in terms of how the program actually works at run time. However, designing large systems by drawing diagrams like this would be very unwieldy and would quickly become unmanageable. Therefore, take this diagram only as a means of setting the stage for the introduction of a better method. This does not say that such diagrams might not be useful in an automated tool to write low-level code by drawing pictures of it instead of writing code statements manually. However, that is not system design.

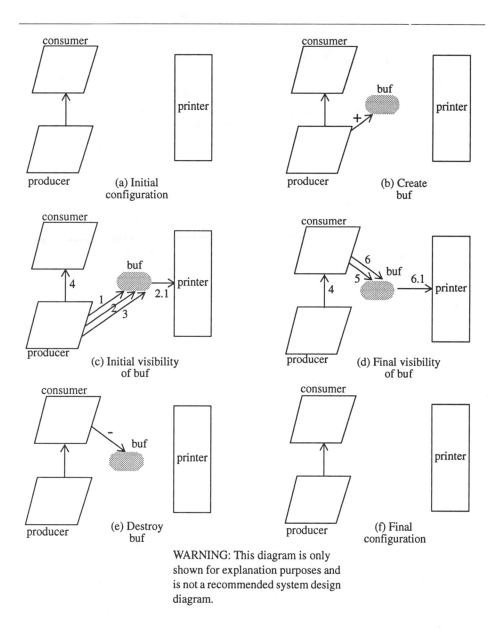

Figure 5.9 Code snapshots of the structurally dynamic producer-consumer.

5.6 HIGH-LEVEL DESIGN, ASSEMBLY (UCM3)

5.6.1 The Slot Model of Structural Dynamics

The slot model shifts our perspective from dynamically changing configurations of *actual* run-time components to fixed configurations of *slots* for them. A slot is a fixed organizational place where a dynamic component can play a role. The concept is that slots are always locally visible where they are shown, but not always occupied. We imagine slots, while they are occupied, as being local components like the local buffer objects in Figure 5.3.

Figure 5.10 is a component context diagram with two slots in it. The slots in Figure 5.10 are intended for a single buffer object that moves from one slot to the other. This is an operational model, not necessarily a description of code (Figure 5.9 provides an accurate description of what actually happens in code, but, as we have observed, is too unwieldy for design purposes). Because component context diagrams are only intended to provide a context for understanding the behavioural fabric, not to describe the fabric itself, we do not get any information from this diagram about behaviour, apart from the fact that slots exist. However, it provides a suitable fixed background for use case maps that show behaviour.

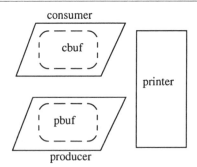

Figure 5.10 Buffer slots.

Figure 5.11 shows that a fixed map can convey the essence of structural dynamics much more compactly than a complicated sequence of snapshots like those in Figure 5.9. Figure 5.11 shows two forms of the map, either one of which conveys the general idea. However (b) illustrates that the form of a map for a static case may have to be changed to accommodate a dynamic version because of the addition of new responsibilities along the path (compare with Figure 5.6(b)).

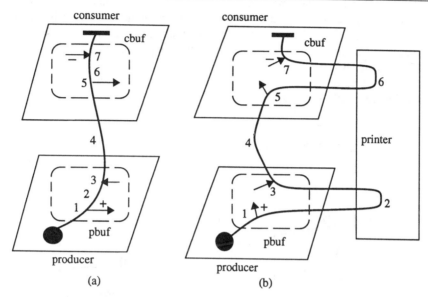

RESPONSIBILITIES:
1. (⟶⁺) An object is created and moves into slot pbuf in producer.
2. Local responsibilities are performed.
3. (⟵) The object moves out of slot pbuf "into the use-case path".
4. The object (implicitly) moves along the use-case path from producer to consumer.
5. (⟶) The object moves "out of the use-case path" into slot cbuf in consumer.
6. Local responsibilities are performed.
7. (⟶) The object moves out of slot cbuf and is destroyed.

Figure 5.11 Structural dynamics with slots and use case paths.

5.7 DETAILED DESIGN, ASSEMBLY (CG2, VG)

Figure 5.12 demonstrates that, because slots are like fixed components when they are occupied, the same collaboration-graph style as for fixed components applies.

Collaboration graphs contain no actual dynamic components, and no create/destroy arrows for them, only the slots that dynamic components may occupy. We showed dynamic components and create/destroy arrows for them in code snapshot diagrams to set the stage, but then recommended these diagrams not be used as system design diagrams because they are too complex and maps make them redundant. This leaves no place for the dynamic components themselves in the design diagrams we have exercised so far. We suggest that in many cases maps and collaboration graphs together provide enough information to write code.

The connections of Figure 5.12 are equivalent to those of Figure 5.3, except with fixed buffers replaced by slots.

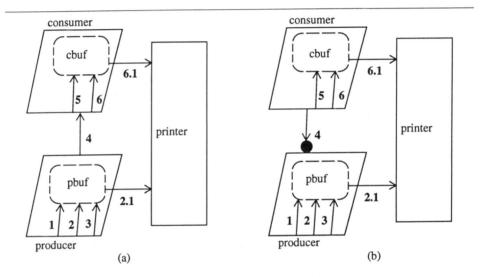

Figure 5.12 Collaboration graph with slots.

Although code snapshot diagrams like Figure 5.9 are redundant for design purposes, now that we can express structural dynamics in a higher-level way with use case maps, a simpler, related diagram can be helpful for programming: a *visibility graph* (Figure 5.13). A visibility graph shows in a single diagram an overlay of the visibility relationships that occur between components over time. Visibility graphs express detailed assembly domain concerns in a way that is close to code. The arrows, called *visibility references*, in these diagrams are drawn with different arrowheads and shown originating *inside* the bodies of components to distinguish them from the connections of collaboration graphs. Fixed visibility references are shown with black arrows and dynamic ones with grey arrows. Visibility references to objects in slots are, by definition, dynamic.

The combination of use case maps, collaboration graphs, and visibility graphs displays all the major design decisions that are needed to get started with conventional programming. Object-oriented programming requires only the addition of classes to provide the fixed components and the dynamic components that will fill the slots.

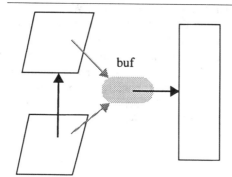

CAUTION:
A view like this is always needed as a mental model, but not necessarily as an actual diagram. However, it useful in complicated cases.

Figure 5.13 A Visibility graph.

5.8 HIGH-LEVEL DESIGN, MANFG. (CRD1)

In this section, we are concerned with showing how to move toward an implementation that includes both object-oriented elements (classes and objects) and real time elements (processes). We are not concerned with using classes as a high level abstraction mechanism for other things (this is an important and powerful use of classes, but is outside the scope of this particular example).

Recall from Chapter 4 that our suite of models aims to help humans reason about how software under design will behave as a system when it eventually runs. Recall also that the role of the manufacturing domain is to provide a design place to put those aspects of infrastructure that enable operational components to be created and to run. Class hierarchies in object oriented programs provide infrastructure of this kind, as do real time executives that support processes.

There are basically two approaches to combining classes, objects, and processes in an implementation. One is to put the processes in the class hierarchy. The other is to leave them out. In either case, a real time executive is required. There are interesting issues associated with the first approach that we defer to Chapter 10 and Chapter 11 . We illustrate only the second approach here. We treat both the real time executive that will support producer and consumer processes and the class hierarchy that will support buffers and the printer as distinct and equal elements of the manufacturing domain.

5.8.1 Processes

Figure 5.14(a) contrasts the treatment of processes with the treatment of the other operational components of the producer-consumer application. Our design diagrams did not include the real time executive as a component, only the processes. This is a decision we made as designers. We could have included it but did not because the diagrams would become black with paths and arrows and thus incomprehensible. We decided instead to treat it as an implicit lower layer, as shown in Figure 5.14(a) (see Chapter 3 for a discussion of layering). The jagged line marks the boundary of a layer on a component context diagram, in this case the boundary between the producer-consumer application and a real time executive. The manufacturing aspect of this layer is that it knows how to create and destroy processes. There is also an operational aspect, namely it schedules processes to run and provides for interprocess communication and synchronization. Part (b) of the figure shows what such an executive would look like if it were included in a collaboration graph in the operation domain.

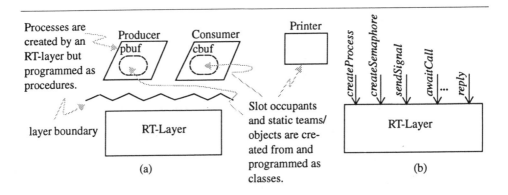

Figure 5.14 Adding concurrency with a real time executive layer.

5.8.2 Classes

Figure 5.15 shows a high-level class relationship diagram that identifies classes for buffers and the printer, without filling in any details. In general, a class relationship diagram identifies classes, inter-class relationships (for example, inheritance), the attributes and methods of classes, and perhaps some relationships between instances of classes (for example, objects of class A use objects of class B). A high-level class relationship diagram omits details (for example, methods).

The printer component is implemented by class `Printer`. The buffer components are implemented by two classes joined by an *isa* relationship: class `PrintingBuffer` and class `BasicBuffer`. The *isa* relationship models inheritance; it means that instances of class `PrintingBuffer` inherit the methods and attributes of class `BasicBuffer`. The advantage of this class organization is that `BasicBuffers` may be used in contexts where printing on devices is not needed. `BasicBuffers` are more general than `PrintingBuffers` because `BasicBuffers` do not need to know about printing devices. The organization of classes has increased the likelihood of reusing the general concept of a buffer in contexts outside this specific example. Class relationship diagrams are primarily concerned with the organization of classes to increase reuse and extensibility. This is the power of object-oriented programming. Later design examples have more interesting class relationship diagrams.

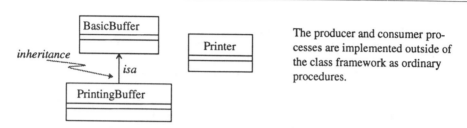

Figure 5.15 A high level class relationship diagram.

Class relationship diagrams are often called "object models" elsewhere and are the central model of many object-oriented design methods [26][3]. A strength of class relationship diagrams for object-oriented design is that they align almost directly with the programming constructs of object-oriented languages. This strength has caused many methods to claim that object-oriented design is seamless because the same concepts can be used for all stages from requirements analysis through to coding. Although it is true that the same *concepts* can be used through all stages, a problem is that the *details* are subject to change once detailed design issues are introduced [18], requiring changing the diagrams that express the concepts.

To insulate high level design diagrams from detailed changes in class hierarchies, we place greater emphasis on models of operation like use case maps in conjunction with relatively sketchy class relationship diagrams like this one, using the latter mainly for recording the concepts that have to be supported. During detailed design we refine such diagrams as a step towards implementation.

5.8.3 Cross-Referencing Manufacturing and Operation/Assembly

Classes are not necessarily synonymous with the teams, processes, objects, and slots of our operation/assembly diagrams. We need to cross-reference them. Any form of cross-referencing that works will do (for example, naming conventions might be sufficient in many cases). To emphasize that some form of cross-reference must be maintained, we show an *allocation table* (Table 5.1). Along the top of the table are operational components (for example, teams, processes, and slots). Along the left side of the table are manufacturing-domain entities (for example, classes). Although the producer and consumer processes are not implemented as classes, the procedures that implement them, namely *producer()* and *consumer()*, are shown as manufacturing-domain entities because they provide descriptions that are analogous to classes. The pbuf and cbuf slots are both filled by instances of the `PrintingBuffer` class. We have included the `BasicBuffer` class in the allocation table and have indented the `PrintingBuffer` class to indicate that it is a subclass of `BasicBuffer`. An entry in the body of table for the superclass `BasicBuffer` means that it is involved in creating operational components (for example, the objects in the pbuf and cbuf slots).

Table 5.1   Allocation Table of Producer-Consumer Example

OP M	Teams	Processes		Slots	
	printer	producer	consumer	pbuf	cbuf
producer() procedure		*			
consumer() procedure			*		
Printer class	*				
*BasicBuffer class				*	*
PrintingBuffer class				*	*

5.9 DETAILED DESIGN, MANFG. (CRD2)

5.9.1 Processes

The RT-Layer has an interface (Figure 5.14(b)) that the application calls to use its services, for example, *createProcess()*, *sendSignal()*, and *awaitCall()*.

Many real time executives are implemented in procedural languages and are linked to an application through call-back procedures that the application registers with the executive. For example, to create a process an application would pass the pointer of a procedure as a parameter to the RT-Layer's *createProcess()* procedure. To run the process, the real time executive would make a call to the procedure that was registered during the *createProcess()* call. Interprocess communication (IPC) provides another example use of the RT-Layer. Recall that IPC is modeled in a collaboration graph using direct connections between processes. This expresses design intent and abstracts from the details of how IPC is implemented. With the RT-Layer of Figure 5.14, IPC would be implemented as follows: A sending process would call *sendSignal()* of the RT-Layer with the identifier of the destination process and the name of a signal as parameters; and the destination process would call *awaitCall()* of the RT-Layer with the name of a signal(s) to wait for as a parameter. The matching of signals, exchange of parameters, and possible synchronization of the processes is implemented by the RT-Layer.

5.9.2 Classes

Figure 5.16 provides a detailed class relationship diagram that is a refinement of the higher level one. The BasicBuffer class has a data attribute called charArray and methods *store()* and *unstore()* for operating on the data attribute. Instances of class PrintingBuffer inherit these properties, but also add a *print()* method for printing the data attribute (see class PrintingBuffer). Through inheritance, instances of class PrintingBuffer can store, unstore, and print their data contents. This is the behaviour that objects filling the cbuf and pbuf slots of Figure 5.12 must support.

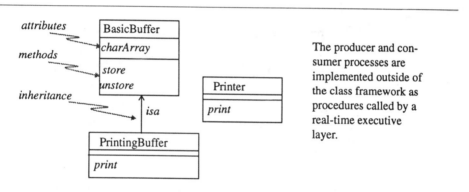

The producer and consumer processes are implemented outside of the class framework as procedures called by a real-time executive layer.

Figure 5.16   Detailed class relationship diagram of the producer-consumer example.

5.10   IMPLEMENTATION (CODE)

This section is for readers who like to follow everything down to the last detail. Other readers may skip it without loss of continuity of the design material. We illustrate implementation-level details using one particular programming language, C++. The ideas are broader than C++, but a concrete example is generally useful to anchor new ideas to something familiar. The source code for the example can be found in Figure 5.17 and Figure 5.18. For more information on C++ see [29] and Appendix B. Section 5.10.1 discusses techniques for writing source code from the models presented in this chapter.

```
// Code shows partial class interfaces. Some scoping issues are
// ignored.

const int max_len = 256;

class BasicBuffer{
public:
    // Interface methods
    void store(char* str);
    void unstore();

protected:
    char charArray[max_len];
};

Printer aPrinter;

class PrintingBuffer: public BasicBuffer{
public:
    // Interface methods
    void print() { aPrinter.print(charArray); }
}

// Identifiers of the producer and consumer processes used
// by the real-time layer to distinguish processes.
ProcessId producerId;
ProcessId consumerId;


// The main body of the producer process. This procedure
// is called by the real time executive.
void producer() {
    PrintingBuffer* pbuf;
    while (True) {
        // Produce an item. Faked here
        pbuf = new PrintingBuffer();

        pbuf->store(ProducerString);
        pbuf->print();
        pbuf->unstore();

        // Send signal named "give" to the consumer process
        // The buffer is a parameter.
        sendSignal(consumerId, "give", (int *)pbuf);
        pbuf = Null;
    }
}
```

Figure 5.17 Source code of producer-consumer

```
// The main body of the consumer process. This procedure
// is called by the real time executive.
void consumer() {
    PrintingBuffer* cbuf;
    while (True) {
        // Wait for the signal "give".
        cbuf = (PrintingBuffer *)
                awaitCall(consumerId, "give");
        cbuf->store("I am in the consumer");

        // Release any callers.
        reply(consumerId); // release producer

        // Local responsibilities
        cbuf->print();
        // Destroy the buffer
        delete *cbuf;
        // Empty the slot
        cbuf = Null;
    }
}

main(){
// Create Processes.
    consumerId = createProcess(consumer);
    producerId = createProcess(producer);
}
```

Figure 5.18 Source code of producer-consumer
cont'd

5.10.1 Guidelines for Developing Code from Diagrams

The technique for developing code from diagrams is to use all the relevant figures jointly as guides: the use case map (Figure 5.11), the collaboration graph (Figure 5.12), the visibility graph (Figure 5.13) and the class relationship diagram (Figure 5.16), selecting information from each as appropriate. For example:

- How to program interactions between components follows from the collaboration graphs (for example, Figure 5.4), and component context diagrams (like Figure 5.14 showing the use of a real time executive as a layer) and how the components are manufactured (for example, the implementation of processes as procedures). The code below shows how the *give* interaction (Figure 5.4) between a producer process and a consumer process is programmed. The code involves a *sendSignal()* call from a producer process to the RT-Layer and an *awaitCall()* call from a consumer process to the RT-Layer. The RT-Layer implements the interprocess communication and

process synchronization. Expert C programmers will recognize the forced type con-
version (coercion) in these lines. Others should consult a programming book if they
are worried about the details.

```
// The main body of the producer process. This procedure
// is called by the real time executive.
void producer() {
PrintingBuffer* pbuf;
while (True) {
   ...
   // Send signal named "give" to the consumer process.
   // The buffer is a parameter.
   sendSignal(consumerId, "give", (int *)pbuf);
   ...
// The main body of the consumer process. This procedure
// is called by the real time executive.
void consumer() {
PrintingBuffer* cbuf;
while (True) {
   // Wait for the signal "give". The cbuf variable is set
   // as a return parameter.
   cbuf = (PrintingBuffer *) awaitCall(consumerId, "give");
   ...
   // Release any callers.
   reply(consumerId);
```

- How to program the dynamic components themselves comes from the interfaces of
  the slots they must occupy (collaboration graphs) and the responsibilities they must
  perform there (use case maps). For example, a buffer object to fill the two slots in
  Figure 5.12 must have an interface to support the operations implied by all the connections to *both* slots (store, unstore, print) and be capable of using these to perform
  the responsibilities required by the use-case paths (in this simple case, the operators
  are one-to-one with the responsibilities, but this is not necessarily true in general).
  The class relationship diagrams indicate how the interfaces are divided among
  classes that are related by inheritance. From the source code:

```
class BasicBuffer{
    public:
    // Interface methods common to cbuf and pbuf slots
    void store(char *str);
    void unstore()
}

//PrintingBuffer is a subclass of BasicBuffer
class PrintingBuffer: public BasicBuffer{
    public:
    / Interface methods
    void print();
}
```

- How to program *interactions* with dynamic components once they are established in slots (that is, once all required pointers are known locally) follows straightforwardly from collaboration graphs. Programming the interactions of Figure 5.12 requires only that the processes have a pointer for referencing buffer objects when needed. The source code below shows how a producer process sends messages *store()*, *print()* and *unstore()* to the buffer object in the pbuf slot.

```
// The main body of the producer process. This procedure
// is called by the real-time executive.
void producer() {
PrintingBuffer* pbuf;
while (True) {
...
    pbuf->store(ProducerString);
    pbuf->print();
    pbuf->unstore();
```

The *sequences* of creating, moving, and destroying dynamic components are determined by paths in a map (for example, Figure 5.11). To help the reader to understand this code in relation to the map, we identify the following responsibility points in the map of Figure 5.11 with specific lines of the code example:

1. ($\xrightarrow{+}$) An object is created and moves into slot pbuf in producer.

```
void producer(){
    PrintingBuffer* pbuf;
    pbuf = new PrintingBuffer();
```

The pbuf variable of the producer procedure identifies the slot pbuf in the source code. The variable is a pointer to instances of class PrintingBuffer. The result of *new* is an identifier of a new buffer object.

2. Local responsibilities are performed.

```
void producer(){ ...
    pbuf->store(ProducerString);
    pbuf->print();
    pbuf->unstore();
```

The calls *store()*, *print()*, and *unstore()* are sent from the producer procedure to the buffer object identified by the pbuf variable.

3. ($\longleftarrow$) The object moves out of slot **pbuf** "into the use-case path".

```
void producer(){...
    // Send signal named "give" to the consumer process with
    // the identifier of the buffer as a parameter.
    sendSignal(consumerId, "give", (int *)pbuf);
    pbuf = Null;
```

The identifier of the buffer object referenced by the pbuf variable is sent to the consumer process as a parameter of the *sendSignal()* call to the RT-Layer. Note the convention of setting the pbuf variable to Null when implementing a move-leave operation (for example, to implement the producer forgetting about the buffer object it is "sending"). This convention (required by the map) helps to avoid mutex problems due to aliasing across process boundaries.

4. The object (implicitly) moves along the use-case path from producer to consumer. The movement occurs as parameter passing in the *sendSignal()* call (see **3** above).

5. (⟶) The object moves "out of the use-case path" into slot cbuf in consumer.

```
void consumer() {
    PrintingBuffer* cbuf;
    while (True) {
    // Wait for the signal "give". The cbuf variable is set as
    // a return parameter.
    cbuf = (PrintingBuffer *) awaitCall(consumerId, "give");
```

The cbuf variable of the consumer procedure identifies the cbuf slot in the source code. The variable is a pointer to instances of class PrintingBuffer.

6. Local responsibilities are performed

```
void consumer() {
    ...
    cbuf->store("I am in the consumer");
    ...
    cbuf->print();
```

Calls *store()* and *print()* are sent to the object identified by the cbuf variable.

7. (⟹) The object moves out of slot cbuf and is destroyed.

```
void consumer() { ...
    ...
    // Destroy the buffer
    delete *cbuf;
    // Empty the slot
    cbuf = Null;
```

The delete statement destroys the buffer object identified by the cbuf variable. The cbuf pointer is set to Null for safety.

5.11 SUMMARY

In this chapter we have:

- Toured some design models to show their nature and relationships.
- Identified the key models as *use case maps, class relationship diagrams, collaboration graphs* and *visibility graphs*.
- Identified that cross reference must be maintained between *use case maps* and *class relationship diagrams*, but the specific technique used in this chapter (allocation tables) is incidental and not fundamental. Interaction sequence diagrams and code snapshot diagrams are derived diagrams in this suite, not primary design ones (they are useful for showing complicated details).
- Showed the power of the abstraction techniques of use case maps for *structural dynamics* by working from the bottom up to demonstrate how matters are much more complicated at the detailed design level without maps. Showed that paths in maps for structurally static cases may have to be rerouted to accommodate structurally dynamic variations because of additional responsibilities along them. Identified *visibility graphs* as useful models to supplement these descriptions.
- Linked the concepts to programming by showing some code fragments.

Case Study: A Conventional Object-Oriented Application from an Unconventional Perspective

*T*he focus of this chapter is on showing how to work with use case maps to help with the design of a representative object-oriented application, a graphical user interface system called BGETool. A set of use case maps expresses the model-view-controller paradigm. The case study uses all the design models in a coordinated way at all levels of design and implementation (some code is also provided).

The design example is a simple drawing tool called Basic Graphical Editor Tool (BGETool), to be built on top of the user interface framework of Smalltalk [16]. The choice of Smalltalk has an effect on the design of the tool because we use the Model-View-Controller (MVC) paradigm of Smalltalk as a design pattern for the tool's organization and behaviour. In particular, we use the MVC use case pattern presented in Chapter 2 as a repeated building block for the high-level design of the tool in the Operation domain. This simplifies design because we are reusing an existing design pattern. The resulting use case map of the tool guides further design. In the case of Smalltalk, use of the MVC pattern also simplifies implementation because the pattern is built into Smalltalk's user interface framework for reuse at the programming level.

Some readers may recognize the similarity between the BGETool presented in this case study and the public domain Smalltalk program called HotDraw [19]. This is not a coincidence. The BGETool case study began as a reverse engineering and re-engineering exercise with use case maps for HotDraw. In the study, we reverse engineered HotDraw into a use case map model (high-level design) and then redesigned and prototyped some aspects of the redesign using the maps as a guide. In this chapter, we present the case study as though it were a forward-engineering exercise, beginning with use cases and pro-ceeding to use case maps through to detailed collaboration graphs. It would be inaccurate to say that the design and design process we present in this chapter is not greatly influ-enced by the existence of HotDraw. We believe, however, that the case study is represent-ative of how use case maps can be used for forward engineering of object-oriented systems.

The design sequence we follow is outlined in Figure 6.1. The purpose is not to be prescriptive about the design sequence but to illustrate one possible approach. The work items we develop during requirements and high-level design are (1) use cases and inter-face mock-ups, (2) class relationship diagrams, and (3) use case maps. During detailed design we develop (4) refinements to class relationship diagrams, (5) collaboration graphs and (6) visibility graphs and source code.

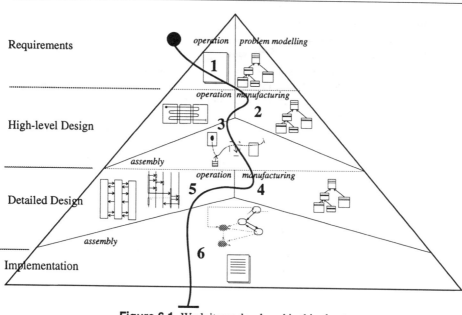

Figure 6.1 Work items developed in this chapter.

6.1 USE CASES AND INTERFACE MOCK-UP

The BGETool behaves similarly to many mouse-based drawing tools. Simple drawings may be created using a number of primitive figures, such as text, circles, rectangles, lines, and arrows. The figures of a drawing may be copied, moved, reshaped, deleted, and shuf-fled on top of one another. Drawings created with the tool may be saved to disk and reloaded for further editing. Commercial drawing tools (and even HotDraw itself) have far greater capability than is outlined here for the BGETool. However, the behaviour of the BGETool is enough to illustrate the design process.

A good place to start design is with a mock-up of the application as seen by the user. This can be done using hand-drawings for simple cases and prototyping tools for more complex ones. The mock-ups can be used for communication between users of the system and the designers of it. For some systems, the user may be another application or even a piece of hardware. This does not make a mock-up of the user interface any less important, it only changes the method of representing it.

A possible user interface of BGETool is shown in Figure 6.2. BGETool has three rectangular areas inside a Smalltalk window. The areas are a drawing area, a menu bar, and a tool palette. The title bar is standard to Smalltalk and provides a quit button (on the left), a full-screen expansion button (on the right), a label (Drawing), and a menu of window operations (not shown). Figures are drawn and manipulated in the drawing area. Tools in the tool palette affect the interpretation of user input in the drawing area. The tools are: a selection tool, a shuffle up tool, a shuffle down tool, an eraser tool, a line creation tool, an arrow creation tool, a rectangle creation tool, an ellipse creation tool and a text creation tool. The operations save, load, undo, cut, copy, paste, move and resize are not part of the tool palette and must be activated through some other means. Undo, cut, copy, and paste are in a pop-up menu in the drawing area. Save and load are in a pull-down menu in the menu bar. These two menus are separated because save and load operate on entire drawings and the other operations effect only the currently selected figures in the drawing area. Move and resize will be invoked by direct manipulation of the figures.

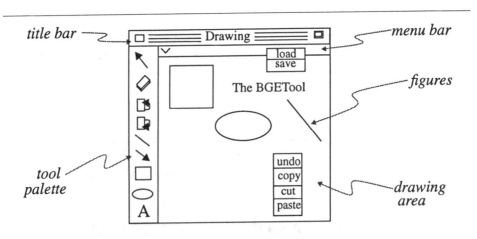

Figure 6.2 Mock-up of BGETool user interface.

Drawing tools are so common that the above discussion gives a good idea of how a user will interact with the BGETool. However, systematic development of use cases is still important to serve as a communication mechanism between designers and users while refining requirements, and to act as documentation of the operation of a system to drive further design. In support of this latter purpose, it is important to find and document the key different use cases that will have a strong effect on future design decisions. This can be a difficult task since the "future design decisions" have not yet been made. This is but one example of the chicken-and-egg problems that designers face throughout all stages of development. To find key use cases, designers rely on experience, iteration, and heuristics, such as "develop use cases for the major functional requirements of a system" or "develop use cases that will exercise all the important paths through the components of the system."

We have selected the following use cases (Figure 6.3): *load drawing*, *select tool*, *select figure*, and *cut figure*. These use cases can be seen as a decomposition of the larger use case: *load drawing and cut a figure from it*. These use cases result in a rather complete set of paths through the high-level organization of the BGETool. This does not mean they cover all uses of the system, for example others might be *save a drawing*, *create a figure*, *shuffle a figure*, *de-select a figure*, *undo a cut*, and so on. However, the ones we have selected cover the paths that drive the key design decisions. Other use cases might be helpful to verify these design decisions.

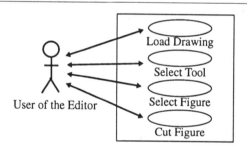

Figure 6.3 Use cases of the BGETool

The use cases are presented in Figure 6.4 along with a sequence of snapshots of the user interface of the BGETool as each use case unfolds. Presenting mock-ups of the user interface like this makes the use cases more concrete and aids in communication.

Implicit in the pictures of these use cases are a number of design decisions. From the *load drawing* use case, the currently selected tool is highlighted in the tool palette by drawing a box around it, the selection tool is the default tool when the tool starts up, and dialogue boxes are used for user input. From the *select tool* use case, tools have different cursor images to provide visual feedback to the user. From the *select figure* use case, a selected figure has handles displayed on the edges of a rectangular box that encloses it. It is by manipulating these handles that a figure may be resized.

A. Load Drawing Use Case

The user of the editor pulls down the menu from the menu bar and selects load, a dialogue box appears, the user enters the name of a drawing file into the dialogue box and the drawing is loaded into the BGETool. Loading a drawing results in the figures being displayed in the drawing area and the title of the drawing appearing in the title bar.

B. Select Tool Use Case

The user of the editor clicks the mouse over the selection tool in the tool palette area. The selection tool is highlighted and the cursor changes to the selection tool image.

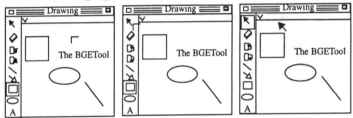

C. Select Figure Use Case

The user of the editor positions the cursor over a figure and clicks the mouse. The figure becomes highlighted with filled rectangular boxes (handles) on its edges.

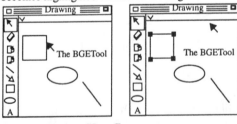

Figure 6.4 Details of use cases.

D. Cut Figure Use Case

The user of the editor selects cut from the drawing area and the selected figure is erased.

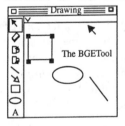
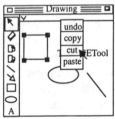
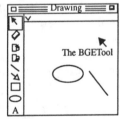

6.2 SOME CLASSES

A purpose of object-oriented analysis during high-level design is to record the classes (and the relationships among them) that model the problem. This aids in problem domain understanding, serves as a vocabulary of essential design concepts and acts as a basis for doing more detailed class-based design in the Manufacturing domain. We keep this analysis rather lightweight (free of detail) at this point, so that the changes that are inevitable during design refinement can be easily made.

Here are some guidelines for the use of class relationship diagrams during early design:

- use class relationship diagrams to document the static entities and relationships of the problem domain,
- use inheritance sparingly, and
- downplay behaviour by ignoring methods — they can be fleshed out later.

It is impossible to completely ignore the behaviour of classes when developing class relationship diagrams. If a class has no behaviour, what is its purpose? The point is that *details* of behaviour must not be allowed to dominate thinking during problem understanding and high-level design with class relationship diagrams. We have found that ignoring methods in class relationship diagrams during early design helps to keep details from entering the picture too soon. For high-level design, employ use case maps to express behaviour because they present a more abstract view of it than details in class relationship diagrams. More detailed class relationship diagrams that include methods are needed at later stages for designing flexible and extensible organizations of classes, perhaps by applying patterns of the kind described in [14].

During high-level design, the first classes may be found in the statement of requirements, user interface mock-ups, and use case analysis. Figure 6.5 presents a first pass at some classes and inheritance relationships for the BGETool (see Appendix A for the complete class relationship notation). At this stage we think there will be two interrelated hierarchies in the BGETool: one for tools and one for figures; and we identify two superclasses for each hierarchy, a Tool class and a Figure class. These superclasses contain behaviour that is common to all their subclasses. The subclasses of Tool and Figure align with the objects seen in the user interface of the tool. The hierarchies seem like good ones because the subclass/superclass relationships read naturally; for example, a RectangleFigure *isa* Figure and a SelectTool *isa* Tool.

Other classes include a Drawing class. An instance of a Drawing will be a container of instances of class Figure. The need for a figure container was identified in the *load drawing* use case. There is also a class identified for each of the rectangular screen areas of the tool, for example, DrawingArea, ToolPalette, and MenuBar classes. These classes highlight the importance of the three areas of the BGETool, but we have not assigned specific behaviour to them yet. Finally, there is a Handles class but its position in the class relationship diagram is left open. With the open issues noted, we proceed.

Notice, that we have not included the user interface classes that we get from Small-talk, such as dialogue boxes, cursors, menus and windows, because we are treating Small-talk as a layer. Experienced Smalltalk programmers can recognize these classes as fundamental to Smalltalk; others must consult documentation.

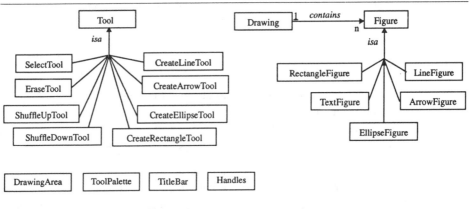

Figure 6.5 A first cut at some classes.

It may be beneficial at this point to add depth to our class relationship diagrams by introducing some intermediate and abstract classes. A benefit of introducing more abstract classes, beyond the reuse opportunities they give, is that the vocabulary of design concepts becomes simpler. However, the reader is cautioned against over engineering the class relationship diagrams at this early stage.

Figure 6.6 is a refinement of the first cut at the classes given in Figure 6.5; the delta between the figures is highlighted in Figure 6.6. The PolygonFigure class is added as a superclass of RectangleFigure and LineFigure to reuse some basic line-drawing behaviour. For similar reasons, the LineFigure class is made a superclass of the ArrowFigure class. Also, we have replaced the separate figure-creation tool classes of Figure 6.5 with a single class, called FigureCreationTool. The FigureCreationTool class has an attribute figureToCreate that will be set at runtime according to the figure selected for creation from the tool palette.

This latter modification was made in anticipation of the types of extensions that the BGETool framework will support. It seems likely that users of the framework would like to add new figures, such as curved lines and triangles. The original class relationship diagram of Figure 6.5 requires that a new tool-creation class be added for each new figure type. The new scheme simplifies the addition of new figures because a new class is not needed to create each new figure. Extensions to a framework are simplified when the additions are localized. The new scheme requires only an abstract protocol between the FigureCreationTool class and the figures it is to create, the details of which we will ignore for now.

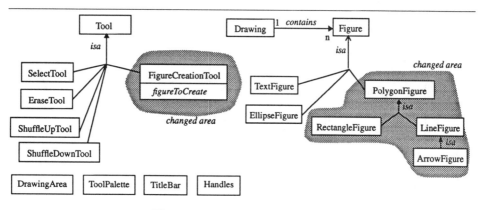

Figure 6.6 A second cut at the classes.

6.3 USE CASE MAPS

The Model-View-Controller (MVC) paradigm is a common one for graphical Smalltalk applications, which we expressed in an uncommon way in Chapter 2 with use case maps. Here we refine and apply the MVC maps of Chapter 2 to describe the high-level design of the BGETool in relation to the use cases of Section 6.1. We will see that applying a reusable design pattern like the MVC is a powerful lever for design and that use case maps can be a useful tool. In this case, the pattern defines the high-level design of the system and thus influences all later design stages. Our purpose here is to show the use of an existing design pattern, not to develop the pattern itself, which is a complex and highly iterative design process of its own.

Before presenting the use case maps of the BGETool, we review the generic MVC pattern (see Figure 6.7, which repeats Figure 2.18). Recall that an MVC team separates concerns into user input, user output and application data management. These concerns are divided among three components as follows: Controllers manage user input, Views display application data on output devices, and Models manage application data. Views must display the current state of the application data managed by the Model, so changes to a Model's data must be propagated to the Views in an MVC team. An AND-fork models the propagation of Model data changes to Views because this expresses the requirement that the outgoing paths that propagate the changes are taken in any arbitrary order. The AND-fork defers the issue of how the propagation is implemented. In Chapter 11 we present a layering pattern for implementing this propagation that takes advantage of a built-in Smalltalk service for propagating changes from sources to dependents called the *dependency mechanism* (to indicate this in a map, the AND fork is replaced by a layer fold). However, for the maps of this chapter we stick with the simple AND fork; Smalltalk experts may read the AND forks in this chapter as implying invocation of the dependency mechanism.

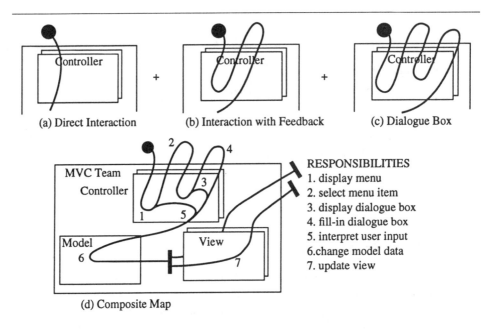

(a) Direct Interaction   (b) Interaction with Feedback   (c) Dialogue Box

MVC Team
Controller

Model
6

View

RESPONSIBILITIES
1. display menu
2. select menu item
3. display dialogue box
4. fill-in dialogue box
5. interpret user input
6. change model data
7. update view

(d) Composite Map

Figure 6.7 The generic MVC pattern.

User interface applications built using the MVC pattern often consist of several interrelated MVC teams. These MVC teams define the high-level organization of a system and act as framework for more detailed design. The individual teams can result from assigning a team to each distinct area of the screen. For example, the BGETool would have an MVC team for each of the tool palette, drawing area and menu bar sections of the tool. Figure 6.8 names the MVC teams, giving an iconic representation of their high-level design, and shows the area of concern for each on the user interface of the BGETool. The teams and their responsibilities are as follows:

- The ToolMVC team manages interactions in the tool palette area. Users select a new tool to use by selecting it with the mouse. The selected tool becomes the new current tool.
- The EditorMVC team manages the sets of figures, called drawings, created with the tool. This includes loading a drawing for editing and storing a drawing away (see the pop-up menu). The team is responsible for displaying the name of the current drawing in the name stripe of the BGETool.

- The DrawingMVC team manages user operations against the figures that are currently selected (that is, have handles displayed). The current drawing changes as a result of a load operation in the EditorMVC team. The team operates in the drawing area of the tool.

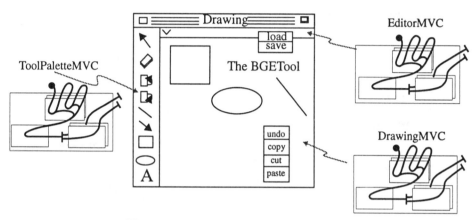

Figure 6.8 Areas of concern for BGETool teams.

Figure 6.9 is a component context diagram for the tool. Aside from the use case map of the generic MVC pattern, this is the first operational design diagram we have drawn of the BGETool. A context diagram shows only the components and their containment relationships. Use case maps are drawn over a component context diagram to express high-level behaviour. In this example, we first describe the component context diagram, we then develop a use case map for each of teams, and then we combine the individual team use case maps into a map spanning the context diagram of the system. We can follow this divide-and-conquer approach because the MVC design pattern has resulted in a nice partitioning of our system into three relatively independent teams. Without such a partitioning, one would first develop use case maps across the system as a whole and, through a process of map factoring and component decomposition, eventually arrive at a point where the major teams of a system can be reasoned about independently. The availability of a tried-and-tested design pattern, like the MVC, has saved us a good deal of work.

The component context diagram of the BGETool, Figure 6.9, is more specific than the context diagram of the generic MVC design pattern given in Chapter 2. In particular, the Controllers and Views of the teams are not replicated. This is because there is only one view of the data in any of the windows. For example, there is only one view of the tools in the tool palette, and only one view of the figures in the drawing area. The use case maps that follow will further refine the components of the BGETool.

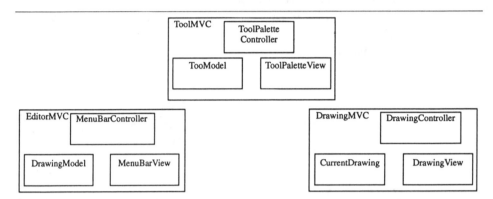

Figure 6.9 Component context diagram of the BGETool.

The responsibilities of the components in Figure 6.9 are as follows:

- ToolMVC: The ToolPaletteController handles mouse operations in the tool palette area, the ToolModel manages the set of tools, and the ToolPaletteView displays the tools — which includes highlighting the currently selected tool.
- EditorMVC: The MenuBarController handles mouse operations in the menu bar, the DrawingModel manages the set of all drawings created with the tool, and the MenuBarView displays the name of the currently selected drawing.
- DrawingMVC: The DrawingController handles mouse operations in the drawing area, the CurrentDrawing manages the set of figures in the drawing area, and the DrawingView displays those figures in the drawing area — which includes highlighting the currently selected figures.

We will now develop a use case map for each of the MVC teams identified. The paths in the maps come from the paths in the generic MVC map (Figure 6.7) and the use cases developed for Figure 6.4. Refer back to Figure 6.4 to see the affect on the user interface at places where the use case paths travel outside a the system boundary. With the aid of use case maps, the components in the context diagram, Figure 6.9, will be refined into more specific types, and their contents and responsibilities will be elaborated. Also, the paths through the generic MVC design pattern will be modified for the specifics of the BGETool. In a loose way, one may think of the MVC design pattern as a class defining the general organization and behaviour of an MVC team, and think of the teams of the BGE-Tool as specific instances of the MVC. The differences in the design of the BGETool from the generic MVC pattern may be thought of as specializations required to use the generic MVC pattern in a specific circumstance.

6.3.1 The EditorMVC Team and Load Drawing Use Case

Figure 6.10 is a use case map of EditorMVC team. The path in the map traces the Load Drawing use case.

The components of the EditorMVC team differ from the generic MVC team in the following ways. First, a pool, called Drawings, has been added to the DrawingModel. This pool contains the Drawings (a drawing is a set of figures) that may be edited with the tool. While in the pool the Drawings are inactive, a Drawing must be taken from the pool and be deposited in a slot elsewhere in the model to become active. Showing the pool in the design diagram makes the management of its contents explicit; we left this detail out of the maps of the generic MVC team. The DrawingModel is modeled as an object, because it is primitive, that is, it does not have any design decomposition at this level of abstraction. Drawing a pool inside of an object means that the object is responsible for managing the pool, not that the object has internal structure for doing so. The MenuBarView is also modeled as an object. The MenuBarController is a team because it has an internal slot, called DialogueBox. An object in the DialogueBox slot is responsible for displaying a form for the user to enter the name of a drawing to edit. The use of a slot makes the MenuBarController a more reusable component because different objects can fill the DialogueBox slot to make the controller behave differently.

The use case path shown is a refinement of the use case path Dialogue Box of the generic MVC map (see Figure 6.7). This path has three interactions with a user. In the first, the user invokes a menu; in the second, the user selects an menu item; in the third, the user fills in a dialogue box (in this case to enter the name a file containing a drawing to edit).

Depending on the name entered by the user a different path will be taken out of the OR fork before responsibility $A6$. The top path is taken if the precondition is that the drawing entered by the user in the dialogue box already exists. The bottom path is taken if the precondition is that it does not exist, in which case the drawing entered by the user must be created and added to the Drawings pool. After the paths rejoin, the selected drawing object is added to the path (move-stay). The Drawings pool has changed as a result of responsibility $A6$, so dependents of the DrawingModel must be informed via the AND fork. The drawing object will flow along all the branches of this fork. The MenuBarView displays the name of the new drawing object. We will return to the lower branch of the fork when we combine the use case maps of the individual teams into a use case map of the system.

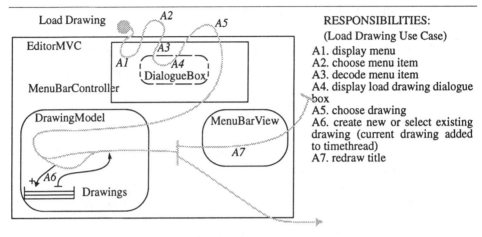

RESPONSIBILITIES:
(Load Drawing Use Case)
A1. display menu
A2. choose menu item
A3. decode menu item
A4. display load drawing dialogue box
A5. choose drawing
A6. create new or select existing drawing (current drawing added to timethread)
A7. redraw title

Figure 6.10 The EditorMVC team and Load Drawing use case.

6.3.2 The ToolMVC Team and Select Tool Use Case

The ToolMVC team and the Select Tool use case path are shown in Figure 6.11. All the components of the ToolMVC team are modeled as objects: We will not examine the internal structure of these components at this level of design.

The Select Tool use case path is a refinement of the Direct Interaction use case path of the generic MVC map (see Figure 6.7). The use case path shows that the only interaction with the user occurs when the user selects a tool from the tool palette using the mouse.

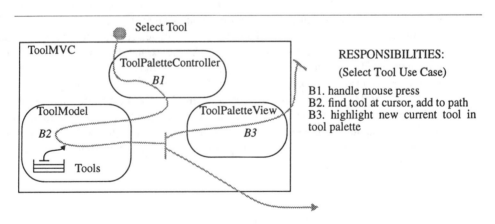

RESPONSIBILITIES:
(Select Tool Use Case)

B1. handle mouse press
B2. find tool at cursor, add to path
B3. highlight new current tool in tool palette

Figure 6.11 The ToolMvc team and the Select Tool use case.

The selected tool object is added to the path at responsibility *B2* (move-stay) of Figure 6.7. This changes the ToolModel data and the AND fork passes on the result. The selected tool object flows along all the branches of this fork. The move-stay of the selected tool object means that it still remains in the pool. This simplifies the management of the pool because the selected tool object need not be returned to the pool when it is finished role playing (in other words, when it is finished occupying slots along the path). We will return to the use case path leaving the ToolMVC team when we stand back to examine the system-level use case map of the BGETool.

6.3.3 The DrawingMVC Team with Select Figure and Cut Figure Use Cases

Figure 6.12 is a use case map of the DrawingMVC team and the use case paths Select Figure and Cut Figure. The DrawingController team has an internal slot for the CurrentTool. The CurrentTool responds to mouse clicks in the drawing area; different tools (selected from the tool palette) react to mouse clicks in different ways. The assumption of Figure 6.12 is that the CurrentTool slot is filled with a selection tool object. The CurrentDrawing is a slot because different drawings may be edited with the tool at different times. We will see how and when the CurrentDrawing slot is filled when we examine the system-level use case map of the BGETool. The Figures pool, managed by the CurrentDrawing, contains all the figures that are in the currently edited drawing. Finally, the DrawingView is modeled as an object.

The Select Figure use case path is a refinement of the Direct Interaction use case path of the generic MVC map (see Figure 6.7). The user selects a figure with a single mouse click and, ultimately, handles are displayed on the figure to mark it as selected. At responsibility *C3*, handle objects for the selected figure are added to the Figures pool and the view notified. At *C4* the new handles are displayed. This behaviour suggests that from the perspective of the DrawingView, handles are to be treated as types of figures, because there are no special responsibilities for displaying handles.

Before *C3* there is a stub along the Select Figure use case path. This stub collapses a piece of the path; the piece will be expanded when we examine the internals of the DrawingController team (Section 6.3.5).

The Cut Figure use case path is a refinement of the Interaction With Feedback path of the generic MVC map. At responsibility *D5*, the selected figure is removed from the Figures pool and destroyed. At *D6* the display is updated to erase the cut figure.

For the BGETool, multiple paths on the same diagram, as in Figure 6.7, do not imply path concurrency. The paths cannot be concurrent because we know that we are designing a sequential system.

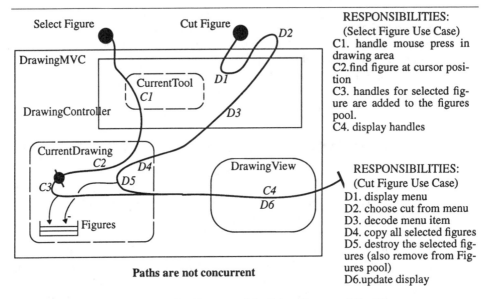

Figure 6.12 The DrawingMVC team and the Select Figure and Cut Figure use cases.

The design of the three MVC teams just presented is a result of applying the standard MVC map to the design of the BGETool. We now use these teams to illustrate two points: that individual maps can be combined into larger composite maps, and that individual maps can be zoomed into to expose more detail.

6.3.4 Linking the MVC Teams into a Composite Use Case Map

A power of use case maps is the ability to represent large portions of system on a single diagram. Figure 6.13 is a high-level use case map of the BGETool. The figure shows how to combine the EditorMVC, ToolMVC and DrawingMVC maps into one map. We only include enough paths to give the general idea (the Cut Figure path is missing).

The teams are linked in the following ways. There is an interteam path from the ToolMVC team to the DrawingMVC team. The purpose of this path is to enable a newly selected tool to be deposited into the CurrentTool slot of the DrawingController. Recall that a newly selected tool flows along the Select Tool path and that the behaviour of the current tool modifies the behaviour of the DrawingController in response to mouse clicks in the drawing area. There is another inter-team path from the EditorMVC team to the DrawingMVC team. The purpose of this path is to enable a newly selected drawing object to flow from the Drawings pool of the EditorMVC to fill the CurrentDrawing slot of the DrawingMVC team. After a new drawing object is installed into the CurrentDrawing slot the AND fork fires to update the display with the figures of the new drawing.

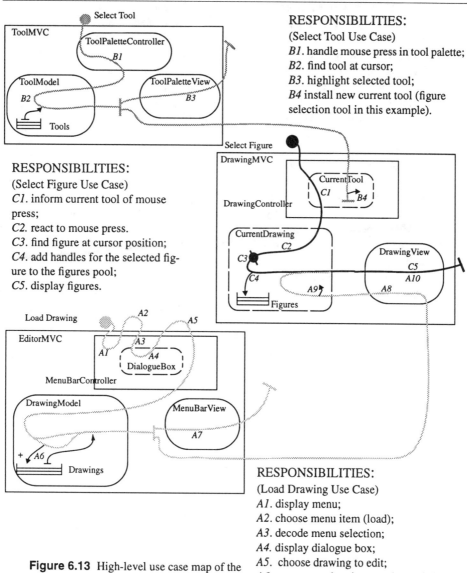

RESPONSIBILITIES:
(Select Tool Use Case)
B1. handle mouse press in tool palette;
B2. find tool at cursor;
B3. highlight selected tool;
B4 install new current tool (figure selection tool in this example).

RESPONSIBILITIES:
(Select Figure Use Case)
C1. inform current tool of mouse press;
C2. react to mouse press.
C3. find figure at cursor position;
C4. add handles for the selected figure to the figures pool;
C5. display figures.

Figure 6.13 High-level use case map of the BGETool.

RESPONSIBILITIES:
(Load Drawing Use Case)
A1. display menu;
A2. choose menu item (load);
A3. decode menu selection;
A4. display dialogue box;
A5. choose drawing to edit;
A6. create new drawing or select existing drawing and add to the use case path;
A7. update name stripe;
A8. update;
A9. install new current drawing;
A10. display figures.

There is another inter-team path from the EditorMVC team to the DrawingMVC team. The purpose of this path is to enable a newly selected drawing object to flow fromt- the Drawings pool of the EditorMVC to fill the CurrentDrawing slot of the DrawingMVC team. After a new drawing object is installed into the CurrentDrawing slot the AND fork fires to update the display with the figures of the new drawing.

Diagrams, like Figure 6.13, are meant to explain the operation and organization of systems as a whole at a high level of abstraction. They are useful for design because they can guide detailed development, as we show subsequently. They are useful for mainte- nance because they document design intentions that can remain stable relative to more detailed changes.

An important issue that may have performance implications is: When should objects to fill slots such as CurrentTool and CurrentDrawing be created? We have presented no use case paths to show the creation of objects to fill the Tools pool in the ToolMVC of Figure 6.13, but have implicitly assumed they would follow a pattern similar to that of the Drawings pool in the EditorMVC in the same figure, in which objects are created as needed and then placed in a pool from which slots may be filled. The question is: Should objects be created as needed in this way, or should default objects be created during a setup phase, leaving it to later to add contents as needed by the path context? The approach of creating them as needed may have performance penalties. The default-object approach requires an initialization path at setup time to create the default objects and to populate the slots with them (an example of such a path for a different example is given in Chapter 10, Section 10.3). We can use portions of the paths we have already designed to fill the slots with default objects during system setup. For example, the portion of the Load Drawing use case path beginning in the DrawingModel may be used to create a default drawing object and install it in the CurrentDrawing slot. In Section 6.6 we show the source code to make this happen.

6.3.5 Zooming into a Map

Figure 6.14 shows more detail of the map for the DrawingMVC team. The figure expands the stub seen in Figure 6.12 and adds more internal structure to the DrawingController team. As seen previously, the DrawingController has a CurrentTool slot. The CurrentTool slot allows the response of the DrawingController to user input to adapt dynamically to the selected tool. For example, the eraser tool causes figures to be deleted, but the selection tool marks figures as selected so that they become the focus of the next operation.

New to the DrawingController is the HandlesFigure team, that in previous diagrams, we choose to suppress as detail. The HandlesFigure team accounts for the behaviour that occurs when a selected figure has one of its handles manipulated. For example, dragging a corner handle on a rectangle causes the rectangle to be expanded or contracted. The Han- dlesFigure team has two slots: a SelectedFigure slot that is filled by a figure object when it is selected, and a Handles slot that is filled by a handle object. The Handles slot is repli- cated because a figure may have many handles. Both the SelectedFigure and Handles slots are filled when a figure is selected and empty otherwise. The HandlesFigure team is replicated because there may be many selected figures at any time.

The use case path through the DrawingMVC team of Figure 6.14 expands the stub along the Select Figure use case path of Figure 6.12. The expansion of the stub explains how the slots of the HandlesFigure team are filled with figure and handle objects. After the selected figure is found at *2*, it is deposited in the SelectedFigure slot. At *3*, handle objects for the selected figure are created and deposited into the Handles slot. The HandlesFigure team can now operate. The newly created handles objects are added to the use case path (move-stay) and then deposited into the Figures pool, at *4*. The change to the Figures pool results in the display of the handles in the drawing area, at *5*.

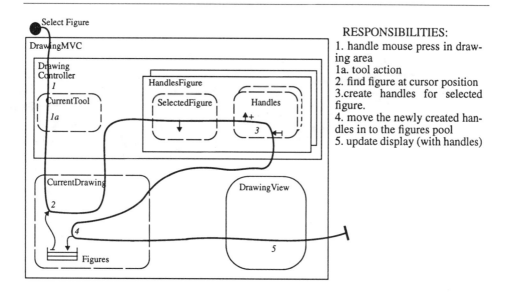

RESPONSIBILITIES:
1. handle mouse press in drawing area
1a. tool action
2. find figure at cursor position
3. create handles for selected figure.
4. move the newly created handles in to the figures pool
5. update display (with handles)

Figure 6.14 Recursive decomposition of the DrawingMVC team.

6.4 CLASS REFINEMENT (DETAILED DESIGN)

Given the high-level operational map of the BGETool, we return to refine our class relationship diagrams. We are dealing with classes that have more to do with solution domain concerns than with problem domain ones.

Figure 6.15 extends our earlier class relationship diagram of Figure 6.6 with classes needed to manufacture the objects to fill the MVC teams developed in the Operation domain. The new classes are: MenuBarController, DrawingController, ToolPaletteController, MenuBarView, DrawingView, ToolPalette-View, DrawingModel and ToolModel. Additionally, the Handles class has been made a subclass of the Figure class as motivated by the discussion of the **select figure** use case path in the operation domain (Figure 6.14).

From our earlier class relationship diagrams we rename the DrawingArea, ToolPalette and MenuBar classes, to be, respectively, DrawingMVC, ToolMVC, and EditorMVC. The MVC classes represent the MVC teams in the BGETool map of Figure 6.13. Having classes to represent teams in the implementation makes the design intent more explicit in the source code. Also, team objects can be used for controlling access to team members and for configuring team members during initialization.

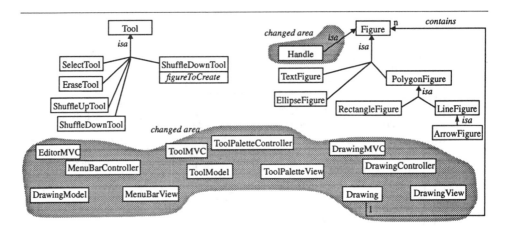

Figure 6.15 Class refinement.

An allocation table (Table 6.1) shows how the classes map to teams, objects, slots, and pools. Abstract classes are marked with an asterisk and the number of subclasses they have is given.

1. The Drawing class identified earlier as a container of figures is now additionally a template for the Model objects to fill the CurrentDrawing slot of the DrawingMVC team.

2. We have designed the system such that the components in the Operation domain align almost one-to-one with the classes in the Manufacturing domain. A line of diagonal entries indicates that the concepts in the domains align. Otherwise the entries would be scattered. There are several design choices that can cause the domains not to align. For example, it may be that teams are not represented as classes; their only presence in a running system are the connections between objects that would be their members. The HandlesFigure team of Figure 6.14 is one example of a team that is not represented by a class. It is also common that a single object will fill several slots in an organization, that is, play many roles. The buffer objects

Table 6.1 Allocation table for the BGETool

M \ OP	Teams						Objects						Slots				Pools		
	EditorMVC	ToolMVC	DrawingMVC	MenuBarController	DrawingController	HandlesFigures	DrawingModel	MenuBarView	ToolModel	ToolPaletteController	ToolPaletteView	DrawingView	CurrentDrawing	CurrentTool	Handles	SelectedFigures	Drawings	Figures	Tools
EditorMVC	*																		
ToolMVC		*																	
DrawingMVC			*																
MenuBarController				*															
DrawingController					*														
DrawingModel							*												
MenuBarView								*											
ToolModel									*										
ToolPaletteController										*									
ToolPaletteView											*								
DrawingView												*							
Drawing													*				*		
*Tool (5)														*					*
Handle															*			*	
*Figure(6)																*		*	

of the MTU case study are an example of this (Chapter 11).

3. We have designed our class relationship diagrams to avoid the sharing of objects across teams. Object aliasing cannot be completely eliminated but it should be kept to a minimum, especially between teams that represent the decomposition of a system into its major parts (subsystems). Teams tend to become too tightly coupled when an alaised object uses information it is privy to in one role to fulfil its responsibilities elsewhere. Information hiding and separation of concerns can suffer as a result.

4. Slots are related to abstract classes because polymorphic behaviour through subclassing from an abstract class is the perfect vehicle for filling the same slot with different objects, at different times, that have different behaviours. For example, the CurrentTool slot can be filled by any tool object that inherits from the `Tool` abstract class, provided the `Tool` class provides the basic behaviour expected of objects in the slot. However, the slot concept itself is separated from whether a slot is always filled by the same object, filled by different objects of the same concrete class, filled by different objects of the same abstract class, filled by objects from different abstract classes, or sometimes not filled at all. We have more to say on the relationship between abstract classes and slots when we develop collaboration graphs in Section 6.5.

6.5 COLLABORATION GRAPHS (DETAILED DESIGN)

Collaboration graphs show operational connections between teams, objects, and slots. In the Smalltalk world of this example, these connections correspond to messages. However, we do not show all messages in collaboration graphs, but only ones that are operational in relation to fixed objects and slots. We exclude the following types of messages (there is enough information in the other diagrams of our diagram suite to guide coding of these messages):

1. *Messages whose sole purpose is to establish visibility between objects to enable further operational messages to be sent.* When designing collaboration graphs, assume the objects can gain visibility of one another as necessary. Installing objects in slots amounts to making them visible where needed. When developing collaboration graphs, assume the slots are filled with objects and are ready to interact.

2. *Messages that are purely a result of functional factoring and the division of behaviour between subclasses and superclasses* (for example, the self messages of Smalltalk that trigger the notification mechanism higher up in the class hierarchy). These messages often come about because of design decisions associated with reuse, where our concern with collaboration graphs is understanding interobject messaging patterns to achieve use case paths.

3. *Messages to create objects and to install objects into slots.* In our conceptual world, creating objects requires going outside the Operational domain of the collaboration graphs into the Manufacturing domain. We do not show in our collaboration graphs the messages to classes that do this in Smalltalk.

This is not to say that the types of messages above are unimportant. In fact, the design intent embedded in them is very important and can account for a large portion of the code in a system (especially the message types dealing with structural dynamics, types 1 and 3). However, we believe that understanding structural dynamics is so important that we provide a means of elevating it to a higher design level than collaboration graphs (slots in use case maps and create-move-destroy responsibilities along paths). Collaboration graphs then only have to model details of the operational interactions between components, assuming slots are occupied.

We give one example of a collaboration graph for the BGETool (Figure 6.16). The components in the collaboration graph shown have been laid out in the same spatial arrangement as used for the use case map diagrams. This helps to keep the organization of the system in mind when developing interobject messaging patterns.

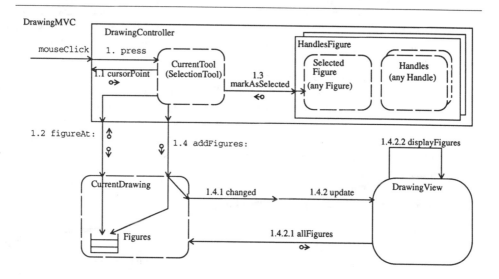

Figure 6.16 A Collaboration graph corresponding to the Select Figure use case.

The collaboration graph in Figure 6.16 is for the Select Figure use case path of Figure 6.14. The CurrentTool slot is filled with a SelectionTool object. The SelectedFigure slot is filled with any figure and the Handles slot is filled with any handles object. The scenario begins with a mouseClick message originating in some lower layer software being sent to the DrawingController. The DrawingController informs the SelectionTool object in the CurrentTool slot of the mouse click by sending it the message *press*. The SelectionTool object then sends the message *cursorPoint* to the DrawingController to find the X,Y position of the mouse. The next message is *figureAt* from the SelectionTool object to the CurrentDrawing (note we are assuming that the SelectionTool can somehow gain visibility of the object in the CurrentDrawing slot). The input parameter to the *figureAt* message is the X,Y position of the mouse, the output parameter is the figure at that position. If a figure is found, the SelectionTool object then marks the figure as selected by sending it the message *markAsSelected*. The *markAsSelected* message returns the handles objects of the selected figure. The SelectionTool object then asks the DrawingModel to add the handles objects to the Figures pool (message *addFigures*). The change to the Figures pool causes a *changed* message to an underlying dependency mechanism and a consequential *update* message from that mechanism to the DrawingView (see Chapter 11 for details on the dependency mechanism as a layered pattern). The remaining messages display the new handles in the drawing area.

Collaboration graphs in the Operation domain are used to develop the method interfaces of classes in the Manufacturing domain. To derive the complete method interface of a class one must consider the union of all collaboration graphs that include instances of the class. Developing enough collaboration graphs that a class method interface can be automatically derived is often impractical. It is more important to develop the collaboration graphs of the key use case paths to get the key interobject messaging patterns correct and to allow some of the detailed support methods to evolve during detailed coding.

Figure 6.17 shows the class method interfaces that can be derived from the collaboration graph of Figure 6.16 for the Select Figure use case path. Note that we have added the *press* method to the interface of the abstract class Tool. The reasoning is that all tool objects that fill the CurrentTool slot must respond to the *press* message sent from the DrawingController. In this way, tool objects can react to mouse events in the drawing area when they are the current tool. We have also added the method *cursorPoint* to the interface of the DrawingController class. These two methods are the beginnings of a protocol between tool objects and drawing controller objects. If new tools are added to the framework of the BGETool they will inherit this protocol.

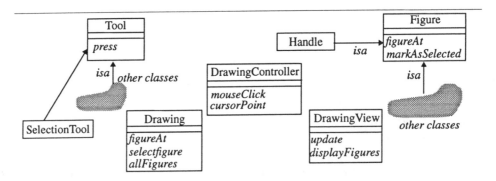

Figure 6.17 Developing method interfaces from collaboration graphs for the Select Figure use case path.

6.6 VISIBILITY GRAPHS AND SOURCE CODE

A visibility graph shows only the visibility *references* between objects. A reference from object A to object B allows A to send messages to B. Visibility graphs are useful because they show the layout of a runtime network of objects.

A visibility graph for the objects involved in the Select Figure use case is shown in Figure 6.16. The model and notation are as follows: Objects and references may be static or dynamic. A static object or reference exists for the length of a program run, after some system initialization phase. Anything static is drawn with a black outline. A dynamic object or reference is created or destroyed during a system's operation. Anything dynamic is drawn as shaded. A dynamic reference may be *mutable*, meaning that the instances of the reference may point to objects of different types (in the context of this case study that means of different classes) through time. A mutable reference is labelled "mutable". For an alternative approach to representing these issues and more see the Fusion design method [13].

Models from the Operation and Manufacturing domains give clues to how to construct a visibility graph. We discuss the clues and how they were used to construct the visibility graph of the Select Figure use case path below.

1. *Interobject messages of collaboration graphs require visibility references between the objects.* We can see from the corresponding collaboration graph (Figure 6.16) that visibility connections are needed between the `DrawingController` and `CurrentTool` object, and the `CurrentTool` object and the object in the CurrentDrawing slot, and so on.

2. *Teams are logical boundaries for scoping the visibility.* One would expect objects within a team to be interconnected to support their collaborative behaviour. To keep systems loosely coupled, it is best to limit visibility across team boundaries. This is especially true of teams that define the major functional divisions of a system (subsystems). Although not shown in Figure 6.16, the DrawingMVC, EditorMVC, and ToolMVC teams are such teams.

3. *References to objects filling slots are dynamic because, by definition, objects move into and out of a slot through time. The references to objects filling slots may be mutable if the slot is filled by objects of different types, that is, from different classes.* In other words, if a slot is associated with an abstract class and instances of subclasses of that abstract class fill the slot, then the reference is mutable. For example, the `DrawingController->CurrentTool` visibility reference in Figure 6.16 is dynamic-mutable because different objects from different classes fill the CurrentTool slot through time.

4. *References between fixed objects within the same team tend to be fixed*, for example, the `DrawingController->DrawingView` reference in Figure 6.16.

5. *Objects filling slots and objects created or destroyed along use case paths are dynamic.* For example, `Figures` and `Handles` are dynamic (see the use case map of Figure 6.14).

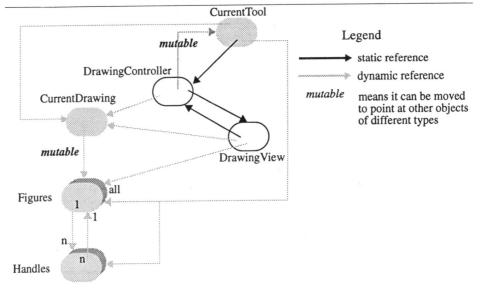

Figure 6.18 Visibility graph corresponding to the Select Figure use case path.

6.6.1 Understanding and Coding Structural Dynamics

This section is for readers who want to follow everything down to the level of code, but may be skipped by others without loss of continuity in relation to design models.

Recall that the collaboration graphs developed in the Operation domain left out several detailed message types. The message types were: messages that establish visibility, messages to self and to superclasses that are solely to support reuse, and messages to create and destroy objects. Figure 6.19 is a code snapshot diagram that includes these message types for the `select figure` collaboration graph of Figure 6.16. The complexity of this figure indicates why we do not recommend drawing code snapshot diagrams as design diagrams in forward engineering (although they may be useful as aids to program understanding if they can be automatically generated from source-code descriptions). The nodes in the diagram are objects and the grey arcs indicate messages that were not part of the original collaboration graph (Figure 6.16). The create arc (the one with a + sign next to it) does not indicate a message to the Handles objects, but rather a message to the classes in the manufacturing domain that will create the objects.

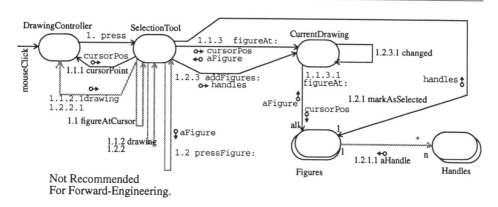

Figure 6.19 Code snapshot diagram showing visibility messages, messages to self, and creation messages.

A code snapshot diagram offers little abstraction above the source code itself. For comparison by those readers familiar with Smalltalk, we include the source code matching the code snapshot diagram of Figure 6.19 in Figure 6.20 and Figure 6.21.

The code snapshot diagram of Figure 6.19 and the visibility graph of Figure 6.16 illustrate how dynamic object-oriented programs can appear at the run-time-object level. The discussion to this point illustrates that much of the dynamics at the object-level is not needed to understand the organization and operation of a system in the large using use case maps, and that maps, collaboration graphs, and class relationship diagrams can be used to infer much of the dynamics at the object level.

Source code associated with object-level dynamics is often scattered throughout many classes. *A helpful technique is to localize the source code associated with dynamic structuring in one place.* This makes code associated with normal operation easier to understand because the code is not dominated by other concerns. It makes the system structure easier to understand from the source code because the pieces related to the system structure—of which code for dynamic structuring is part — are in fewer places. Teams are a good place to localize structural dynamics. If teams are implemented as a classes, then instances of teams can initialize themselves, create their members, and connect their members together. For example, an instance of an MVC team could be created with code that looks like this (assuming Views create the Controllers):

```
anMVC := MVCTeam model:aModel viewClass:View
```

If teams are not part of the implementation, then the dynamic formation of collaborating groups of objects tends to become decentralized among the members.

```
Class DrawingController
instance vars: "currentDrawing, currentTool..."
"Methods follow"
mouseClick
    ...
    "Send message press to currentTool object"
    currentTool press
    ...
drawing
    "Return the current drawing object"
    ^currentDrawing

cursorPoint:
    "Return the cursor point"
    ^self sensor cursorPoint

Class Tool
instance vars: "controller"
press
    | aFigure | "An automatic variable"
    "Send myself the figureAtCursor message"
    aFigure := self figureAtCursor.
    aFigure is Nil
        ifTrue:[ ... ].
        ifFalse:[self pressFigure:aFigure]

figureAtCursor
    "Send drawing the figureAt: message with
    argument cursor point"
    ^self drawing figureAt: controller cursorPoint

drawing
    "Get the current drawing"
    ^controller drawing

pressFigure
    "Subclasses must implement this method"
    self subclassResponsibility.
"SelectionTool is a subclass of Tool"

Tool subclass: #SelectionTool
pressFigure:aFigure
    |handles|
    "Send figure markAsSelected"
    handles := aFigure markAsSelected.
    "Send drawing addFigures with newhandles"
    self drawing addFigures: handles
```

Figure 6.20 Pseudo Smalltalk code for the select figure use case.

```
Class Drawing
instance vars: "figures, ..."
addFigures: someFigs
    figures addAll:someFigs.
    "Invoke the dependency mechanism"
    self changed

Class Figure
instance vars: "handles, ..."
markAsSelected
    "Create handles and return them"
    handles := self createCornerHandles.
    ^handles
```

Figure 6.21 Pseudo Smalltalk code for select figure use case cont'd.

System initialization is full of dynamic structuring in an object-oriented system. It is during system initialization that the static objects in a system are created and connected together, and slots are filled with default objects if needed. *Localizing system initialization code can result in the code documenting the system structure*. This is very important for system understanding and maintenance. Figure 6.22 gives some Smalltalk code for those with familiarity with Smalltalk that could serve as the initialization code of the BGETool. The source code is in a method called *openOn:withLabel:* with parameters aCurrentDrawing and aLabel. The code has the following sequence: create model objects, create MVC teams, size the window to hold the teams, create the inter-team dependencies, fill the slots with default objects, and start.

```
"In Class EditorMVC"
openOn: aCurrentDrawing withLabel: aLabel
  "This is the method that starts an instance of the BGETool tool"
  "The following list are automatic variables"
  | container toolPaletteSize aDrawingModel aToolModel
  anEditorMVC aToolMVC aDrawingMVC|

  "Create the model objects for all Teams. The new message
  creates objects. (CurrentDrawing already exists)"
  aDrawingModel := self new.
  aToolModel    := ToolModel new.
  aDrawingModel label: aLabel.

  "Create the MVC Teams. Class MVCTeam is sent the message model:
  viewClass. (Views create their own controllers.)"
  anEditorMVC    := MVCTeam model:aDrawingModel viewClass:MenuBarView.
  aToolMVC       := MVCTeam model:aToolModel viewClass:ToolView.
  aDrawingMVC    := MVCTeam model:aCurrentDrawing viewClass:DrawingView.

  "Size the window that will hold the tool and open it."
  aDrawingModel sizeWindowForEditorMVC:anEditorMVC toolMVC: aToolMVC
  drawingMVC:DrawingMVC.

  "Create inter-team dependency relationships. The controller of
  the DrawingMVC team is made a dependent of the model in the
  ToolMVC team. The view of the DrawingMVC team is made a depenedent."
  aToolModel     addDependent: aDrawingMVC controller.
  aDrawingModel addDependent: aDrawingMVC view.

  "Set the Current Drawing to aDrawing. The  DrawingModel to DrawingView
  dependency will fire and the CurrentDrawing slot will be filled."
  aDrawingModel setDrawing: aCurrentDrawing.

  "Set the Current Tool. The ToolModel to DrawingController dependency
  will fire and the CurrentTool slot will be filled."
  aToolModel setCurrentTool ! !
```

Figure 6.22 Initialization code of the BGETool.

6.7 SUMMARY

In this chapter we have:

- Applied use case maps to the design of a common type of object-oriented application.
- Demonstrated how use case maps may be used as part of an object-oriented design process that includes use cases (Operation), class relationship diagrams (Manufacturing), collaboration graphs (Operation), and visibility graphs (Assembly) down to the source code level.
- Used a standard use case map definition of the MVC pattern to design a system-level use case map. An MVC team was designed for each screen area of the BGE-Tool and then configured together to form a system-level use case map.

The case study demonstrates that class relationship diagrams are affected by design decisions in the Operation domain. For this reason one should not over engineer class relationship diagrams during problem domain understanding. The case study also demonstrates that the dynamic structuring of systems at the object-level is ancillary to understanding the system-level organization and operation of a system in use case maps, and that the maps, together with collaboration graphs, can be used to infer many of the detailed decisions at the object level.

Many different models and diagrams were used to both design the BGETool and to present it as a case study. The central models are: use cases, use case maps, class relationship diagrams, collaboration graphs, and visibility graphs.

Advanced *Use Case Map* Model

*T*his chapter extends the use case map model of Chapter 3 to include concurrent scenarios that may proceed at unpredictable rates relative to each other, may influence each other, may conflict with each other, and may fail before completion. It presents design at this level as an activity that positions concurrent components (processes, ISRs, and teams of them) along paths to create bound maps that imply appropriate solution properties to realize the scenarios.

Identifying influences of concurrent scenarios on each other is a difficult and important issue in both requirements analysis and high-level design. There are several kinds of influences that we can identify, some of which are amenable to path techniques, and others of which are not. Cases that are amenable are as follows: direct coupling can be identified between paths at specific points along them; indirect coupling can be identified between paths through responsibilities (and the components that perform them); and failures can be associated with specific points along paths. The case where failures can occur anywhere along paths can be helped by path techniques, but solutions cannot be developed solely in terms of paths. Outside the scope of path techniques is the case where scenarios interact with each other at random points along paths in a way that depends heavily on local results as they progress. Scenarios like this may be signs either of a need to reformulate the requirements, or of a problem that has too much ripple to be modeled by paths (recall Chapter 2).

A difficult problem in system design is the possibility of conflicts between concurrent scenarios that paths allow but that we did not have in mind when we developed maps.

We may have expected scenarios to reach coupling points in some specific order when they may be able arrive in a different order. We may have made a wrong assumption about what is happening globally on another path based on local information; for example, what if a timeout occurs on the incorrect assumption that another path has failed, when it is only slow? A concern of this chapter is to lay the groundwork for using maps to reason about such issues during high-level design and for avoiding building conflicts into solutions.

When multiple scenarios are possible along paths, the convention mentioned in Chapter 3 of saying *a path is in progress* instead of *a scenario is in progress along a path* could be ambiguous. Generally we shall say it the short way if what we mean is clear from the context.

We caution the reader to remember that we are not aiming to define a model that can specify behaviour in detail, only one that provides a thinking and idea-capture tool for use during requirements analysis and high-level design. This is particularly important when reading about path coupling, in order not to misinterpret the coupling notations.

7.1 UNBOUND MAPS

In general, even with the simplest maps, more than one scenario may be in progress at the same time. As illustrated below, we recommend having a mental model of scenarios in terms of snapshots of multiple pointers moving along paths, remembering that such snapshots are not design diagrams that you would actually draw.

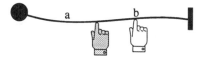

The number of concurrent scenarios that is possible along the same path is constrained by the environment, if the path starts there (such information is part of the context of a map), and by the nature of the components of the system, if the path starts in an internal component. Typically we assume the number of concurrent scenarios to be small, often equal to one. The model of unbound maps does not provide any information about the relative progress of multiple different scenarios along a path. They could, in principle, overtake and even pass each other. These matters can only be resolved in bound maps, by positioning appropriate system components along paths..

In general, we want to identify all couplings between concurrent scenarios explicitly in maps, to avoid the problem that occurs with prose use cases of having coupling buried in detailed prose descriptions. Being able to distinguish the main different types of coupling is also useful, even if details are left uncommitted. We distinguish two main types of coupling (direct path coupling and coupling through responsibilities) and two subtypes of direct path coupling (synchronous and asynchronous). We also have notations to indicate failure points along paths and the aborting of paths that are stopped, or possibly progressing incorrectly, after a failure. These notations will now be explained.

7.1.1 Direct Synchronous Coupling

Synchronously coupled paths are indicated by a bar cutting across the different paths at the points where they are to be synchronized. This is not just ripple in a single path as described in Chapter 3 but explicit synchronization of concurrent paths.

AND join   *Pure synchro-nization*   *Rendezvous*

The default meaning when there is a lot of concurrency is that one scenario per path is synchronized (this may be overridden by labeling the diagram to indicate how many along each path will be synchronized).

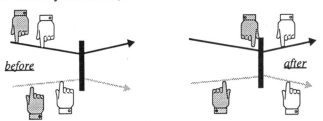

before   *after*

The meaning for a rendezvous is that one entering scenario per incoming path is synchronized to follow the shared path as one.

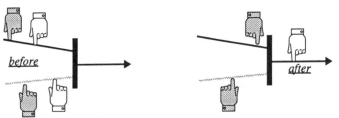

before   *after*

Scenarios along a single path may be synchronized but, unless the context tells us how many, the number to be synchronized must be indicated by labeling the bar. Note that a single path like this may actually be several superimposed paths that have come together at an OR join not shown here. The preface of this book has an example of several people reading this book together in which the synchronization is of this kind, with the paths before the OR join providing the context.

before   (2)   (2)
                                                      after

Data may be exchanged during synchronous coupling. We often assume it implicitly because of context, but it may be indicated explicitly by using standard data flow arrows. Synchronous coupling offers the possibility of exchanging data in either direction, or even working on data jointly before separating again. Data includes dynamic components moving along paths, such as from a pool to a slot, from a slot to another slot, or from a slot to a pool.

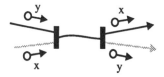

Note that there may be some cases that look like ripple that can be resolved by rendezvous, because the shared rendezvous path in effect allows the scenarios to interact at all points along it. The constraint is that the scenarios must follow the same route, in synchronization.

7.1.2 Direct Asynchronous Coupling

Asynchronous coupling is basically simple and is complicated only by the multiplicity of interpretations that are possible when there is lots of concurrency. The simplest form is indicated by positioning a filled circle along a main path (this is called a *waiting place*) and touching a triggering path to it tangentially (either the body of a triggering path is tangential or the end bar is). This identification of paths as *main* and *triggering* is relative to

one waiting place only. A main path for one waiting place may be a triggering path for another.

The basic interpretation is that progress along the main path *may* have to pause until

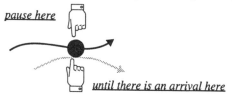

there is an arrival along a triggering path. We say "may", because factors other than just the existence of the coupling determine whether a pause is actually required in some specific case. We think of a waiting place as being *open* or *closed* at different times, open meaning a pause is not required and closed meaning a pause is required. The coupling is asynchronous because the pause occurs only along the main path, not mutually; the trig-

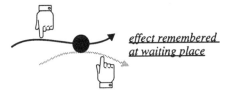

*effect remembered
at waiting place*

gering path does *not* pause. The effect of the trigger is assumed to be remembered at the waiting place, whatever the effect is; it may be to change the state of the waiting place from open to closed or vice versa, and/or to leave some data for pickup.

As with synchronous coupling, data may be transferred, but only in one direction, from the triggering path to the waiting path, and it cannot be worked on while in transit.

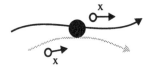

When multiple triggering paths exist, they have an OR effect (an AND effect may be indicated by AND-joining paths together before touching the waiting place).

OR   *AND*

The assumption is that the main path progresses with knowledge of which trigger occurred.

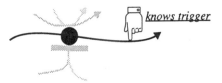

knows trigger

Beyond this simple interpretation are nuances that the notation does not model. Initial conditions may have an effect not indicated by the notation, for example, a waiting place may be assumed initially open. The rules for opening and closing a waiting place are not specified. The implications of multiple arrivals along main and triggering paths are not specified, such as how arrivals along main and triggering paths accumulate at the waiting

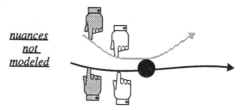

nuances
not
modeled

place, and how their leaving it affects the accumulation. In other words, most of the rich detail that would be needed to model actual behaviour or that would have to be built into implementations is missing. As is appropriate for high-level design, maps provide a framework for reasoning about these issues but do not themselves resolve them.

7.1.3 Direct Coupling with Timeout

Replacing the waiting place in any of these asynchronous coupling configurations with a timer indicates a timed waiting place. Everything is the same as before except the timer is

timeout on
asynchronous
coupling

alternate timeout path

assumed to be set by an arrival along the main path. If the timer does not run out before a trigger arrives, then everything is still the same as before. If the timer runs out, things are still much the same if the same main path is taken out of the waiting place, except that the scenario continues with knowledge that a timeout occurred, not an ordinary trigger. An alternative timeout path may also be provided. The rules for setting, clearing and resetting the timer when multiple scenarios are in progress along the main path are not specified.

The notation also provides for timeout on synchronous coupling.

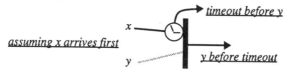

timeout before y

x

assuming x arrives first

y

y before timeout

7.1.4 Coupling Through Responsibilities

If the coupling is of a kind that does not require at least one path to wait, then direct coupling between paths of the above types is not suitable. The solution is to couple paths through responsibilities. Ultimately, a stronger commitment will be made by binding the responsibilities to the same component in a bound map. However, we need a visual notation for use in unbound maps, because we do not want to be forced to read responsibility definitions expressed in prose to discover that such coupling is intended.

The notation for coupling through responsibilities is shown below: Outline the coupled responsibility points with small circles and join the circles with a curve, using a line style that is distinguishable from ordinary use case paths. If the paths and associated responsibilities are close together, simply overlap the small circles. This notation would normally disappear from a bound map because a component would replace it.

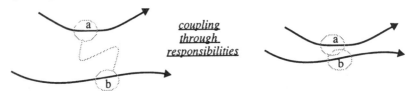

7.1.5 Failure Points

Failures in the underlying system may cause progress along a path to stop, leaving the system in an incomplete state and possibly jeopardizing other paths in progress. Failures may occur at predictable points along paths, or anywhere along paths. In the former case, a notation to indicate failure points is a useful aid to discovering recovery mechanisms that may be built into maps around failure points. The failure-point symbol (a ground symbol borrowed from electrical engineering) is an annotation like a layer fold that is placed on

maps for information. This symbol marks points where a path *may* end abnormally, due to some failure in the underlying system. This puts some knowledge of the underlying system organization into maps, but not in a strongly component-specific way.

If failures can occur at any point along a path, the situation is not so simple. Discovery must be indirect, for example, by monitoring critical state variables for indications of failures, and recovery mechanisms cannot be structured around specific points along paths.

In either case, recovery may involve trying to abort paths in progress, either ones stopped by the failure, or ones that may do damage if they continue after the failure. For

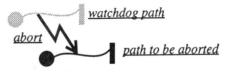

this purpose, we use an abort symbol that looks like a lightning stroke drawn from one path (the so-called watchdog path, meaning the one that discovered the failure) to the path to be aborted. The intent of an abort would be to put the system back into a state before the aborted path started. Of course, this may be impossible in practice, particularly in distributed systems, in which case compromises must be made. However, the notation provides a framework for reasoning about the issues involved.

7.2 AN EXAMPLE: TIMEOUT AND RECOVERY

Suppose we extend a basic producer-consumer pattern from Chapter 2 to include a report back that consumption was successful (Figure 7.1). We might want to do this if produce-consume was a distributed transaction taking place, say, across a network. In Figure 7.1 we imagine the transaction as being at the scale of information exchanges between people over the Internet, with the Internet itself modeled as an unreliable conduit and the people providing the timeout-recovery mechanism.

The problem with distributed transactions is that the path may fail in either the forward or return direction—i.e., on the bc segment of the path, or de one—so we cannot be sure that the simplistic pattern on the left will work. However, we can combine some of the techniques we have learned to produce the pattern shown on the right that allows for the possibility of retry after timeout on waiting for an acknowledgment at responsibility e. The AND fork after responsibility b expresses the concept of both propagating the transaction to the other end and waiting for an acknowledgment, concurrently.

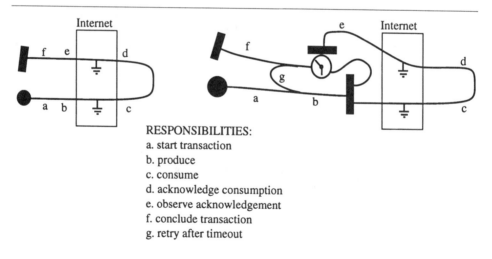

RESPONSIBILITIES:
a. start transaction
b. produce
c. consume
d. acknowledge consumption
e. observe acknowledgement
f. conclude transaction
g. retry after timeout

Figure 7.1 Timeout-recovery in a distributed transaction.

There are a number of possible scenarios in relation to this map highlighted in Figure 7.2:

(a) This is the intended correct operation scenario, with no failures or timeouts.

(b) This scenario fails, times out, and retransmits. As is, it implies failure occurs again (but see (d)).

(c) This scenario is similar to (b) except the failure is in the return path instead of the forward path. It ends up with the consumer thinking the transaction is completed and the producer thinking it is not. A step to solving this problem is uniquely identifying transactions so that retries can be distinguished from new transactions. However, if there are no retries, the two sides end up with an inconsistent view that is not resolved by this pattern. The assumption of this pattern is that retries continue until success is seen by both sides. If this assumption is not valid, something more must be done (however we will stop at this point with this example).

(d) This scenario starts from a timeout, without showing how we got there, and shows successful completion.

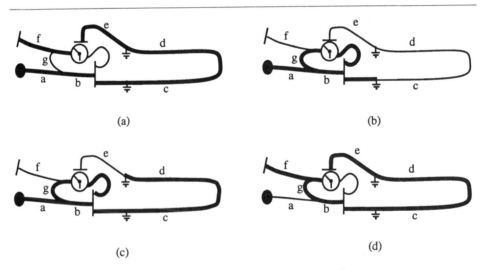

Figure 7.2 Some timeout-recovery scenarios.

The map of Figure 7.1 does not look different in kind from the mouse double-click map of Chapter 3, emphasizing the point that the maps by themselves have no scale. A map like this can be useful for guiding the design of the components of the system that will make the scenarios happen. Chapter 8 presents a case study of the design of systems of collaborating processes inside the black boxes of a distributed application to implement a map like this one.

7.2.1 Another Application of Timeout-Recovery

Timeout-recovery patterns may be used in many places. Another application—to part of the producer-consumer map of Figure 2.8 from Chapter 2—is shown in Figure 7.3. In this map, the consumer terminates the temporary produce-consume agreement unilaterally after nothing is heard from the other side for a time. This prevents the consumer from sticking forever in consume mode when some glitch prevents completion of the producer-initiated teardown sequence. The map assumes that the producer path failed at the marked failure point. If it did not fail, but was just slow, then the assumption of this map is that stale action along the producer path will be ignored by the consumer.

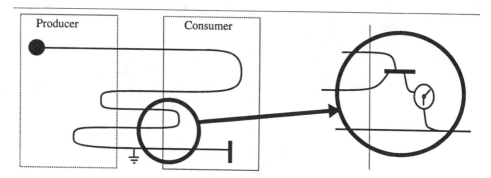

Figure 7.3   Another timeout-recovery application (refinement of Figure 2.8 from Chapter 2).

7.3 BOUND MAPS

New design issues for bound maps are raised by unbound maps expressing concurrent scenarios that may proceed at unpredictable rates relative to each other, may influence each other, may conflict with each other, and may fail before completion. Designing bound maps to resolve these issues boils down to positioning concurrent *components* (processes and ISRs) on paths in different ways to provide different types of control (supplementing the type of design of bound maps outlined in Chapter 3 and illustrated in Chapter 6). This design approach exploits the fact that different positioning patterns imply different properties. We will first explain the properties of processes and ISRs and then develop the properties of different positioning patterns for them in maps.

7.3.1 Processes and ISRs as System Components

Processes and ISRs realize *and* control the concurrency of paths in bound maps. To lay the groundwork for understanding how they do this, we will now enlarge on the brief explanation of their properties as system components that was given in Chapter 3 (for completeness, we repeat the properties from Chapter 3).

Processes /⬜/ A process is an autonomous, self-directed component that may operate concurrently with other processes. Its internal logic is sequential; in other words, there are no concurrent elements inside processes, the only concurrent elements are the processes themselves. If a designer needs multiply concurrent components (sometimes called multithreaded, a term we avoid here because of possible confusion with threads—a synonym for paths—in our maps), active teams are the way to go. Active teams are teams with multiple processes in them.

For most design purposes (except evaluating performance) we imagine processes as fully concurrent. Software processes are pseudo-concurrent when many of them share a single processor, but the pseudo-concurrency is hidden from the programmer and does not need to be modeled by the designer (except for performance issues).

Our design model views processes (and ISRs) as the ultimate source of all control in concurrent systems. The model distinguishes between *perform* and *control*. All components *perform* their own responsibilities. However, processes (and ISRs) *control* when passive components perform their responsibilities through call chains that are below the level of maps. We do not need to show the call chains in design diagrams at this level to understand this. The bottom line is that when we bind a single process (or ISR) to a path, we imply that the other components along the path will be under its control to make the path progress. When we bind multiple processes to a path, we imply that, between them, the processes will control the other components (we would not normally bind multiple ISRs to a path, unless it spanned multiple physical processors). To simplify discussion from now on we shall usually use processes as the exemplars, leaving the qualifying "and ISRs" implicit.

In principle, the design model of a sequential program has one controlling process (corresponding to the mainline program) that causes the action to unfold through chains of calls.

Processes are sufficiently coarse-grained components that they may be regard as teams of a kind. This is done by allowing a subset of component types, namely objects and passive teams, to appear within the process outline. This meaning is that the bounding process is the only one that interacts with these components (regardless of where they are located in code).

Interrupt Service Routines △   Readers may wonder why we bring interrupt service routines (ISRs) into the high-level picture. We do not require them to be brought in, only offer the option. For many purposes they are lower-level details; we can simply regard them as implicit partners of processes that link processes to the physical world. However, as we pointed out earlier, maps can be at any scale and it is often useful to develop maps that include details at the scale of interrupt processing along with other components like processes and objects. This makes them high-level components in that context.

An ISR is a software routine that acts as a link between hardware devices and higher levels of software. It is activated by a stimulus called an interrupt that arrives from hardware. Our design model is that ISRs are triggered directly *only* from hardware. However, software may also trigger them indirectly by issuing special commands to hardware components that will force interrupts.

An ISR may perform responsibilities over a series of interrupts before communicating with higher levels of software.

An ISR is half like a process and half not (the triangle shape symbolizes this—a triangle is half a parallelogram): The half that *is* like a process has the following characteristic: ISRs run autonomously and therefore are autonomous sources of control, just like processes. The half that *is not* like a process has the following characteristics: ISRs are primitive components that do not have a team-like character (in other words they have no decomposition in our design diagrams). They do not have any interface elements that are accessible from software. ISR-to-process and ISR-to-ISR communication is very constrained. ISR-to-process communication is possible only by means of shared data and/or asynchronous interactions. Process-to-ISR communication is not possible through software. ISR-to-ISR communication is possible only through shared data.

Typically, an ISR runs in a short burst that steals cycles from the currently running process, although this is a detail like process pseudo-concurrency that is below the level of our design model.

For simplicity, we shall speak in most of the rest of this chapter as if processes are the only controlling elements of paths, leaving "and ISRs" implicit.

7.3.2 Designing by Positioning Processes on Maps

Concurrency of paths in maps introduces extra issues, such as overtaking along paths, congestion at coupling points, and races between paths. Concurrency is both realized and controlled by processes. Processes collectively ensure that progress along paths is orderly and that congestion and races are taken care of by queuing or other means (as well as, of course, ensuring that paths are made to happen correctly). The question is, to what extent can solutions be indicated at the level of maps? There are three issues: How can we arrange processes to control concurrency *across* paths? How can we arrange processes to control concurrency *along* paths? How can we arrange processes to provide suitable coupling *between* concurrent paths? In this section we hit only the highlights, leaving details to examples (for example, Chapter 8).

Concurrency Across Paths The issue is controlling concurrency of scenarios across different paths that traverse the same passive team or object. For illustrative purposes, we use the team notation to represent nonprocess components of any kind and refer to them just as "components". Everything we say here applies also if the components are specifically identified as objects.

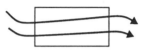

Unless a nonprocess component is intended to be reentrant in a global sense (that is, its responsibilities have no effects that are detectable in the future along any path), serial ordering must be imposed on the performance of its responsibilities along all concurrent traversing paths, or errors may occur. Here are representative patterns.

Serialization. One solution is to put the component under the operational control of a single process. This is indicated simply by placing one and only one process along the set of paths.

Mutual exclusion. Another solution is to indicate that mutual exclusion protection is required for the component by showing the component with a double outline. The

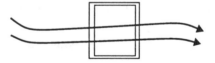

interpretation is that its responsibilities must not be exercised concurrently by processes. When we do this we have in mind that the protection will likely be provided by a mutual exclusion semaphore. (If ISRs can also access the component, interrupt lockout would be required instead). Processes and ISRs are not candidates for double outlines because they already have mutual exclusion protection by definition (no other component can get at their internals).

Positioning processes in different ways in relation to AND forks or AND fork-joins makes commitments as follows:

"Don't care" ordering. This pattern implies that there is no concurrency across the forked path segments, only "don't care ordering" of the responsibilities between the segments. The implication is that the process will internally interleave the advancement of the paths in some order of its own choosing.

Fork concurrency. This pattern implies that the processes implement the concurrency of the forks.

Fork-join concurrency. This pattern implies that the processes somehow synchronize themselves at the AND fork and subsequent join, and advance the path segments concurrently in between.

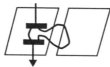

Concurrency Along Paths When individual paths are required to be concurrent (in other words to have concurrent scenarios progressing along them), multiple processes may be positioned along the path to control the action. Otherwise we get into intricate, tricky, and inefficient sequential programs that advance progress along the path in an interleaved way for previous stimuli while at the same time polling periodically for new stimuli at the start of the path.

Process stack. One approach is to use a *stack* of processes. However, this is potentially difficult to control (processes could race each other along the path).

Process pipeline. A pattern with more built-in control is a *pipeline* of processes along the path. Each process controls a segment of the path sequentially. Several path segments can be in progress concurrently. This in turn means that several sce-

narios can be in progress concurrently, because the processes in effect hand them along the path to each other. Process IPC mechanisms (not shown in maps) will be used to constrain the rate at which scenarios propagate along the path. For example, synchronous IPC imposes a stronger constraint than asynchronous IPC. However, a path like this by itself makes no commitment to the IPC mechanism, it just provides a framework for thinking about it.

Interprocess excursion. A pattern that can be carelessly interpreted as severely constraining concurrency is an *excursion*. The excursion bight appears to require forcing the first process to wait while the second one is busy performing its respon-sibilities along the path. This may be called *procedurizing* because it is like proce-dure call-return. Why do we need processes if we make them act like procedures?

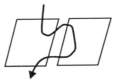

However, add another path traversing the first process and we get a different per-spective. We can now see that an excursion does not *require* procedurizing. The first process may do other things along a different path while the excursion bight is being handled by the second process.

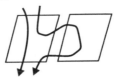

Coupling Between Paths Positioning processes in different ways in relation to the coupling between paths makes commitments about how the coupling must be realized by process IPC mechanisms.

Paths coupled through responsibilities. For design clarity, paths should be cou-pled through responsibilities only when there is no intent to assign the responsibili-ties to different processes that would use IPC to realize the coupling. If this rule is

followed, there are two patterns of interest. In one, the coupled responsibilities are
assigned to the same process, so there is no concurrency issue. In the other, the cou-

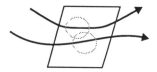

pled responsibilities are assigned to a nonprocess component that is shared between
different processes. This may call for use of the mutual exclusion pattern.

Private asynchronous coupling. This pattern suggests an asynchronous IPC mechanism directly between the processes.

Shared asynchronous coupling. This pattern suggests an asynchronous IPC mechanism, that is implemented by a shared mechanism such as a public semaphore or
mailbox.

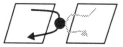

Private synchronous coupling. This pattern indicates a rendezvous not only
between paths but also between processes. It requires a procedurizing IPC mechanism.

Shared synchronous coupling. This pattern might be used to indicate that there are
responsibilities along the rendezvous path requiring back-and-forth interaction

between the processes at a more detailed level (so procedurizing of the entire rendezvous would not be acceptable).

Performance of Paths Paths with processes along them provide a handy common denominator for mentally adding up the qualitative, end-to-end effects of IPC overheads, IPC queuing delays, time required to execute responsibilities, and so on. Thus maps
can be used to make rough, qualitative judgments during high-level design about performance trade-offs between different candidate organizations, for example between ones
with fewer or more processes along the paths. Making such judgments based on general
domain knowledge, without knowing specific details of how everything will be connected
together or programmed, is part of a designer's job during high-level design. Quantitative
performance analysis is, of course, only possible when details are known, for example, we
know the precise nature of inter-process communication, the real time required by detailed
computations, the hardware configuration/performance, the event arrival rates and distri-
butions, and so on. However, strategic trade-offs can be made during high-level design,
without knowing all these things in detail.

Robustness of Paths Processes are arbiters of robustness of paths because they
are the active components that control the paths (apart from ISRs) and are generally associated with physical components that may fail, for example, they run on physical processors and manage interactions with physical i/o devices. From a path perspective, the effect
of failures is to break paths, in other words, to cause paths to stop or to proceed incorrectly. In general, many paths may traverse a single process and many processes may control a single path, so there is lots of opportunity for problems.

For robustness of paths, the first and most obvious rule is that paths must never be
broken by the processes that control them. This may seem to be a small matter of programming. However, errors can easily creep in if programmers do not understand the end-to-
end picture represented by maps.

If we can identify specific failure points along paths, then we can design for robustness by positioning processes on either side or on top of the failure points and giving the
processes responsibility for discovering the failures and taking action to keep the paths
going correctly. Recovering from breakage of paths between processes may require, for
example, timeout-recovery mechanisms managed by the processes themselves.

If we cannot identify specific failure points along paths, then we can design for
robustness by positioning watchdog processes off to one side and assigning them the
responsibilities of monitoring system state variables for evidence of path breakage and
taking action to abort broken paths (and perhaps to destroy the processes that control the
paths, in case the processes are damaged), or to somehow keep the paths going through
interactions with the processes that control them.

7.4 ORIGINATION-TERMINATION PATTERNS

This section provides basic patterns for originating and terminating paths in components of all kinds, along with implications of the patterns in relation to the active components in maps, namely processes and ISRs.

7.4.1 Processes

- Paths originating in processes are controlled by them, meaning the processes may

start paths at times of their own choosing. The control extends as far as the next

process along the path. If a process originates only one path, the convention is that the process carries the path all the way to the end of the segment it controls, before starting the path again.

- Many paths originating in the same process indicate don't-care ordering of starts, and arbitrary interleaving of responsibilities along each path afterwards.

- Ending a path in a process implies that some other process (or ISR) farther back along the path hands over responsibility for completing the path.

- Locating a concatenation point between paths inside a process indicates that the ultimate source of the action is in the first path and that the process will only start action

along the second path as a response. However, because processes are autonomous, consequential action down the second path may be started at a time of the process's own choosing. In other words, there may be a period determined by this process during which no progress takes place along the second path. The normal design assumption would be that the process would not arbitrarily delay progress along paths.

7.4.2 Interrupt Service Routines (ISRs)

- When a path begins in an ISR, our viewpoint is from the software side of the ISR. From this viewpoint, the occurrence of an interrupt is the only thing that can start action along the path.

- When a path ends in an ISR, our viewpoint is from the hardware side of the ISR. From this viewpoint, only the hardware can start action along the path (to result in the delivery of an interrupt).

- When paths are concatenated in an ISR, we are linking the above two situations together. Because an ISR gets its autonomy from hardware and has no autonomy as a software component, it cannot arbitrarily delay action along the ongoing path like a process can.

- A path that begins in an ISR may end in process, possibly one at the end of a chain of processes.

- A path that begins in an ISR may end in an object or team shared between the ISR

level and the process level. The meaning usually is that passages of the path deposit intermediate results that are being accumulated for eventual handover to a process.

7.4.3 Objects

- Paths originating in objects indicate the picture is incomplete; there must be an

implicit path originating elsewhere, in some process (or ISR), and concatenated to this one, that starts the action going.

- When a path ends in an object, it implies that there is some process (or ISR) farther back along the path that is using the object to perform the responsibilities along the path.

- Paths concatenated in objects chain the above circumstances together. The separation into two paths is the result of factoring a map and has no behavioural semantics of its own.

7.4.4 Teams

- When a path starts or ends in a team, or when paths are concatenated in a team, the meaning depends on the composition of the team, using the above rules.

7.5 SUMMARY

In this chapter we have:

- Extended the basic use case map model to include concurrent scenarios that may proceed at unpredictable rates relative to each other, may influence each other, may conflict with each other, and may fail before completion.
- Identified path interaction, conflict, and failure as important issues that maps help to raise to a high level of visibility. Pointed out that maps should be constructed so that coupling occurs at well-defined points along the maps (identified either by direct coupling or by indirect coupling through responsibilities and components).
- Presented design at this level as an activity that positions concurrent components (processes and ISRs) along paths to create bound maps that imply appropriate solution properties to realize the scenarios.
- Provided standard process-positioning patterns to resolve concurrency across and along paths and coupling between paths.
- Explained the rudiments of using process bindings in maps to design for performance and robustness.
- Provided standard origination-termination patterns for paths in relation to components in bound maps.

CHAPTER 8

Case Study: High-Level Design of a Real Time, Distributed System

This chapter focuses on issues in high-level design of a simple distributed application that is intended to be implemented using real time techniques, that is, concurrent processes, timers and interrupt service routines. It focuses on issues in the operation domain, including discovering processes from maps, factoring maps to give smaller maps for subsystems, using maps as invariants for making design trade-offs, and working with maps at different scales in a coordinated manner. The example is a computer communications problem called the MTU (Message Transfer Utility) that, although superficially simple, exemplifies many of the characteristics that make designing real-time systems difficult.

Whether or not the application will also be implemented with object-oriented techniques is not an issue in this chapter, which focuses on the operation domain.

We do not aim in this chapter to be prescriptive about design steps or to provide a balanced treatment of all design issues. We do not even attempt to resolve all design issues in relation to the case study, because this would require selecting a particular solution and developing it in depth, whereas our thrust is more toward reasoning about different possible solutions (this is, after all, high-level design).

This case study is continued in Chapter 10, where many of the issues glossed over in this chapter will be addressed in more depth.

The order of presentation of topics in this chapter should not be interpreted as a prescribed order for design steps. The presentation order was chosen to separate issues for tutorial purposes. The techniques of the chapter are intended to be used for reasoning about design issues in a high-level way at any point where such reasoning is required.

8.1   DISCOVERING PROCESSES

8.1.1 The Application

The application we shall study here is a specific version of the two-way producer-consumer problem that was introduced in Chapter 2. Two computer systems called MTU1
and MTU2 send one-line messages to each other over a communications link joining
them. To refer to the computers, we shall say "MTU1" or "MTU2", to refer to the software in either one, we shall say "MTU". Unlike the fax system treated in Chapter 2,
MTU1 and MTU2 may send and receive at the same time (this is known as full-duplex
operation in computer-communications parlance). The map that we shall use as a starting
point is shown in Figure 8.1. It shows a pattern that assumes the link is reliable. The path
shape is distorted compared to the corresponding earlier figure because we want to visualize reception and transmission responsibilities as progressing up and down *inside* the system black boxes, instead of across them. There is no technical reason for this, it is purely
for ease of visualization.

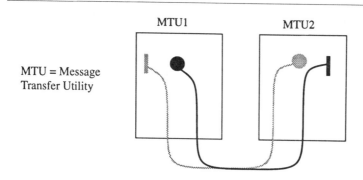

Figure 8.1 The initial problem: communication over a reliable link.

Figure 8.2 adds responsibilities to the map. In this simple map, the numbers that are
the names of the responsibilities also indicate the sequence in which the responsibilities
are performed. However, that is only incidental. When we extend the map to cover a more
general version of this problem, some paths may have the same responsibilities in nonnu-
merical sequence. The responsibilities that need explaining are as follows (the others are
the inverses of these):

> **packetize**: For generality, data is assumed to be sent as a data packet, which is a
> fixed-length, fixed-format byte string with space for data and a header containing
> identifying information.

form-data-buffer: For simplicity, each one-line message is assumed to be put in a fixed length data buffer that exactly fits into the space for data in a packet.

send: This is a unilateral responsibility that sends the entire packet without any interaction with the other end.

By now, this should be enough information to give the essence of the required scenarios without having to write a use case out in prose as well. The only open issue is, how much concurrency do we require along the paths? In other words, how fast can senders be allowed to start new scenarios while old ones are still in progress along the paths? Assuming the link is reliable, the main issue is the possibility of overrunning available buffer space at the sending end if physical transmission is too slow, and at the receiving end if it is too fast. Generally, these matters are constrained by communications protocols. However, let us imagine for the moment that there are no constraints and then add them later.

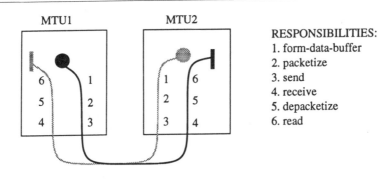

RESPONSIBILITIES:
1. form-data-buffer
2. packetize
3. send
4. receive
5. depacketize
6. read

Figure 8.2 Initial map.

Why are we starting out with such a simple view of this problem? We saw a timeout-recovery pattern in Chapter 7 that looks like it might be applicable here to handle communication over an unreliable link. Why don't we start with that? The answer is we could (and we shall a bit later), but we first need to exercise the process-discovery issue in a simpler context.

8.1.2 Factoring

Recall from Chapter 3 that factoring is a way of treating black boxes like the MTU ones in Figure 8.2 as systems with their own, smaller use case maps derived from the larger map. The factored maps are distinct maps in their own right that can help humans to reason about local design issues in local terms, while still maintaining the association with the larger map to provide context. This can be particularly useful when the black boxes are to be organized internally as systems of collaborating components, as is the case here (the components will be processes).

Figure 8.3 does the required factoring: First, cut the large map between the teams as shown by (a) and then put start and end terminations on the dangling ends of the paths in an obvious way as shown by (b) to give a smaller, local map. This gives a local picture of independent tx and rx paths, the first starting inside the team and ending in the environment, and the second, vice-versa. The details of what the paths do in other teams has vanished from this picture (though it still forms an important part of the design context).

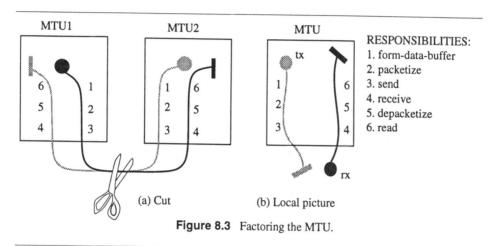

Figure 8.3 Factoring the MTU.

8.1.3 From Problem to Solution Concurrency

In this section we are concerned with discovering processes to satisfy the factored map of Figure 8.3. We also want to compare different configurations of processes (a configuration is a set of processes with a specific number of processes in it and a specific positioning of them in relation to the paths of the map). We say this is going from problem to solution concurrency because the paths express problem concurrency and the processes express solution concurrency.

We know from Figure 8.3 that the 1-2-3 and 4-5-6 paths are, at a minimum, required to be concurrent relative to each other. We have left open the issue of how much concurrency there will be along each of them. There are many possible process configurations with different degrees of process-level concurrency.

Figure 8.4 makes a first pass at identifying some possible process configurations. The issue here is not which configuration is the "right" one, but the fact that diagrams like these display the configurations in a way that helps us, with experience, to assess tradeoffs between them by inspection. They are the high ground where requirements meet physical constraints.

We want to give a sense here of how to use diagrams like this to reason about the issues at a high level.

The first thing to notice is that the physical sending of a packet needs only to be *started* by a process, leaving the actual sending to an ISR. Similarly, actual receiving would be the responsibility of an ISR, with a process entering the picture only when a complete received unit was available. Therefore, the start and end points of the paths in this figure should be interpreted the way the processes see them, meaning they do not include physical transmission and reception. We could add explicit ISRs to the map (Section 8.4.2), but there is no need as long as we keep the above interpretation in mind. It tells us that at the process level, the send and receive responsibilities will take very little real time.

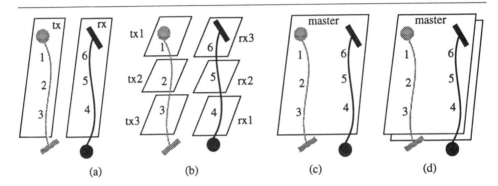

Figure 8.4 First candidate process configurations.

With this in mind, we can analyze the different configurations in a qualitative fashion as follows:

(a) All responsibilities along a path are allocated to one process. This mirrors in the solution domain exactly the minimum required concurrency in the problem domain. The tx process is responsible for the whole 1-2-3 path and the rx process for the whole 4-5-6 path. Thus the processes give the paths concurrency. The implication is that each path is run through from beginning to end by the process before it revisits the beginning. There are several variables with which to juggle, for example, the average rate of path completion, the average rate of path starting, and the ability for the ISR level to handle the rate of path completion. In this application, the rate of tx path completion could be too high for the ISR level unless the rate of tx path starting is constrained. The rate of rx path starting could also be too high for the rate of rx path completion if, for example, the path had to store messages in files. If neither of these issues arises, this would be a good solution. We shall return to these issues later.

(b) Each responsibility is allocated to a separate process. This also satisfies the minimum problem-domain requirement that the 1-2-3 and 4-5-6 paths be concurrent, but it also allows progress along each path to be concurrent, for example, tx3 could be transmitting one packet, tx2 preparing a second one, and tx1 preparing a message to go into a third one, all concurrently. However, given the above interpretation of the send and receive responsibilities, there is likely to be very little practical difference in concurrency between this configuration and the first one. This is because a single process can probably work through the path end to end faster than packets can be physically transmitted or received. The main effect of adding processes along the path to increase concurrency may be to add IPC overhead along the path. This conclusion would be invalidated if we decided to use a multiprocessor configuration in which different physical processors handled the top and bottom ends, for example, one processor handled everything up to and including packet processing and another one handled everything above that. We have observed that novices tend to design organizations like this for uniprocessors under the erroneous impression that processes are a good way of achieving code modularity. They are not; they should be used to modularize behaviour, as here, not code.

(c) This is a strawman configuration. A single master process is effectively a mainline sequential program. Path concurrency could only be achieved by the process explicitly interleaving the execution of responsibilities along the different paths. The process would have to check periodically (poll) for stimuli at different start points in order not to lose stimuli.The process would also have to maintain the path context for all paths (when we use a process for each path, we effectively hand this administrative burden over to the executive that supports the processes). All of this could be very inefficient.

(d) Some successful solutions in industrial practice use an approach where an interrupt-driven executive determines the responsibilities and queues them up for a *stack* of master processes.

We will now set the stage for adding a little more structure to the organization. Figure 8.5 shows that processes can seem to cut across team structures that make sense in nonprocess terms, for example, teams at the level of message, packet, and link processing. A different binding of processes to paths gets around this problem without affecting the level of concurrency.

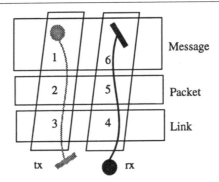

Figure 8.5 What does it mean to have processes cutting across other structures?

Figure 8.6 shows two different bindings with the same concurrency as Figure 8.4(a) that have more flexibility. In the binding of (a), tx would directly *perform* 1 and would *control* 2 and 3, and rx would directly *perform* 4 and would *control* 5 and 6. In the binding of (b), tx would *control* 1, 2, and 3, and rx would *control* 4, 5, and 6, but neither would directly *perform* any of them. We would add teams or objects along the paths to perform the responsibilities that the processes do not directly perform. Process bindings like the ones of Figure 8.6 or Figure 8.4(b) are easily aligned with team structures like the one in Figure 8.5 simply by making the processes part of the teams.

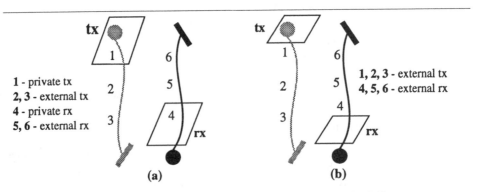

Figure 8.6 Process bindings with some organizational flexibility.

Figure 8.7 shows another process configuration that is different from all of the ones we have seen so far. It adds one extra process to the rx path of Figure 8.6(a). The motivation would be to give a higher priority to the beginning path segment (by giving the rx1 process a higher priority) to ensure that a new arrival could start along the rx path before the single process of Figure 8.6(a) had finished traversing it end to end. We already pointed out in our discussion of Figure 8.4(a) (which has the same level of concurrency as Figure 8.6(a)) that one process along the reception path could not cover this situation adequately.

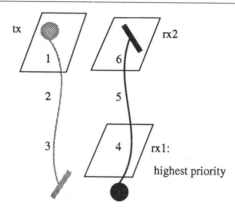

Figure 8.7 Distributing processes along a path to give its parts
different priorities.

8.2 MAPS FOR PERFORMANCE AND ROBUSTNESS

We now turn to the development of an unbound map to express a timeout-recovery scheme for communication failures in the MTU. This map will be free of commitment to any specific process configuration. However, in developing it, we shall have a family of configurations in mind, as hinted at by Figure 8.8. Having a family of component configurations in mind like this when developing unbound maps is the usual case. The result is that maps express large-grained behaviour patterns in a way that is invariant over different members of the family. We do not recommend trying to develop free-form maps that can be adapted to any arbitrary component configuration.

Figure 8.8 follows the suggestion in Chapter 7 that design for robustness be done by associating processes with failure points. Figure 8.8 brackets communications failure points along the main end-to-end paths of the MTU system as a whole by pairs of processes that are intended to be jointly responsible for detection and recovery of failures at those points. Such failures consist of loss of all or part of transmissions. The design intent is that the processes will keep the paths going in the presence of such failures, which would otherwise cause the paths to stop permanently at the failure points. A designer might quickly scribble this type of diagram on a whiteboard, on the traditional "back of an envelope", or just hold it as a mental model as a basis for reasoning and discussion, not documentation. This particular process configuration happens to be one we identified for completely different reasons in Figure 8.6(a) in the context of a local map for half of the MTU. The property that characterizes the family of configurations we have in mind is that there is one process on each side of each failure point to handle detection and recovery.

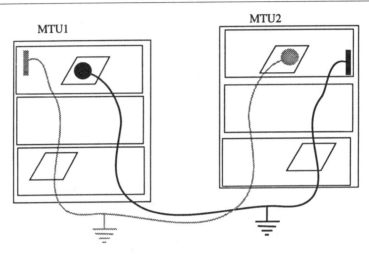

Figure 8.8 A view of the whole.

Now let us turn to the problem of developing a refined, unbound map.

8.2.1 Adding Timeout-Recovery to the Original Map

We now add a requirement for synchronization between the two directions of communication of the MTU as follows: acknowledgment (ack) packets are sent for received data packets and negative acknowledgment (nak) packets are sent for packets that are received but cannot be understood. To be sure of identifying acks with correct data packets, the packets include space for an "alternating bit" that changes value for each new data packet (excepting retransmitted ones). Thus the computers send not only data packets to each other, but also ack and nak packets. At the level of actual transmission and reception, there is no observable distinction between the three types of packets, they are all just sequences of bytes or bits. Only one outstanding transmission is allowed in either direction; in other words, no further transmissions can be made until either an ack is received or the transmission is abandoned. In each MTU there is a timeout facility that enables retransmission to take place if no ack is received within a certain time period. Retransmission may also take place after a nak is received. There is a limit on the number of retransmissions, after which the attempt to transmit that message is abandoned.

As before, data messages are prepared, placed in buffers, packetized for transmission, sent and received as packets, received in buffers and depacketized after reception for processing and storage.

We have already seen a timeout-recovery map in Chapter 7 that looks like it could satisfy these requirements, if properly interpreted. Maps can provide reusable patterns! However, we only developed that map for one direction whereas here we need a bidirectional map. Futhermore, for tutorial purposes we want to show a variety of approaches to developing maps and using them for design. One approach is that of Chapter 7: Develop an unbound, whole-system map first, leaving the issue of process bindings for later. Another approach is the one we are following here: develop a simple end-to-end map first, develop some promising process bindings in relation to it, and then refine the unbound map and see how it affects the bindings. To continue as we started out in this chapter, we shall now refine the simple map we have been working with, instead of adapting the one from Chapter 7. However, we will end up in the same place and we are not aiming to be prescriptive about the order of the steps to get there.

Figure 8.9 builds up map (e) as a composition of a pair of alternative maps (c) and (d) that are refined from the simple success and failure maps of (a) and (b).

The key is recognizing in (c) that achieving remote success is not enough, success must also be recognized locally (that is, at the transmitting end) through receipt of an acknowledgment. The map machinery to do this requires a pair of AND forks, one at each end, as shown in (c). These enable a local path at the transmission end to wait for an ack while a normal tx path proceeds to the remote end, and also enable a local path at the reception end to proceed normally while an ack path proceeds back. Failure to receive an ack is then easily handled by making the waiting place at the transmission end a timed one.

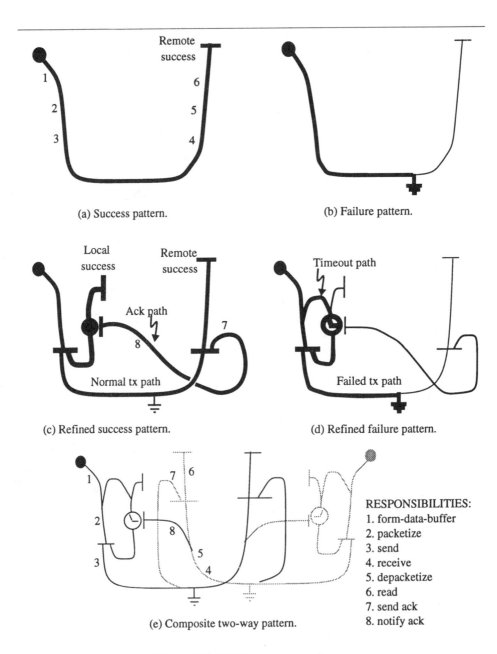

(a) Success pattern.

(b) Failure pattern.

(c) Refined success pattern.

(d) Refined failure pattern.

(e) Composite two-way pattern.

RESPONSIBILITIES:
1. form-data-buffer
2. packetize
3. send
4. receive
5. depacketize
6. read
7. send ack
8. notify ack

Figure 8.9 Building up a composite map.

8.2.2 Path Conflicts in Maps

This section identifies some important issues in the use of maps to guide not only system thinking but also detailed design and implementation.

Because maps are formed as compositions of end-to-end paths with some shared path segments, there may be conflicting sequences in the composition. For example, we may follow one end-to-end path into a shared segment and then inadvertently switch to another path going out. Our purpose in this section is not so much to point out conflicts in the MTU example, although they are interesting, but to make the following two points: Exploring maps for conflicts is an important part of the high-level design process; making sure conflicts don't get into code is an important part of the detailed design and implementation process.

Figure 8.10 identifies conflicts in the MTU map. Note that two interpretations of conflicts are possible. Either they are truly conflicts that should not occur—and therefore should be explicitly prevented in the implementation—or they identify valid, variant paths that were not thought of in constructing the map, that must be correctly supported in the implementation. There is no map *notation* to denote conflicts; they must be recorded by listing conflicts or highlighting conflicting paths.

In Figure 8.10:

- Conflicts (a) and (b) could occur if noise on the communications link could alter transmitted bits sufficiently. However, usually this is prevented by mechanisms below the level of this map, such as checksums or cyclic redundancy codes.
- Conflict (c) could be a critical race if it is not handled properly. Retransmission after timeout when the other end has already received and acknowledged the original transmission could result in the other end seeing the retransmission as something new. Abandonment of transmission due to too many timeouts could result in a late ack being interpreted as an ack for a later transmission. There is also the issue of whether or not a nak should be included along this path to allow the other end to ask for retransmission if it receives a garbled transmission. The *possibility* of critical races is widespread in concurrent systems. Maps are helpful for spotting them. Critical races are hard to see at the level of the software components that implement segments of the paths.

The requirements that we started with anticipated both of these problems. They prescribed a negative acknowledgment to enable the other end to ask explicitly for retransmission and also specified an alternating bit field in packets to prevent the race described above from becoming critical. However, not all issues are resolved by requirements that come spelled out from higher authority. Sometimes designers must analyze the situation themselves to anticipate problems like these. As indicated by these examples, maps are helpful for this purpose.

(a) Transmitted data received as ack.

(b) Transmitted ack received as data.

(c) Race between timeout and ack.

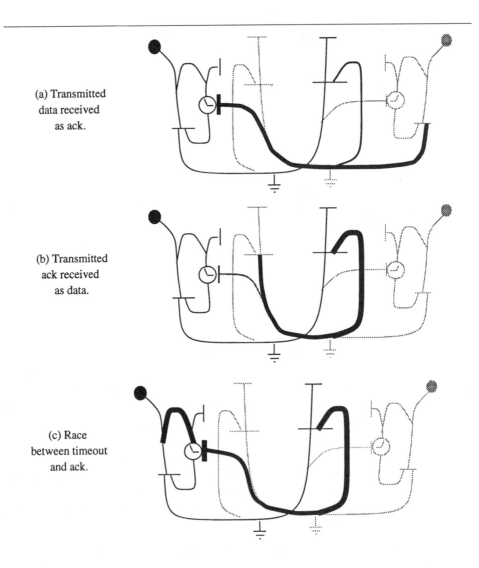

Figure 8.10 Path conflicts in maps.

8.3 MAPS AS INVARIANTS FOR EVALUATING TRADE-OFFS

Figure 8.11 repeats the earlier factoring process for the refined map to produce a local map
that can be used as an invariant against which to evaluate different candidate local component organizations (Figure 8.12).

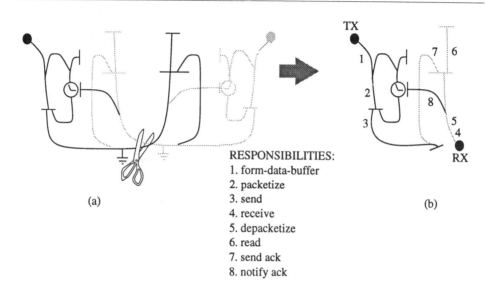

(a)

RESPONSIBILITIES:
1. form-data-buffer
2. packetize
3. send
4. receive
5. depacketize
6. read
7. send ack
8. notify ack

(b)

Figure 8.11 Factoring the refined map.

In general we are interested in more than just processes. We are also interested in
teams. We focused on processes first in this case study because we wanted to look at them
independently. Teams may be discovered from maps by looking for functional relationships among responsibilities. For example, in the MTU it seems obvious to group sending
responsibilities with receiving ones, packetizing with depacketizing ones, and message
preparation ones with message storage ones. This grouping could have been done first.
The important point here is that the discovery of processes and teams may be based on
quite different criteria, so they can be done independently of each other. (We are not saying that grouping responsibilities in maps is the only criterion for discovering teams.
However, we do not explore other ways here. See Chapter 12 for a discussion of the ways
use case maps can complement other methods to give a balanced design approach.)

The result in this case study (and we think in many practical problems) is that the designer has three independent things to juggle with initially: maps, teams, and processes (and later, objects and ISRs). It is useful in design to fix some aspects as invariant while other aspects are varied, to evaluate trade-offs. In this particular example, we may regard the map and the teams as invariant relative to the processes. A helpful way of viewing the trade-off picture is shown in Figure 8.12. Different component context diagrams showing different process organizations, but invariant team organizations, are evaluated using an invariant use case map as a common denominator. The particular set of process organizations in the figure was chosen to give a sense of the range of choices, not to be exhaustive. Observe that because the criterion for discovering teams did not include a requirement to have processes in them, some teams may not have any (such teams are not empty because they will have objects in them that have not been discovered yet). Responsibilities can often be left out of such diagrams as assumed detail. The presence of the teams serves to remind us of the responsibilities.

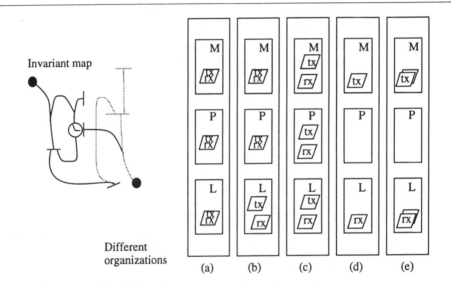

Figure 8.12 Maps as invariant patterns to help evaluate design trade-offs.

Think of the map on the left superimposed on the organizations on the right, assuming the relative sizes and form factors are adjusted to make this possible (for example, Figure 8.13 for case (d)).

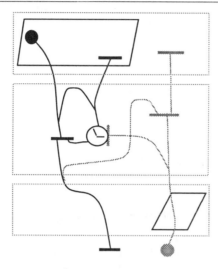

Figure 8.13 An example of superposition in relation to Figure 8.12(d).

The different configurations of processes in Figure 8.12 all have pros and cons:

- Configurations (a) through (c) maximize flexibility in relation to the possible use of a multiprocessor for this problem. They do so by providing active processes in teams that might be allocated to different processors. Configuration (d) and (e) minimize overhead along paths by minimizing the number of process interactions along the paths.

- Configuration (d) follows directly from the fact that processes are needed for concurrency of reception and transmission. It is a natural one when the software will run on a single processor because it enables control of entire paths to be centralized in one process instead of decentralized among several, thereby minimizing overhead along paths. However, it is not a natural one when the software is split among several processors.

- Configuration (e) is a variation of (d) that would enable multiple transmissions and receptions to proceed concurrently along the same path, under the control of distinct processes. This configuration introduces interesting issues associated with process coordination. For example, processes may overtake other processes and even pass them along a path, unless detailed means, below the level of the map, are put in place to prevent it. The map warns of the possible problem and provides a context for thinking about it, but does not resolve the problem.

- The other configurations come from anticipating that the teams might be allocated to different physical processors (for example, L might be in a front end processor, or perhaps both L and P). The minimum configuration if each team is in a separate processor is (a). The others are variations to provide full transmission and reception concurrency in each team.

8.4 SCALEUP ISSUES

8.4.1 Complexity

Is the MTU example complex enough to be realistic? Have we somehow stacked the deck in favour of our method by presenting only examples like the MTU to which it easily applies? We respond to these questions as follows:

- Complexity is not necessarily a function of size only. The tricky end-to-end coordination issues, the race conditions, and the failure-recovery techniques in this example are all representative of practical systems. Practical systems may have a lot of functional detail in them that is excluded from this example and that makes them large (in terms of size of code). However, the impact of such detail on the big picture represented by use case maps can be kept small by modelling functionality in terms of point responsibilities along paths.
- The MTU, like all the examples in this book, has been chosen because it has the characteristic of displaying large-grained behaviour patterns that are primarily point to point. For such patterns, the map model seems such a common-sense one that is hard to imagine it not being applicable to a system of any size or complexity. However, there may be systems characterized by patterns with substantial ripple that are too complex to be represented by use case maps. We think they are not broadly characteristic of the kinds of systems we see in practice, but we are not claiming they do not exist.

8.4.2 Scaling the MTU: Stubbing and Layering

Our treatment of the MTU has so far focused on issues only at the scale of message and packet communication. This is why we have not yet introduced interrupt service routines; assuming the MTU will be interrupt driven at the character level, they can be viewed as invisible at this scale. Furthermore, the whole MTU system might be regarded as detail in some much larger system. We explore these issues below.

We remind the reader that stubbing is a map-drawing technique that implies the existence of off-diagram detailed maps and that layering is a component-decomposition technique that does not. The fact that we illustrate both with maps is a by-product of the fact that our examples are all presented with maps. We do not mean to imply that maps are required to define layers; they are not.

Stubbing the Whole MTU Figure 8.14 illustrates how to treat a whole system like the MTU as a stub:

(a) The MTU map could be connected into local user teams as shown. However, this map is full of detail that is not relevant to local users.

(b) From a user perspective, the entire MTU (end-to-end) could be regarded as a pair of stubs for message transmission and reception. The transmission stub is in-line because the user path does not come back until transmission is completed end to end. Reception is assumed to happen spontaneously from the user perspective.

(c), (d) The stubs would be expanded in a separate diagram. Observe that any stub may have side effects due to internal end points of forks that are not visible in the higher-level diagram and never come back to the starting point. For example, in the TX stub, one of these end points is associated with the end of the reception path and the other is an internal abnormal ending.

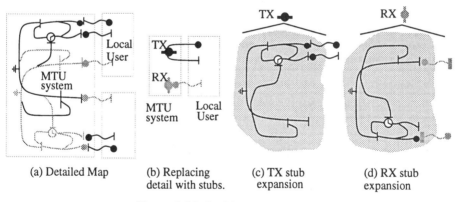

| (a) Detailed Map | (b) Replacing detail with stubs. | (c) TX stub expansion | (d) RX stub expansion |

Figure 8.14 Stubbing the whole MTU.

Layering the Whole MTU Alternatively, we might view the whole MTU as a layer (Figure 8.15). The MTU layer could be made visible with folds for explanation purposes (b) but would be invisible in ordinary design diagrams (c), just as the existence of the executive to support concurrent processes is invisible in our design diagrams.

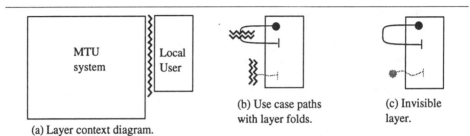

(a) Layer context diagram.

(b) Use case paths
with layer folds.

(c) Invisible
layer.

Figure 8.15 Layering the whole MTU.

Layering I/O Details in the MTU We have implicitly layered the physical i/o aspects of transmission and reception in our maps by simply leaving them out. The actual communication lines have bits flowing over them. The interrupt-level software processes characters. However, these are layered details in relation to our maps. Although bit rates are typically fixed by hardware (and so are synchronous), stimuli at the level of our maps are asynchronous. For example, the stimulus that marks the start of a reception use case path is the arrival of the last character of a packet in L, an event that is completely asynchronous as far as the software is concerned. Similarly, we assume that the end point of the transmission path is determined by the sending of the first character of a packet in L, with transmission of the rest handled by interrupt software in a lower layer.

Stubbing I/O Details in the MTU If we want to view physical i/o as stubbing *instead of* layering, we need to do a bit of map manipulation first (Figure 8.16) to get separate paths that may be stubbed.

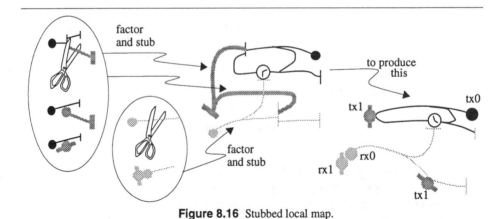

Figure 8.16 Stubbed local map.

- Character-by-character reception and transmission of packets is represented by stubs labeled rx1 and tx1. These consolidate the L-team character processing that has to take place to start the incoming paths and end the outgoing ones.
- The two primary paths are tx0 and rx0. The tx0 path is the same except that the AND fork has been factored so that L-level responsibilities along it are handled by the stub tx1 as an offshoot from the main path, which itself curves back to the waiting place. A similar factoring has taken place on the reception side.
- The start of rx0 is triggered by the rx1 stub. The tx1 stub appears as an offshoot in two different places, but represents the same L-team responsibility path in both places.

Figure 8.17 gives an example of how the character-level stubs in Figure 8.16 may be expanded and integrated with L-team componentry, including interrupt service routines. We identify this as high-level design because it fills in details in a high level way with maps. In this figure, in addition to buffer objects, there is a software uart team to provide a software interface to the hardware that would process the characters in an application like this in a personal computer (this team would read and write characters and control interrupts). Action at this level would be interrupt-driven on a character-by-character basis following the paths shown here. For example, the tx1 path brings in packet data to be transmitted, proceeds to txL where the data is stored, proceeds to uart software and then out to the physical environment for transmission, returns to the software via the **isr** when the transmission is finished, cuts across txL again to pick up another character, and keeps looping around in this way until the last character is transmitted. In the meantime, more data to transmit may be placed in the double txL buffer.

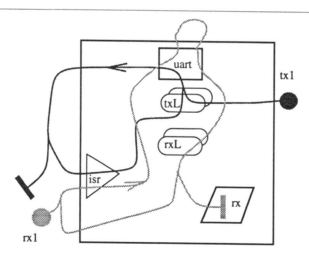

Figure 8.17 Filling in details of interrupt processing in a high level way.

8.5 SUMMARY

In this chapter we have:

- Showed how to discover processes and teams from maps by thinking along and across paths.
- Showed how to reason about whole-system issues with maps. The issues are performance and robustness here, but the approach of using maps as a framework for reasoning is quite general.
- Given examples of how maps can be reusable and extensible patterns of a high-level kind, and invariants for evaluating alternative component organizations.
- Demonstrated how maps may be used to bounce back and forth between requirements and high-level design, using simple maps to express basic requirements to get started and then refining them as insight develops.
- Showed how to factor maps to treat components in them as systems in their own right.
- Given examples of techniques that should be reusable for other problems.

Detailed Design Notation

*T*his chapter provides a general collaboration graph notation that is both particularly simple and particularly widely applicable to a range of object-oriented and real time implementation techniques. It is positioned here to set the stage for detailed developments in the following two chapters. However, except for an overview section, the focus of the chapter is rather detailed and most of it is not needed to understand the essence of the following chapters.

An overview of the collaboration graph notation is provided in Section 9.1; this is new material that gives the essence of the notation. The rest of the chapter is new material for detailed design specialists that may be skipped without loss of continuity in relation to the main ideas of the book.

The collaboration graph notation has specific features for processes, interrupt service routines, objects, slots, and teams. It is also quite simple, employing only five additional symbols

beyond the components themselves (which are the same ones that have already made their appearance in relation to use case maps). The combination of wide range and simplicity makes the notation interesting and useful in its own right, which is why it is in the body of the book instead of in an appendix (other standard notations used in the book are summarized in Appendix A).

Where use case maps are a high-level expression of the purposeful behaviour of a system of collaborating components, collaboration graphs are a detailed expression of the *interfaces* and *connections* that enable them to collaborate. Our use of the terms "collaboration" and "interaction" is not quite the same. When we speak of a set of components as a whole, we use the term "collaboration". However, when we speak of activity over a specific connection, we use the term "interaction".

9.1 THE COLLABORATION GRAPH NOTATION

Figure 9.1 gives the essence of the notation.

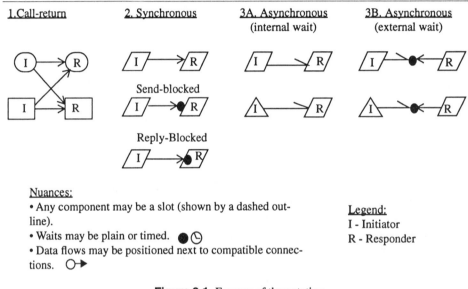

Figure 9.1 Essence of the notation.

Components at the ends of connections are referred to as *initiators* and *responders*. An initiator is the component that starts any interaction over a connection (for example, makes a call, sends a message). A responder is the component at the other end of the connection from the initiator. The direction from initiator to responder is referred to as the *control* direction. When a connection is composed of a single arrow, the initiator is at the tail and the responder is at the head. However, when the connection is composed of two arrows (asynchronous with external wait), the seemingly counter-intuitive situation occurs that both initiator and responder are at the tails of arrows. This is because both have to go outside themselves to interact over a connection that implicitly has interaction machinery embedded in it that is separate from both the initiator and the responder. This separate machinery is explicitly not modeled by separate components in this notation.

Legal initiators and responders are the same components as before, namely objects, teams, processes, slots, or interrupt service routines. Excluded from the class of initiators and responders are lower-level units of software like functions, methods, semaphores, mailboxes, or entries that in some cases provide the interfaces of components and in all cases are the means of implementing the connections between them. Such units are not separately represented in the notation. They are implied by the connections. Therefore, although simple *arrows* may be easily associated with calls and message sends in sequential software, *connections* may require a deeper interpretation. For example, autonomously generated accepts and replies are implied by synchronous connections, and interaction machinery positioned *between* components is implied by asynchronous ones with external waiting (for example, semaphores, mailboxes).

All we need for design of sequential object-oriented programs are call-return connections. The other connection types are needed for designing real time programs in terms of processes and interrupt service routines.

9.1.1 Attributes of Connections

We will now characterize the connections in terms of the attributes in Figure 9.2, to enable their semantics to be defined in a general way, without reference to specific software implementation technologies. Attributes are assumed to be supplied by the implied interfaces and interaction machinery.

Connection type	Attributes		
	Control	Interaction	Synchronization
Call-return	Initiator	Round trip	Unsynchronized
Asynchronous	Shared	One way	Unilateral
Synchronous	Shared	Round trip	Bilateral

Figure 9.2 Attributes of connections.

Control The control attribute indicates whether or not the initiator and responder ends share control or not. If control is not shared then, by default, it is solely in the hands of the initiator. This means there is nothing to stop multiple concurrent action at the responder end due to multiple concurrent initiators.

Interaction Whether or not control is shared, interactions may be round trip (meaning a response is possible from the responder in the same interaction) or one way (meaning no response is possible in the same interaction).

Synchronization Synchronization types are as follows:

Unsynchronized means there is no synchronization of any kind, because the responder is not capable of participating in it (for example, passive teams, objects).
Asynchronous means unilaterally synchronized, because only the responder may have to wait for an initiator, but never vice-versa.
Synchronous means bilaterally synchronized (both ends have to wait for each other); this is often called *rendezvous*.

9.1.2 Exclusions from the Collaboration Graph Notation

There is no representation for dynamic components except indirectly through slots. This is not an oversight; we rely on other diagrams to convey structural dynamics (use case maps, visibility graphs).

We provide no representation for broadcasting calls or messages to many places at once (analogous to AND forks in use case maps that indicate paths may go in many directions at once). Object-oriented and real time implementation technologies that we aim to cover with this notation do not support broadcasting directly, so we have not felt the need to include it. However, it may be useful to have a notation for broadcasting in relation to distributed operating systems that support it. In such cases, we encourage readers to invent their own.

9.2 USING THE NOTATION FOR DESIGN

9.2.1 General Properties

We illustrate the general properties of the notation with team boxes in the following diagrams to signify "any component".

Keep in mind that, although the *system* interface of a component in a collaboration graph is the set of all connections pointing to and away from it (the set of heavy and light arrows in the figure below), the *programming* interface is associated with the set of all

connections pointing *to* it (the heavy arrows only). There may be more to it than this if the component is a slot, because the actual programming interface of a slot occupant may require additional elements to support run-time structural dynamics expressed in maps at a higher level of abstraction.

Data flows may be associated with any connection consistent with the connection

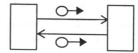

type. They imply parameters of interfaces and interactions. Because data flow is second-ary information in collaboration graphs, we often leave it out when giving examples to explain the notation, but it should never be left out of actual design diagrams used for doc-umentation. In general, flows need to be both named and typed. Data flows may be used to provide information about structural dynamics (Section 9.2.2).

Connections may be annotated with sequence numbers to indicate standard interac-

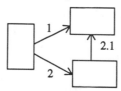

tion sequences. There is no notation to distinguish connection *names* (which may also be numbers) from sequence numbers, so it must be resolved by context. An indented number-ing notation may be used to indicate causally related sequences of interactions in cases where they can be conveyed clearly this way. Otherwise, interaction sequence diagrams may be required to show such sequences.

9.2.2 Structural Dynamics

Section 4.6 explained the relationships between slots, dynamic components and classes in terms of visibility graphs and class relationship diagrams. Collaboration graphs do not show dynamic components, but they show slots. Slots are used in collaboration graphs to show different contexts in which dynamic components may be visible at different times, without showing the dynamic components themselves. For example, in the collaboration graph below, the effect of the slots could be to make components like C4 and C5 visible to C1 and C3 at different times. C4 may be in S1 at one time and in S2 at another, and C5 may be in S2 while C4 is in S1 and in S1 while C4 is in S2.

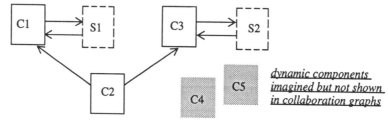

When developing collaboration graphs, we assume that the slots are occupied and ready to interact. Therefore, collaboration graphs normally have no connections in them specifically for creating/deleting components like C4 or C5, or filling slots with them. This is one of the reasons why we said above that the programming interface is only partially determined by collaboration graphs. Leaving out these things actually makes collaboration graphs more useful, because the remaining collaboration patterns are easier to see. Recall that we leave them out not because we think they are secondary scaffolding but because our whole approach to design relies on using maps with slots in them to give a view of structural dynamics at a higher level of abstraction.

The required interfaces of dynamic components come from design diagrams as follows: All dynamic components filling a slot must support the slot interface. Another way of saying this is they must all be of the same type (in a programming-language sense). Dynamic components filling multiple slots must satisfy multiple interfaces. Additional interface elements beyond these may also be required if the dynamic component must be acted on while in transit between slots, to satisfy some responsibility along a use case path (in such case there is no slot to indicate interface elements, they must be derived from responsibilities).

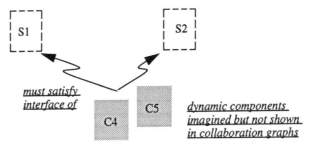

The only place we show dynamic components explicitly in collaboration graphs is adjacent to connection arrows to indicate they are passed as parameters, for example, when a component contains data that is required elsewhere and the whole component is passed instead of just the data.

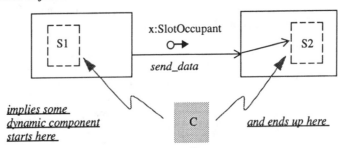

The grand strategy for creating dynamic components and making them visible in different places is best conveyed by a use case map, not by a collaboration graph. This map, together with the collaboration graph, possibly supplemented by visibility graphs, may be used to determine programming details. A considerable amount of detailed programming may be required to manipulate and pass around pointers to ensure that this knowledge is in the right place at the right time. This detail is, in general, below the level of the collaboration graph.

9.2.3 Processes and ISRs

The notation has been designed to express in a generic fashion the essence of a wide range of interprocess and ISR-process interaction mechanisms that exist in practice. Key issues are synchronicity, waiting, and timeout. To model these things we use two styles of arrows and borrow the waiting place and timer symbols from use case maps. The borrowed symbols indicate a more detailed kind of waiting/timeout than for maps, namely waiting for control interactions at interfaces, so there are detailed nuances that do not exist with maps. Otherwise the meanings are consistent. Using the same notation has a beneficial effect once you get used to it because the symbols give essentially the same cues, with nuances obvious from context.

Waiting for Arrivals An *arrival* is something that comes to a responder R at an unpredictable time, like a call, a message or a signal. It may be information it needs or a request for some service. Initiators *cause* arrivals, but are not *themselves* the arrivals.

The *waitany* case is the default for R waiting internally for any arrival. A responder may also wait *externally* for an arrival over a *specific* asynchronous connection (remember that the connection in this case is the composition of arrows plus waiting place, and that the individual arrows are not themselves "connections").

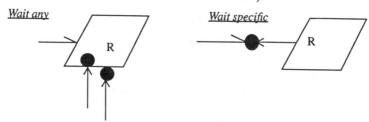

Timed waiting means that R will get either an ordinary arrival before the timeout occurs (in which case the timer is cancelled) or notification of timeout, whichever comes first.

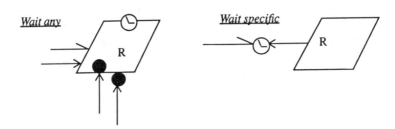

Waiting for Round-Trip Responses (Send-Blocked and Reply-Blocked)
Asynchronous interactions do not have round-trip responses by definition, so this only applies to synchronous ones. Waiting place markers are used in a supplementary way to characterize synchronous interactions as *send-blocked* or *reply-blocked* (this adds additional meaning to the nature of the synchronization beyond the bilateral synchronization that is already an inherent attribute of such connections). The supplementary notation indicates that a specific connection is used by the initiator to make a request that may not be immediately satisfiable, forcing it to wait, for example, because satisfying the request requires input from another process. Note that, although the waiting and timeout symbols are placed at the responder end, they apply to the initiator; this is indicated by associating them with *specific* connections, not the responder process as a whole.

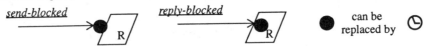

In *send-blocked* interactions, the initiator waits externally, implying that the initiator's request can be ignored by the responder. In this case, the connection itself defines the request. The intent of the timeout is that the initiator may give up after a time, without ever interacting with the responder. Thus the initiator will return from the interaction with either a response or a notification of timeout.

In *reply-blocked* interactions, the initiator waits internally, implying that the initiator's request cannot be ignored, but must be processed by the responder to see what the initiator wants, before determining whether or not an immediate response is possible. The responder may delay a response until it can satisfy the request, perhaps in consequence of a subsequent interaction with some other process. The meaning of the timeout is that the responder will return an indication of timeout if a timeout period elapses before the response is available. Thus the initiator will return from the interaction with either a response or a notification of timeout.

9.2.4 Connection Patterns

The notation may be used to express connection patterns spanning several connections (patterns of many kinds exist in systems). Sometimes it is useful to have special symbols for these (although we do not show any here).

Asynchronous Request-Response: This is roughly equivalent to a reply-blocked syn-

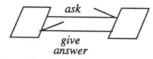

chronous interaction, except that it allows the process sending *ask* to do something else while the answer is being prepared. Because there is no round trip in either case, neither knows whether or not the other got anything or acted on it, so this is a bit shaky in an environment where attempts at asynchronous interactions might be lost.

Futures: Here the process sending *ask* assumes, some time after asking, that the

responder will have the answer, and so does a synchronous *get* to get it. The interaction is not shown as reply-blocked because the presumption is that the other process is ready. Caution might suggest adding a send-blocked style of timeout in case the other process is, for some reason, unavailable.

9.2.5 Connection Rules

Consistent and Inconsistent Attributes Attributes of connections must be consistent with the components they connect. The following combinations are illegal because of inconsistent attributes:

- This combination is illegal because the connections are asynchronous, but objects

and teams require connections with an unsynchronized attribute. Replacing the half-sided arrow with a two-sided one renders them legal because the latter is interpreted by context to have an unsynchronized attribute.

- This combination is illegal because the implied synchronization could require the

interrupt service routine to wait for the process, which, although it might be programmable, would be dangerous.

- This combination is illegal because interrupt service routines cannot be called by

software.

Connection Chains Connections may be chained together between components and across component boundaries. Chains have the combined attributes of their parts; as long as the combination of attributes makes sense, the chain is legal.

- The following chains of arrows are legal; the first because it represents either

chained call-returns, or a call-return with a synchronous interaction chained off the end; and the second because it represents a call-return with an asynchronous interaction chained off the end. These combinations make sense.

- The following combinations are illegal; the first because asynchronous is asynchronous,

nous, no matter how many arrows there are; and the second because there is no path for a round trip if the second arrow is interpreted as call-return (the other interpretation, that this implies an interaction with both asynchronous and synchronous attributes, is meaningless).

Chaining Connections Across Interfaces Connections may be chained across component boundaries to show external-internal connections, where appropriate. The attributes of the connections in relation to the components determine legal and illegal combinations:

- Any outgoing arrow from an object implies an outside initiator, chained through the

object. The ultimate initiator must be a process (or ISR), somewhere at the start of a continuous chain leading to the object, whether or not it is shown in the particular figure. This process (or ISR) is required to act as the ultimate initiator, because the object itself is not an autonomous component. Concurrent programs may have many ultimate initiators, sequential programs may have only one (for a sequential program, the single initiator process would correspond to the mainline).

- Discontinuities in the chain between internal and external connections of a process

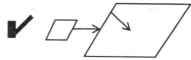

indicates the process acts as an autonomous initiator for the internal connections at times of its own choosing.

- Discontinuities across team or object boundaries are meaningless because neither

can be autonomous initiators in their own right.

- Discontinuities across process boundaries of connection chains originating in objects that are operationally internal to the processes are illegal because they would imply that the process is interacting with itself (implicitly, the interaction would be chained through the internal object in the figure).

- If a team contains processes, the connection chains crossing the boundary may have

different attributes as a whole from the parts that appear outside. This may give a misleading impression of connection attributes if the team is shown as a black box. It is not wrong to show such a team as a black box, but diagrams that aim to give an accurate picture of the connection attributes of the whole need to expose internal processes.

Fan In and Fan Out The fact that connections implicitly contain collaboration machinery has implications for fan in, as described below. The fanned-in connections are shown offset in the diagrams below, for visual clarity, but the meaning is the same as if all connections were joined at the same point on the responder. The interesting fan in issue arises when the initiators are processes, either directly, or indirectly through some cascaded set of call-return connections. (If you use process stacks, remember that connections that are drawn only to the top actually represent fan in to, or out from, all.)

- Fan in of *call-return* connections from different processes implies possibly concur-

rent execution at the responder. There is no implied mutual exclusion, serialization, or queuing.

- Fan in of *asynchronous* connections from different processes implies nothing new.

Arrivals are implicitly queued in first-in-first-out order at the responder, whether there is fan in or not. The responder implicitly dequeues them one at a time, waiting if nothing is there.

- Fan in from different processes may occur at the both ends of asynchronous con-

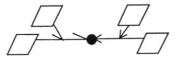

nections with external waiting. There is nothing new at the initiator end, but, at the responder end, it implies multiple responders may have to wait in first-in-first-out order to get arrivals.

- Fan in of *synchronous* connections from different processes implies that *both* arriv-

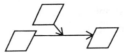

als and initiators are queued in first-in-first-out order. Arrivals are assumed to be dequeued in this order. Initiators are dequeued in this order to return with responses. There is assumed to be no possibility of responding in different order to initiators for the *same* connection (although there is *between* connections).

- Fan out always means that the initiators interact with the connections one a time in

some sequential order determined by their internal logic.

9.3 COLLABORATION GRAPHS AND USE CASE MAPS

Here we provide some guidelines for inferring relationships between local patterns in maps and ones in collaboration graphs. Don't be misled by the fact that *local map patterns* and *local IPC patterns* appear to be at approximately a similar level of visual complexity. The appearance is misleading because end-to-end information that is in the map as a whole is lost in the collaboration graph. This is not important for fragments like these, but it is important for whole systems. When going from maps to collaboration graphs during design, the lost information has to be added back via the internal logic of the components. But this loses the big-picture view that is explicit in maps. To recover the big picture requires putting together a lot of scattered detail. The notations have different purposes and in fact are complementary at different levels.

9.3.1 One-Way Paths and Excursions

This section illustrates how one may use IPC mechanisms to control overtaking and congestion along paths. Generally, there are many possibilities along one path, and more than one has to be considered to make an informed design decision.

One Way Paths The minimum connection required for a *one-way* path is a single asynchronous one in the direction of the path. Such a connection enables maximum concurrency along the path, because the first process does not have to wait for the second one. In other words the rate of progress along the path is determined by the first process. However, it is also dangerous because the second process could be overwhelmed. The IPC mechanism is assumed to provide queuing but the queue could overflow.

Some implementation technologies allow data to be transferred as part of an asynchronous interaction (for example, mailboxes), whereas others do not (for example, semaphores). Unless explicitly drawn as below, the default assumption would be that data transfer is possible. With semaphores, data may be transferred somewhat cumbersomely through a shared object, as in the example shown below (forgetting about the use of dynamic objects and slots for the moment, because they do not affect the issues being discussed here). This leaves the shared object open for access by both processes, requiring that it have mutual-exclusion protection.

A synchronous connection puts control of progress along the path in the hands of the second process. Assuming the connection is used only momentarily to transfer data, this should not slow up the first one too much but it may slow it up somewhat. Care has to be taken not to "procedurize" the second process by locking the two together while it performs its responsibilities along the path. Otherwise, why have more than one process?

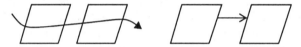

Another possibility is to use a synchronous connection in the opposite direction to the path. This puts control of progress along the path back in the hands of the first process. The send-blocked or reply-blocked notation indicates that it may have to wait if the first process has nothing for it.

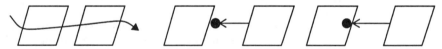

An interesting case is where there are paths in both directions and we innocently use the same connection pattern in both directions, for example, as shown below for a synchronous pattern. Connection patterns like this can cause deadlock. This is an example of needing to see more than one path to make design decisions about connections.

Excursions The case of an *excursion* requires two-way interaction, which may be accomplished in many ways. The most obvious way is to use a synchronous connection in the direction of the excursion. However, this may procedurize the first process in an unintended fashion.

An excursion may be implemented with bidirectional synchronous or asynchronous interactions, one in the forward direction to signal its start and one in the reverse direction to signal its end. This avoids procedurization.

Another way of avoiding procedurization is to implement the forward path of the excursion with a send-blocked or reply-blocked synchronous interaction in the opposite direction to the path, requiring the destination of the excursion to anticipate it. The closing of the excursion loop would be accomplished by a second interaction in the direction of the return path (shown synchronous here, but it could be asynchronous).

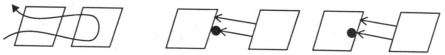

Deciding between these alternatives will likely depend on issues other than just single paths.

9.3.2 Path Forks, Joins and Waiting Places

This section summarizes patterns for various positionings of processes in relation to forks, joins and waiting places in paths.

AND forks and fork-joins wholly inside processes imply don't-care ordering. There is no implication for collaboration graphs. The code of the process may interleave the responsibilities of the paths in any arbitrary fashion.

Asynchronous coupling between paths inside a process calls for an asynchronous connection, with the triggering process the initiator and the other process the responder. The connection may be one with either external or internal waiting. If there is timeout (not shown), the internal-waiting solution below places responsibility for it directly in the responder process.

Asynchronous coupling between paths may be *between* processes instead of inside them, implying some sharing of responsibility. This suggests an asynchronous connection with external waiting. The coupling may be positioned inside an intermediate team or object, in which case its operational nature is hidden from the processes.

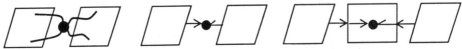

Fork concurrency as below calls for an asynchronous connection. Since there is no consequent join in this map fragment, no other connections are needed.

Fork-join concurrency as below calls for a nonprocedurizing pattern.

Private synchronous coupling is the only case that demands procedurizing.

Shared synchronous coupling may require several connections, including one or more connection-level rendezvous.

With these examples in mind to give guidance, the reader should be able to devise suitable connection patterns for other cases.

9.4 SUMMARY

In this chapter we:

- Identified unique characteristics of the collaboration graph notation, namely that it is both simple and broadly applicable to real time and object-oriented design.
- Gave an overview of the collaboration graph notation.
- Explained fine points of the notation relating to teams, structural dynamics, processes and ISRs.
- Provided guidelines on how to proceed from local patterns in use case maps to local ones in collaboration graphs.

Case Study: Rounding Out the Real Time, Distributed System Example

*T*his chapter rounds out the case study of Chapter 8, not only in its own terms, but also in object-oriented terms. This chapter shows how to make the transition from high-level use case maps to detailed collaboration graphs containing processes. It also shows how to deal with a realistic case of structural dynamics (dynamic buffering) in a high-level way using use case maps, and how to bring the results down to the detailed design level. In a number of ways, this chapter illustrates how the use case map approach enables object-oriented and real time issues to be treated independently in a first-class manner, yet easily integrated at any time: It shows how to add class hierarchies and detailed class structures that cover all the components in the maps, including processes, slots, teams, and fixed objects. Although it treats the issue of object-orientation as if classes were being designed from the ground up, the issues and approaches are also applicable when using classes that already exist, because of the fact that use case maps and class relationship diagrams are equal design partners that can be developed in any order relative to each other. It illustrates the employment of use case maps as a common denominator for evaluating trade-offs between real time and object-oriented issues.

For those who like to follow everything down to the last detail, code examples following the design diagrams of this chapter are included in Appendix B.

Although this chapter touches on highlights of many issues and approaches that span both object-orientation and real time systems, it does not aim to dot every "i" and cross every "t" either for this particular case study or for methods in general; it only aims to lay the groundwork for readers to develop approaches that can be used on other problems.

10.1 FROM MAPS TO COLLABORATION GRAPHS

In this section, we are concerned with making the transition from maps to collaboration graphs. The transition in part requires human judgment and in part is relatively mechanical. Purposes of this section include giving helpful hints about the judgment part and guidelines about the mechanical part.

10.1.1 Team-Process Configurations from a Collaboration Graph Perspective

Figure 10.1 sets the stage by showing a sample of the different types of collaboration graphs that might follow from Chapter 8. The reason for putting this diagram first is to point out the tensions that arise between high-level use of teams as operational groupings and implementation-level use of them as code containers, such as packages, modules, classes, and so on. Once diagrams like Figure 10.1 start to be drawn, the tendency will be to view the teams in them as code containers. Our design model does not *require* this but, once effort has been put into details of the diagrams, there will be a natural tendency to carry them through to implementation as far as possible. Only if the programming technology has no convenient means of implementing containers of the required scale will the diagrams likely remain as abstractions that are not explicit in the code.

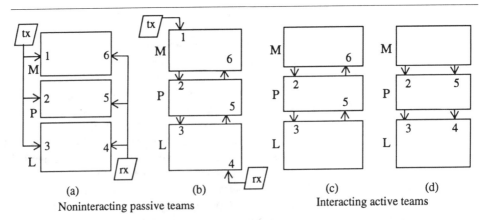

(a)   (b)   (c)   (d)

Noninteracting passive teams   Interacting active teams

RESPONSIBILITIES:
1. form-data-buffer
2. packetize
3. send
4. receive
5. depacketize
6. read

Figure 10.1 Different interteam connection structures.

Before going on to discuss these issues, we will first explain how to interpret Figure 10.1 in relation to Chapter 8. The numbers in the figure are responsibility identifiers taken directly from the use case maps of Chapter 8; they are neither connection names nor interaction sequence numbers. We use the responsibility names this way to keep the maps in mind. The phrases characterizing the responsibilities are not necessarily indicative of names we would give to the connections. For example, the connection from M to P at 5 in (d) would likely be called "get data" rather than "depacketize" because M is only interested in data, not in all packets; the connection from tx to M at 1 in (d) would likely be called "send data" rather than "form data buffer"; and so on. The responsibility identifiers are positioned near where the responsibilities have to be performed, either in an external interaction or in consequential internal ones. Some responsibilities do not appear in some configurations in this figure because they are associated with internal components and connections, for example, responsibility 4, "receive", is an internal responsibility of L in (c). In general there is not a one-to-one mapping from responsibilities in use case maps to elements of collaboration graphs, as will become clearer when we open up the team black boxes.

There is tension, illustrated by Figure 10.1, between using connection structures to express the underlying operational nature of the application and obeying software conventions for connection structures that require control to be hierarchical.

When we make teams passive servers and keep processes outside of them as controllers, as in Figure 10.1(a), we have a structure that expresses very little about the operational nature of the application. Although the processes are in control, in the sense that they initiate all calls to the teams, all the detailed knowledge of the application is in the teams. Large-grained behaviour patterns of the kind expressed by use case maps may be deeply buried in internal details of the teams. However, the passive-server nature of the teams is a convenient one for software construction.

We may try to put a little more information into the connection structure as in Figure 10.1(b), but this seems an unsatisfactory compromise. We may give a little more meaning to the structure by placing the processes inside the teams, thus making some or all of the teams active, as in Figure 10.1(c) and (d).

The configuration of Figure 10.1(c) provides a symmetrical peer-to-peer connection structure that expresses the operational nature of the application, because the bidirectional call chains correspond to the bidirectional, concurrent paths in the corresponding use case map. It is also a flexible structure because it does not force unwanted processes on us. We need a process in the bottom team that can make up-calls when input arrives at the bottom via ISRs (we would never have an ISR make up-calls for the obvious reason that ISRs must do as little processing as possible), but we would likely position a process there in any case. However, the connection structure does not require any additional processes along the up-call path to act as controllers for the calls. All the calls can be controlled by the single reception process at the bottom.

In spite of its flexibility, the container structure of Figure 10.1(c) is often avoided as a way of organizing code, at least for largish teams. One reason is that the code-level containers that implement the teams must have mutual visibility of each other, so that linking independently compiled code for the teams becomes a problem. Another reason is that established programming conventions in a company may require a one-way hierarchy of control at the interface level between containers. Such conventions may be adopted to constrain software complexity, but as we shall see below in the discussion of Figure 10.1(d), they cannot succeed in doing this for active teams that have peer-to-peer, bidirectional operational relationships.

The configuration of choice for container structures in code is likely to be along the lines of Figure 10.1(d) because it presents no compilation-order problems and has a clear hierarchy of control. However, it expresses a top-down client-server relationship that masks the bidirectional operational nature of the application and makes implementing it awkward. In particular, it provides no direct means for the bottom to spontaneously send new receptions upwards. Getting new receptions requires down-calls from the top, requiring the presence of at least one process at the top to make the initial down-call. Because that process may get stuck at the bottom waiting for input, it may have to be a special process whose only purpose is to wait for and return input. Such processes are often called transporters (or listeners, or messengers). Transporters are extra processes, introduced to get around a constraining control structure. As such, they make the implementation more complex, rather than simpler. Maybe the configuration of Figure 10.1(c) is not so bad!

To deal with issues like this, we need to have clear in our minds at the use case map level what fundamental processes are required by the nature of the problem. Then we can evaluate whether extra processes required to meet programming conventions are harmful or not.

A Note for the Advanced Reader The advanced reader will know that a common trick to avoid the consequences of having only down-calls in a structure like Figure 10.1(d) is to implement dynamically bound up-calls that bypass the fixed, interteam connection structure. This is done at the code level by passing a pointer, to a process at the top, downward to the bottom, enabling the pointer to be used at the bottom for spontaneous delivery of new input directly to the process. In our design model, this would be represented by placing process slots in the top and bottom teams that would be initialized to contain the same process (thus aliasing the process between the slots). Spontaneous delivery of new input to a process at the top would be modeled by showing it delivered to the slot at the bottom.

This adds weight to our observation above that trying to simplify the implementation by choosing a one-way connection structure like Figure 10.1(d) cannot succeed for applications of this kind in which there is operational symmetry. The operational symmetry must be achieved somehow, either by extra transport processes or by dynamically bound up-calls that bypass the external fixed connection structure. In either case we have made the implementation more complex, rather than simpler. There may be good implementation reasons for choosing a one-way interteam connection structure, such as compilation order, but the choice should only be made with a clear understanding of the consequences.

Introducing slots as a fix for an awkward interface structure, as we have suggested here, seems to have the design order backwards. Our design philosophy is that slots should enter the picture at the use case map level first. In fact, the slots we introduced above may make good sense at the higher level—and therefore also at the detailed level of the above discussion—if processes at the higher level are modeled as dynamic components that may move into slots as required. Making processes dynamic components may often be sensible in practical applications. For example, device drivers may be installed at run time by creating their processes on the spot, or communications subsystems that are installed at run time to provide new services to replace failed services may have their processes created on the spot.

We leave it as an exercise for the reader to develop the slot solution described above in use case map terms by extending the MTU maps of Chapter 8, using as a guide the producer-consumer example with buffer slots in Chapter 5. In doing so, we suggest exploring the tradeoffs between aliased and nonaliased process slots in the bottom team, remembering that Chapter 5 used nonaliased slots but that the solution described above requires aliased slots.

10.1.2 Examples of Collaboration Graphs

In this section we shall open up two of the teams in Figure 10.1, to get a perspective on how to design their details to realize higher-level maps. Figure 10.2(b) opens up Figure 10.1(a) and develops its internal connection structure to realize the simple map of Figure 10.2(a). There are some new things in map (a) that need explanation first.

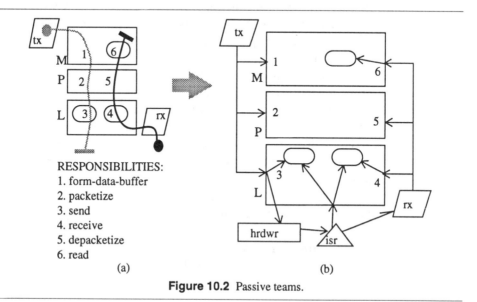

(a)   (b)

Figure 10.2 Passive teams.

The map of Figure 10.2(a) proposes a very simple data buffering scheme that uses three fixed objects to store data. This scheme is here just to have one in place to serve as a basis for filling in collaboration graph details. This simple scheme is not capable of handling more than one in-progress transmission in either direction (Section 10.3 develops a more interesting and realistic dynamic buffering scheme). There is one fixed buffer object for transmission and one for reception in L and one fixed buffer object for reception in M. There is no transmission buffer object in M or any buffer objects in P. The responsibilities 3, 4 and 6 are shown as belonging to buffer objects. The absence of a transmission buffer object in M and of any buffer objects in P does not mean there is no manipulation of communications data in these places, it simply means the data just passes through and any manipulation is done "on the move" (meaning that in code, the data would be manipulated as parameters). The processes are off to the side in the map to align with Figure 10.1(a).

The following sequence is not only helpful for understanding how the particular collaboration graph of Figure 10.2(b) is intended to implement the map of (a), but is also helpful as a reference for remembering in general how collaboration graphs may implement maps:

Transmission path starts: The tx process starts.

Transmission path passes through responsibility 1: The tx process calls the M team at 1; control returns to tx with the message data as a returned parameter.

Transmission path passes through responsibility 2: The tx process calls the P team at **2**, passing the message data as a parameter; the call adds packet headers; control returns to **tx** with the modified data as a returned parameter.

Transmission path passes through responsibility 3: The tx process calls the L team at 3, passing the packet data as a parameter; the call is chained through to the buffer object to store the packet. Then the L team triggers hardware to start interrupt-driven transmission (the buffer object could also do this). Control returns to the tx process. Note how responsibility 3 is implemented by a number of interactions.

Transmission path ends: On successive interrupts the isr calls the buffer object to get successive characters to transmit. The path ends when the last character is transmitted.

Reception path starts: On successive interrupts, the isr calls the buffer object to store successive characters. After the last character is stored it sends a signal to the rx process.

Path passes through the rx process: The rx process returns from waiting for a signal from the isr (presuming it has performed a call to wait previously, otherwise nothing happens until it does).

Path passes through responsibility 4: The rx process calls the L team to read the buffer. This call is chained through to the buffer object which returns the data as a parameter.

Path passes through responsibility 5: The rx process calls the P team at 5, passing the contents as a parameter; the call depacketizes it; control returns to rx with the message data as a returned parameter.

Path passes through responsibility 6: The rx process calls the M team at 6 with the message data as a parameter.

Path ends: Control returns from the call at 6 to the rx process.

Figure 10.3 shows a detailed collaboration graph that might be used to implement the configuration of Figure 10.1(c) for a slightly different map. The same buffering scheme is employed but now the processes are part of the teams.

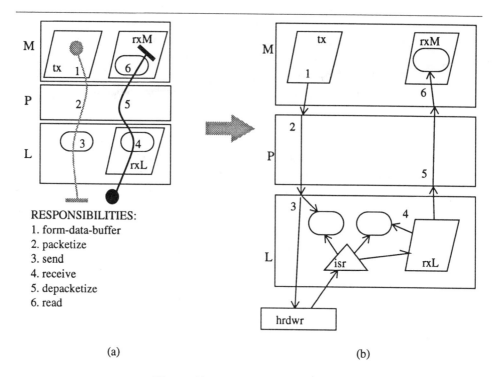

RESPONSIBILITIES:
1. form-data-buffer
2. packetize
3. send
4. receive
5. depacketize
6. read

(a)   (b)

Figure 10.3 Collaborating active teams.

Points to note in Figure 10.3 are:

- The connections are in the same direction as paths, implying that all paths are achieved by chains of *calls*. This is not necessary. The configuration of Figure 10.1(d) can be achieved with the same processes, except with the connections on the rx side reversed (using a send-blocked synchronous connection), implying that path is achieved through a chain of *returns*. The general rule is that path direction in maps does not impose constraints on control direction in collaboration graphs.
- The reception buffer object, although viewed as operationally local to the rx process in the map, is actually shared with the interrupt service routine and must be shown as such in the collaboration graph.
- Again, the responsibilities are positioned near where they must be performed but local detail determines how they are performed. For example, responsibility 4 would be performed by waiting for a signal, returning from the wait when the signal arrives, and then retrieving the data from the reception buffer.

10.1.3 Refining the Details

Figure 10.4(a) refines the map used in Figure 10.3 to add the cross coupling developed in Chapter 8. The added parts are shown with darker lines. Here follow some points to note about this map that are also helpful as general reminders of how to develop detailed maps:

- Both the start and the end of the local transmission path are positioned inside the transmission process in M to make clear that this process sees transmission as a path excursion that loops back to report end-to-end success.
- The OR join between the two transmission paths going from P to L is positioned in P to make clear that L does not see them as separate paths.
- The retransmission path segment is confined to P to make clear that M is not aware of retransmission.
- The asynchronous coupling with timeout at A is positioned inside P to make clear that it is P's responsibility to do all the ack-timeout processing. Because there is no process in P, this places constraints on the collaboration graph to implement this map.

The collaboration graph in Figure 10.4(b) shows how to add refinements to cover these additions to the map. Here are a few points to note about it that are also helpful as general reminders of the nature of collaboration graphs vs. use case maps:

- The new one-way sendack path and the original one-way path to send data are implemented as a shared call-return connection to L.

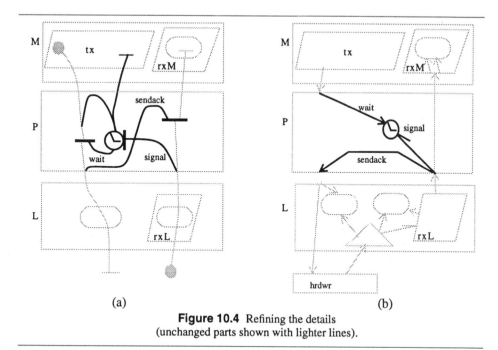

(a)   (b)

Figure 10.4 Refining the details
(unchanged parts shown with lighter lines).

- The wait (with timeout) path and the associated signal path are realized with an asynchronous interprocess connection that spans the distance between the reception process in L and the transmission process in P through connection chaining from both places.
- With three processes and an interrupt service routine, there is enough software concurrency to make the four path segments that exit from the AND forks in the map concurrent, in spite of there being no processes in P where the forks are shown.
- The slightly simpler look of the coupling in P in the collaboration graph is misleading because all the end-to-end information in the map has disappeared. In the collaboration graph we have to rely on the internal logic of components (which at this point in the design process does not yet exist).

10.2 EXPLORING COLLABORATION GRAPHS

High-level design is not the only place to make trade-offs. In this section, we give examples of trade-off issues that arise at the collaboration graph level.

In Figure 10.4(b), the use of a synchronous connection between the rxL and rxM processes where the map really only requires an asynchronous one has its dangers. We put the connection there to illustrate that decisions about connections in collaboration graphs may follow from other considerations than just the maps. In this case the consideration is that synchronism generally makes for reliable transfer of data. A possible performance implication is as follows: If rxM could get tied up for a long time while storing a received message, say in a file (not shown), the synchronous interaction could force rxL to wait, possibly causing it to be so slow that new receptions could be lost. The ultimate consequence could be a slowing down of the whole system due to need for the other end to retransmit. In choosing synchronous interaction here, we have implicitly made a judgment that there will be no important performance effects of this kind. We rely on the programmer not to program rxM in such a way as to cause such effects (for example, by delaying reply until after file storage is completed).

This figure leaves open the issue of multiple reception scenarios along the reception path. The question is, should these be handled one after the other or interleaved? Normally a good design rule that decides the issue is *processes do not poll*. Interleaving is thereby excluded because it requires polling. This means that in the collaboration graph, rxL should not return from its call to P until all consequential reception actions have been completed in P and M. However, the collaboration graph itself does not yet constrain this. As it is, a programmer could include returns from this call at selected points to poll for new input. The danger of this is that if nothing is there, the polling is pure overhead. We would need to specify parameters of the calls and give examples of interaction sequences to make it clear there is to be no polling (or *no polling* could be established as a programming rule).

Figure 10.5 gives two examples of technically acceptable ack-timeout collaboration graphs that must be rejected because they do not fit the requirements of the map of Figure 10.4(a). Both could accomplish the purpose of txM waiting with timeout for an ack. Both are unsuitable because they violate the requirement of the map that all responsibilities associated with acks and timeouts belong to P. This is a sensible requirement that should not be violated, because it centralizes all packet-level processing in one place, which is desirable for modularity.

- The solution of Figure 10.4(b) had txM waiting for an ack in an intermediate place between it and the source at rxL, namely in P.
- Figure 10.5(a) has txM waiting for an ack "at home". The notation indicates that txM sets a timer before waiting for any events (there is only one possible event here, a signal from rxL) and then waits with timeout.
- Figure 10.5(b) has txM waiting for an ack at the source at rxL. We show the interface of rxL as supporting the means by which txM may wait, with timeout, for an ack; however, the same effect could be achieved by moving the shared semaphore implied by Figure 10.4(b) into L.

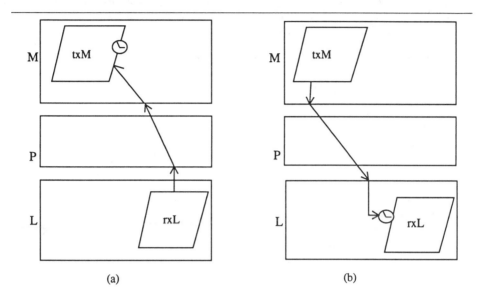

(a)   (b)

Figure 10.5 Legal but unsuitable ack-timeout collaboration graphs.

While rejecting the solution of Figure 10.5(a) for this specific problem, we note that it has one nice property that the other two do not, including the selected one of Figure 10.4(b). It offers the possibility that, for a slightly more general version of this problem, all waiting that txM might have to do for interactions with any other processes (including with ones not shown, for example, one bringing new messages requiring sending) could be centralized in txM. In this specific problem, in which only one message may be outstanding (that is, awaiting an ack) at a time, there is no advantage because, when a message is outstanding, txM has nothing else to do but wait for an ack, so having it wait at a specific place outside itself (in P) causes no problems. In a slightly more general case, multiple messages could be outstanding, and the transmission process might be torn between waiting for new messages requiring sending and waiting in P (or elsewhere) for acks or timeouts for outstanding ones.

A good design rule for processes is *one place to wait*. This rule prevents the possibility of a process being stuck in one place while missing things at another.

Figure 10.6 shows one possibility for guaranteeing that txM has one place to wait. Put a process in P, txP, to do all transmission-oriented processing in P. This enables us to satisfy the one-place-to-wait rule for txM while also satisfying the requirement that all ack-timeout processing be the responsibility of P. The new process txP acts as a switchboard for all transmission-related action in P. The price we pay is more components and more interactions. This is not an unusual price to pay for greater flexibility, but care must be taken not to carry it so far that the additional overhead causes performance problems and the additional complexity causes errors.

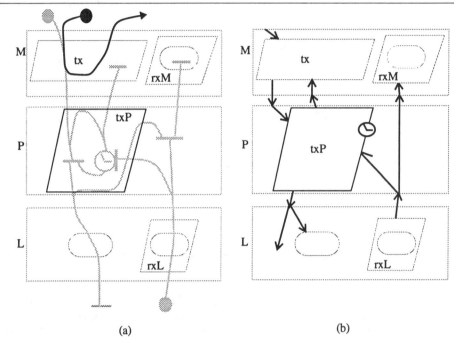

(a)   (b)

Figure 10.6 Satisfying the rule of one-place-to-wait.

10.3 A REALISTIC EXAMPLE OF STRUCTURAL DYNAMICS

In this section, we make a foray back into high-level design with assembly-domain use case maps to develop a dynamic buffering scheme. While this section is on the surface about dynamic buffering in a relatively small-scale communications problem, keep in mind that, apart from the specifics of this particular problem, it illustrates general map techniques that are not restricted to such small scale problems. Here the structural dynamics is displayed by dynamic buffer objects, but on a larger scale it might be displayed by teams at the whole-system level.

One big issue that this section illustrates is how a map allows us to check visually that a structurally dynamic scheme is correct, in the sense that it balances creates, moves and destroys that occur at different places across a system of collaborating processes, teams, and objects. Although buffering may seem like a detailed issue, such system-wide concerns are hard to get right at the detailed level and can result in many errors. Maps help to get them right by enabling us to reason about them in a high-level way.

Dynamic allocation of data buffers is often used in real time software to provide flexibility in dealing with variable loads on the system from different sources when there are memory limitations.

The approach we shall illustrate is one in which one class of buffer object satisfies all buffering requirements. Buffer objects of the same class move from team to team where they play different roles. At the map level, the roles are identified by slots operating in the context of teams (later they will be identified with different sets of interface methods of the class that provides objects to fill the slots).

There are many possible dynamic buffering configurations, one of which is shown in Figure 10.7. The slots in Figure 10.7 are for the buffer objects. The slots provide double buffering for reception in both the L and M teams and for transmission in the L team. There is a buffer slot in P to hold a current buffer object for possible retransmission (txmP) and one to hold an ack/nak object (txaP). Note that pools are not used to represent multiple buffering because we need objects to be active in slots; pools are not places where they can be active. An initialization pattern is shown in (b).

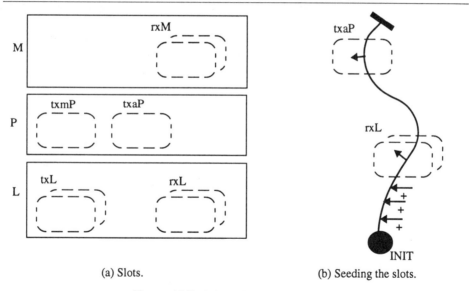

(a) Slots.   (b) Seeding the slots.

Figure 10.7 A dynamic buffering configuration.

In general, multiple buffering (of which double buffering is a special case) is used to accommodate transient differences in the rates of writing and reading data. The idea is that data may be written into one buffer while previously written data is read from other buffers (in double buffering, from one other buffer). The storage capacity and number of buffers must be set to accommodate the worst transient difference in writing and reading rates, to prevent data overruns (data being overwritten while it is being read). There are many variations of multiple buffering possible, from static schemes in which a fixed number of static buffer objects are positioned for reading and writing, and data is copied from them when it is needed elsewhere, to dynamic schemes in which variable-length queues hold dynamic buffer objects in particular places and the objects themselves are moved when data is needed elsewhere. In double buffering, there are no queues, but only two fixed objects (in the static case) or two fixed slots (in the dynamic case) in places where writing could overrun reading. Multiple buffering is only one way of dealing with varying rates of writing and reading data. Another way is using explicit flow control (obtaining permission to write before writing).

The salient features of our model of dynamic double buffering are: slots in double configurations alternate between writing and reading (the writing process or ISR uses one slot and the reading process the other and then they switch slots next time); buffer objects in slots are the destinations of written data; and reading may consist of moving a buffer object out of a slot to somewhere else where it may be read on the move or placed in another slot and read. Note that this model does not permit a single interpretation of phrases like "emptying a buffer", so be careful not to use such phrases; emptying might mean moving a buffer object out of a slot, or destructive readout of the data in a buffer object.

The rationale for this particular slot configuration has more to do with illustrating different design possibilities in one example than with trying to come up with the "best" design:

Reception

L: Double reception buffering is provided in L (double rxL slots) because overruns can occur due to the other end sending a message and an ack close together in time. The assumption is that at the communication rates anticipated, double buffering is good enough. In general, interrupt-lockout protection of the buffer objects is required wherever they are accessed by processes in case the assumption is occasionally violated.

P: No reception buffering is provided in P, because buffer objects containing receptions just pass through (or are discarded, after analysis). One ack buffer slot is provided in P, which is intended to be reused for all acks. The idea is that a standard ack object that may be modified for individual acks is prestored in txaP, aliased between txaP and txL during transmission, and remains in txaP afterwards for reuse. The assumption is that the aliasing is safe. It would be unsafe if an ack of a new data reception was required while an ack was being prepared for a previous one. This is an example of an apparently reasonable design decision, made for simplicity in a particular case, being potentially dangerous in a more general case. Designers must always juggle such trade-offs. More generality could be achieved by, for example, using multiple txaP slots.

M: Double reception buffering is provided in M in anticipation that incoming messages might be stored in an external file (not shown in the figure), file i/o might be slow, and a new buffer object containing a message might arrive at M while it is being performed. Designing in anticipation of requirements not actually expressed is something all good designers must practice.

Transmission

M: No transmission buffering is provided in M because, although buffer objects are created there, there is no reason for them to do other than pass through.

P: Single transmission buffering is provided in P to hold buffer objects for retransmission.

L: Double transmission buffering is provided in L to cater for the case where a message and an ack need to be sent so close together in time that the corresponding objects overrun each other arriving at L.

Figure 10.8 shows with use case paths how this buffering configuration is intended to operate, following the approach and notation of Chapter 3. The control of which slot to use in a double-buffered slot configuration is left to program detail.

The paths show create-move-destroy responsibilities along them in relation to dynamic transmission and reception objects (responsibilities other than create-move-destroy are assumed to be the same as before).

Transmission

a. An object is created (it is assumed to be initialized with a message).

b. The object moves into txmP (where a packet header is assumed to be added).

c. The object moves out of txmP, using the aliasing move-stay operation (it stays in case retransmission is required later).

d. The object moves into txL for transmission. While transmission is in progress, the object is aliased in both txmP and txL, but only plays an active role in one of them, namely txL.

e. The object moves out of txL when transmission is completed, implying txL loses all knowledge of it. It is not shown moving anywhere else before the end of the use case path. If it were not aliased, this would indicate that it should be destroyed. However, it is aliased, so the implication is that it is only forgotten in relation to txL, not destroyed, and is still available through txmP.

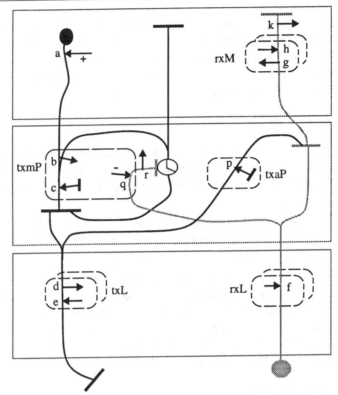

Figure 10.8 Dynamic buffering map.

Data Reception

f. A full reception object moves out of rxL.

g. After being recognized in P as containing data, it moves into rxM.

h. After message reception responsibilities are completed, the object moves out of rxM.

k. The object is recycled back to an empty rxL slot. The map does not show the recycling explicitly as a path, but only shows a move of the object out of the use case path; the move must be commented (the previous sentence is such a comment) to indicate that it means recycling. We could have shown the same thing either by stretching the move arrow all the way to rxL or by routing the path back to rxL , but this keeps the maps simpler and suffices.

p. Along the concurrent acknowledgment path, an ack object is moved out of txaP, using the aliasing move-stay operation (the assumption is that the object's data would be properly filled in first to identify the specific packet received).

d. The ack object moves into txL where it is seen as just another object to be transmitted. This could occur while a message is being transmitted, and we have therefore provided a double-buffered txL slot to take care of this case. While transmission is in progress, the object is aliased between txaP and txL.

e. The object moves out of txL and is forgotten there (but not destroyed).

Ack Reception

f. The ack is just another full reception object that moves out of rxL.

q. The original transmitted object is moved out of txmP and destroyed (because it is no longer needed for transmission).

r. The ack object came out of an rxL slot and has to be recycled back into an empty one.

All this takes much more time to explain in prose than it does to absorb by reading the map, once you are used to the notation.

Note how such a map allows us to check visually that our scheme is correct, by matching creates, moves, and destroys that occur at different places across the system as a whole. For example, the transmission object that is created along the transmission use case path (at a) is explicitly destroyed along the ack-reception use case path (at q). As another example, there are no destroys of reception objects, which means that they must either be recycled (at k and r) or aliased for reuse (at p). (The different approaches for transmission and reception—transmission performs continual creation and destruction, while reception recycles—were taken in this example for illustrative purposes. The transmission side could equally well recycle the same transmission object. Generally, recycling is faster than continual creation and destruction, but may require an initial allocation of more storage space.)

Processes   We have developed this scheme with an unbound map without processes, although with processes in mind. Now we must put the processes back explicitly. The dynamic buffering scheme requires some changes in the M team from our earlier static configuration because having multiple slots for this purpose operationally nested in a single process does not make sense. When the rxM process is busy with one slot, the other slot would be inaccessible. Either both slots must be outside the rxM process as in Figure 10.9(a) or we must have a stack of rxM processes with one slot nested in each. Recall that a process stack positioned on a use case path can result in race conditions along the path. This may make (b) less desirable in some circumstances. This skeleton map is enough to give the nature of the map; the rest follows straightforwardly from Figure 10.8

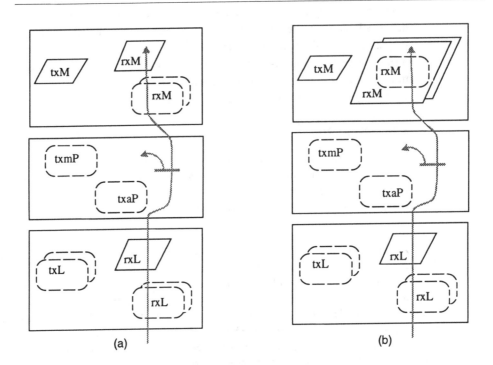

Figure 10.9 Skeleton map showing possible process/slot arrangements
(rest of map follows from Figure 10.8).

10.3.1 Back to Collaboration Graphs

We use Figure 10.9(b) as an example. Refining the collaboration graph of Figure 10.4(b) (repeated in skeleton form in Figure 10.10(a)) to satisfy the requirements of the map of Figure 10.9(b) produces the collaboration graph of Figure 10.10(b).

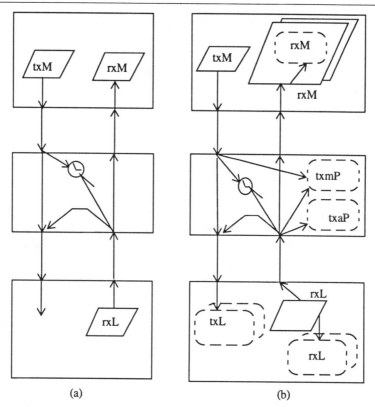

(a)   (b)

Figure 10.10 Collaboration graph for a dynamic buffering scheme.

10.4 CLASSES FOR PROCESSES AND OBJECTS

To round out the chapter, we show how classes for processes and objects may be included
in the design process in a coordinated fashion, using implementation-oriented class rela-

tionship diagrams (manufacturing domain) that are cross-referenced to components in the maps and collaboration graphs (operation/assembly domain). In this section we proceed as if classes have to be designed from the ground up to implement the maps and collaboration graphs we have developed. However, this is a side effect of the order in which we decided to present topics in this case study, not a constraint of the design process. Because use case maps and high-level class relationship diagrams are first-class design elements in our approach, either can come first, or both can be developed together. Many of the classes we shall identify would probably already exist for this type of application and would simply be reused.

10.4.1 High-Level Class Relationship Diagrams for MTU Buffering

If we had used class relationship diagrams in our earlier high-level treatment of this case study, we would have used them to keep a dictionary of important classes. Such class relationship diagrams would have been kept "light" because they would have been likely to change [18]. For this reason we would not have annotated them with methods, and would have made limited use of inheritance. Figure 10.11 shows a diagram along these lines that we might have developed earlier.

The relationship arrows between the boxes of Figure 10.11 model relationships between instances of classes, not relationships between the classes themselves. The instance relationships can be read as follows: An instance of PacketTeam *contains* an instance of Message, an instance of MessageTeam *contains* an instance of Message, and an instance of LinkTeam *sends* and *receives* an instance of Message.

We think of class relationship diagrams like this as recording the basic vocabulary of design concepts during high-level design. In our approach, class relationship diagrams are *not* used for modeling the dynamic properties of the concepts or relationships. In particular, a class relationship diagram does not answer the following questions explicitly:

- How many instances of a class will be created at run-time? For example, is there one LinkTeam object or many?
- When will an instance of a class be created? In other words, does a class represent a fixed or a dynamic component? Or both? For example, does a MessageTeam object create an instance of a Message for each message or are the Message objects reused?
- When will an instance relationship be created? On a class relationship diagram an instance relationship implies that the relationship *may* exist, but under certain operating scenarios the relationship *may not* exist. For example, a LinkTeam object may never receive a Message object if the node is never sent anything.
- How are objects and different instance relationships related? For example, is the same Message object created by the MessageTeam contained in the PacketTeam or are these different objects?

Design methods centered on class relationships, for example, [26], [3], have extended notations for class relationship diagrams that can express some of the issues listed above. These methods make use of multiway relationships and constraints on relationships.We keep our class relationship diagrams simple by not using these extensions. This makes early class relationship diagrams relatively lightweight and thereby easy to change.

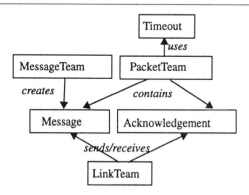

Figure 10.11 A high level class relationship diagram for an aspect of the
MTU application.

10.4.2 Detailed Class Relationship Diagrams for MTU Buffering

At the detailed design level, class relationships naturally become more detailed. Methods, derived from collaboration graphs, are added to classes and more use is made of inheritance to factor common behaviour into superclasses. Also, solution domain classes begin to emerge, as do issues for reusability and extensibility. For example, Figure 10.12 shows a class relationship diagram for the dynamic buffers of the MTU that were discovered in our development of use case maps. The classes of Figure 10.12 subsume the initial classes, `Message` and `Acknowledgment`, shown in Figure 10.11.

The class hierarchy on the left of Figure 10.12 comes from considering the different types of buffers needed in the MTU. There is a `MessageBuffer` class for data messages that are sent by a node, an `AckBuffer` class for acknowledgments sent by a node, and a `ReceiveBuffer` class for data messages and acks that are received by a node. The *italicized* text strings in the class boxes are the methods supported by each class. These methods mostly come from previously developed collaboration graphs. For example, the methods of the `AckBuffer` class come from the connection arrows to the txaP and txL slots in Figure 10.10(b). The methods of the `MessageBuffer` buffer class come from connection arrows to the txM and txL slots of Figure 10.10(b). The methods of the `ReceiveBuffer` class come from the connection arrows to the rxL and rxM slots in

Figure 10.10(b). (We have given names to the methods associated with the connection arrows of the earlier collaboration graphs.) Additional methods—for example, methods of the ReceiveBuffer class that are needed in P—come from responsibilities along use case paths that indicate that buffer objects moving along them need to be acted on as objects while in transit (there are no slots to provide interfaces in such cases, because details have been pushed down to a lower layer).

The buffer classes are arranged to have a common superclass so that some basic behaviour of the buffers is reused. The superclass Buffer has a data attribute for holding the contents of a buffer, for example, message data, packet header, link header, or acknowledgment. The class also has some methods for manipulating the data, e.g, *addBytes()* and *getNext()*. These methods were not part of the earlier collaboration graphs because they are not called by clients of the buffers. They are lower level interclass methods used to support the connection arrows of the collaboration graphs.

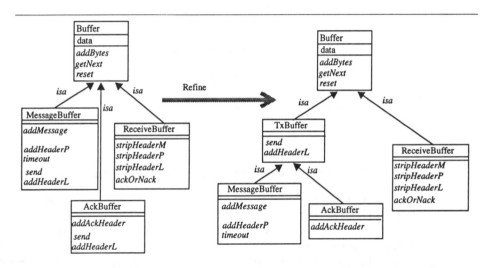

Figure 10.12 A detailed class relationship diagram for buffer classes of the MTU.

The class hierarchy on the right of Figure 10.12 shows a useful refinement to the class hierarchy on the left. The refinement is to introduce a superclass that factors common behaviour out of two or more subclasses. The new superclass, TxBuffer, supports the interactions with the txL slot of Figure 10.10(b). The methods have been removed from the MessageBuffer and AckBuffer classes. In relation to our slot organization, the TxBuffer class defines the interface of the txL slot; the MessageBuffer class defines the interface of the txmP slot and the AckBuffer class defines the interface of the txaP slot. From earlier use case maps, we know that objects in the txmP and txaP slots must also fill the txL slot. The class hierarchy on the right of Figure 10.12 guarantees this because the behaviour needed to fill the txL slot is inherited by `MessageBuffer` and `AckBuffer` objects.

The approach taken here results from a straightforward application of the *isa* (or supertype/subtype) relationship between classes. In Chapter 11 we will demonstrate that there are other ways of organizing the buffer classes of the MTU to follow standard patterns. The patterns there result from pragmatic concerns like ease of partitioning software for separate delivery, and ease of managing object creation and destruction.

10.4.3 Modeling Processes as Classes

In the producer-consumer example of Chapter 5, processes were implemented as procedures outside of a class hierarchy. Here we follow a different approach: We model processes as classes in class relationship diagrams. The advantages are the resulting source code becomes more regular (a class is identified with each operational component) and classes provide a good packaging mechanism for processes.

We still assume, as in Chapter 5, that concurrency is added by a real time executive that our application uses as a layer (RT-Layer). However, we also assume that there is a layer above RT-Layer, called OO-Wrapper (Figure 10.13). The purpose of OO-Wrapper is to hide RT-Layer from our application and ease the integration of concurrency with the object-oriented programming model of our implementation language. In particular, OO-Wrapper contains classes for the concepts used for concurrent programming, for example, a Process class, a Semaphore class, an ISR class, and so on. The classes define a *Concurrency framework* that users extend. For example, a specific process is built by subclassing from the Process class. The Process class hides the details of creating a process with RT-Layer. As another example, if a process is to wait on a semaphore it must first create an instance of a Semaphore class and then send the semaphore object a *wait()* message. The semaphore object would interact with RT-Layer to suspend the process that called it.

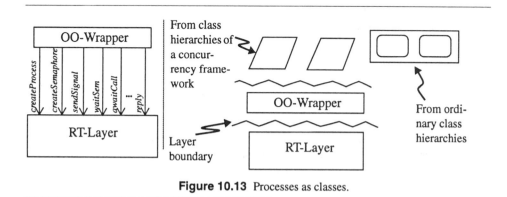

Figure 10.13 Processes as classes.

Actually building OO-Wrapper for a particular object-oriented language and real time executive may not always be straightforward. A fundamental problem that can occur are clashes between the run-time system of the object-oriented language and the real time executive. The use of inheritance between process classes and the implementation of

interprocess communication are two common trouble spots. We will discuss these issues
in more depth in Chapter 11. In the meantime we assume that these issues can be dealt
with in a satisfactory way.

10.4.4 Putting the Pieces Together for the MTU

In Figure 10.14, we propose a relatively complete class relationship diagram for the MTU.
The relationships have been developed to support the map of Figure 10.9(b). There is
duplication of information in these diagrams that shows where standard object-oriented
diagrams and our diagrams come together; we leave it up to the reader to judge whether
such duplication in design diagrams in an actual project would be useful or not. The concurrency framework is highlighted in Figure 10.14 because it is considered as separate
from the application we are developing. The classes of the Concurrency framework implement the OO-Wrapper layer of Figure 10.13.

In Figure 10.14, there are classes for teams, for example, class `MessageTeam`,
class `PacketTeam` and class `LinkTeam`. With this collaboration pattern, each team has
a *send()* method, called from above to transfer data downwards, and a *receive()* method,
called from below to transfer data upwards. The abstract class `MTUTeam` defines these
methods to ensure that all subclasses (teams) have a common interface.

There are classes in Figure 10.14 for each of the processes shown in Figure 10.9(b):
class `TxProcess`, class `RxLProcess`, and class `RxMProcess`. The processes all
inherit from the `Process` class of the Concurrency framework. Inheriting from the `Pro-
cess` class makes instances of a subclass autonomous and concurrent relative to other
components.

The classes for the dynamic buffer objects are as in Figure 10.12.

The *contains* relationships between instances of classes in Figure 10.14 comes from
the operational nesting shown in Figure 10.9(b). For example, the relationship which
reads a `LinkTeam`-*contains*-2-`ReceiveBuffer` objects comes from the two rxL
slots nested in the team in Figure 10.9(b). Notice that we have annotated the ends of some
contains relationships with a slot name. For example, the `ReceiveBuffer` end of the
`LinkTeam`-*contains*-`ReceiveBuffer` relation is labeled rxL. This labelling identifies the role that the object at the end of the relationship plays, for example, the
`ReceiveBuffer` object plays the rxL role in its relationship with an `RxLProcess`
object. However, a `ReceiveBuffer` plays role rxM in its relationship with an `RxM-
Process`. Adding role names to the ends of relationships arrows can help to cross-refer-
ence class relationship diagrams to slots.

The differences between conventional class relationship diagrams and our diagrams
are as follows. Class relationship diagrams show inheritance and the position of methods
in the class hierarchy, use case maps do not. Use case maps show behaviour sequences and
structural dynamics, class relationship diagrams do not. For example, one cannot tell from
the class relationship diagrams of Figure 10.14 whether it is the same or different
`ReceiveBuffer` objects that play roles in the rxL and rxM slots; nor can one tell if the
slots are filled at the same time or at different times. The answers to these questions come

from the a case map. As noted earlier, class relationships can be extended to include things like three-way relationships and constraints to answer some of the questions. But we have found that overuse of these extensions can lead to complex class relationship diagrams that are difficult to read. We separate concerns by limiting what is represented in class relationship diagrams.

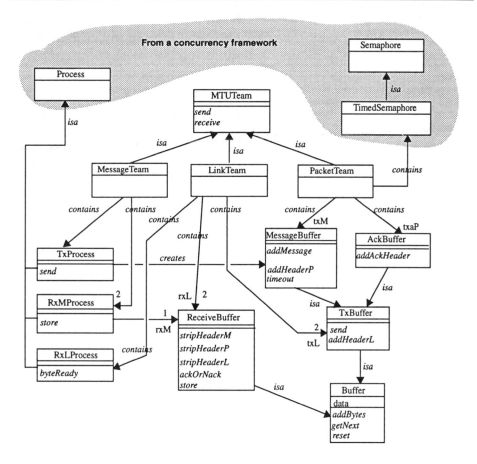

Figure 10.14 Detailed class relationship diagram
of the MTU.

To cross-reference the class relationship diagram of Figure 10.14 to the map of Figure 10.9(b), we use an Allocation Table (Table 10.1). Along the top of the table are the operational components in the map. Along the side of the table are the classes that provide them. Abstract classes (and superclasses) are annotated with an asterisk. An entry in the table means that the class provides an instance of the component at run time, either in whole or in part. For example, the M component comes solely from the `MessageTeam` class. The interesting part of the table is the classes associated with dynamic buffer objects. Note that every object that fills a buffer slot is derived from the abstract class `Buffer`, and that every object in a transmission slot is derived from the abstract class `TxBuffer`. For concrete classes and slots, an entry in the table means that an instance of the class fills the slot. For example, `MessageBuffer` objects fill the txmP and txL slots, `AckBuffer` objects fill the txaP and txL slots, and `ReceiveBuffer` objects fill the rxL and rxM slots. These are several examples of instances of the same class playing multiple roles (filling multiple slots).

Table 10.1   Relating the Operational Domain to the Manufacturing Domain

OP / M	Teams			Processes			Slots				
	M	P	L	Tx	Rx M	RxL	txm P	txaP	txL(2)	rxL(2)	rxM (2)
MessageTeam	*										
PacketTeam		*									
LinkTeam			*								
TxProcess				*							
RxMProcess					*						
RxLProcess						*					
*Buffer							*	*	*	*	*
*TxBuffer							*	*	*		
Message Buff							*		*		
AckBuff er								*	*		
ReceiveBuf fer										*	*

10.4.5 Extending and Reusing the MTU

Figure 10.15 provides some hints of how classes developed for the MTU could be extended to provide new capabilities. For example, an instance of a `PacketTeam` may contain an instance of a `FragmentationPolicy` class for breaking messages into packets. Fragmentation of messages is needed when a message is too large to fit in a single outgoing packet. The fragmentation policy is one aspect of the use case map responsibility *packetize message*. An instance of a `RouteFinder` class may be used for directing packets through a network when the communicating nodes are not directly connected. The `RouteFinder` object would add information to the packet header that would be used to forward a packet to its destination. Route finding is again part of the use case map responsibility, *packetize message*. A `ProtocolStateMachine` class may be added for encapsulating the inter-node protocol. This would localize the logic of the protocol and make changes to that logic easier. The `LinkTeam` instance may contain an instance of an `ErrorCorrecting` class for checking the incoming data streams. Error correcting is part of the use case map responsibility *receive packet*.

These new classes separate concerns by localizing specific behaviour into individual classes. The system becomes more flexible and easier to change as a result. For example, it is possible that there would be subclasses of these classes if there were different ways that their behaviour could be implemented, for example, different `ErrorCorrecting` subclasses for the different ways of finding and correcting data errors, or different `RouteFinder` subclasses for different network layouts.

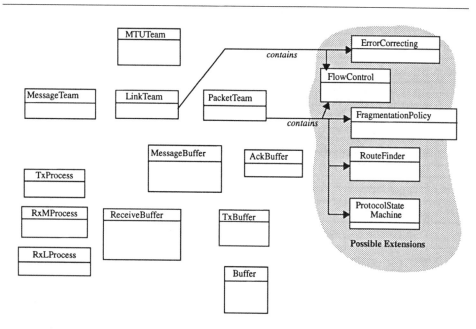

Figure 10.15 Class relationship diagram for a
more complex MTU.

Enough design has been done that we can now develop some source code for the MTU system. Skeleton code sufficient give a sense of the organization of a C++ implementation is given in Appendix B. The next step would be to fill in method details, using the design diagrams for guidance. We leave this as an exercise for the interested reader.

10.5 USE CASE MAPS AS A COMMON DENOMINATOR

Some of the diagrams developed in this chapter provide an excellent basis for understanding how, in general, use case maps may be employed as common denominators for making trade-offs between real time and object-oriented issues. Figure 10.9 (when put together with Figure 10.8) and Figure 10.14 provide examples.

The presence of multiple processes along paths alerts us to the possibility of overhead that will degrade end-to-end performance due to IPC mechanisms in an underlying real time executive or operating system. An example is the reception path spanning the rxL and rxM processes in Figure 10.9 (with Figure 10.8). If we judge that overhead along some path is likely to be a problem, we might decide to reduce the number of processes along the path.

The presence of create arrows and slots along paths alerts us to the possibility of overhead that will degrade end-to-end performance due to the slowness of run-time mechanisms for creating objects. An example is the transmission path in Figure 10.9 (with Figure 10.8). Dynamic-creation overhead can be a serious problem in practical real time systems implemented with object-oriented techniques; it may be alleviated by creating a suite of necessary objects *before* the path starts (as is done for the reception path of Figure 10.9).

The presence of components along paths that are derived from class hierarchies alerts us to the possibility of overhead due to object-oriented implementation techniques. For example, the slots in Figure 10.9 are associated through Figure 10.14 with inheritance paths that may have to be traversed at run-time, causing overhead. To point to one specific case, adding bytes to a buffer object in the txmP slot may imply run-time overhead due to traversal of the inheritance path between the `TxBuffer` class and the `Buffer` super-class to get at the *addBytes* method in the superclass. Although the design model in the world of use case maps is that the inheritance hierarchy is collapsed into a single object that occupies the slot, the actual implementation may or may not do this. If we judge that overhead will be a problem, we might decide that we are willing to put up with a bit less reuse potential by getting rid of the `Buffer` superclass. Alternatively, we might decide that we need the superclass but that we require an implementation technique that collapses the superclass and subclasses into single objects at run time.

We may employ use case maps as common denominators to make qualitative judgments about trade-offs, because everything is pinpointed in relation to the paths in the maps. For example, the maps provide a common denominator for making tradeoffs between the number of active components along paths, the degree of dynamic creation of components along paths, and the amount of traversal of inheritance hierarchies implied by responsibilities along paths that are implemented by classes.

10.6   SUMMARY

In this chapter we have:

- Showed how to make the transition from use case maps to collaboration graphs.
- Illustrated how to explore the collaboration-graph solution space for a real time problem.
- Provided a realistic example of structural dynamics with use case maps (dynamic buffering).
- Pointed the way to working with use case maps, collaboration graphs and class relationship diagrams in an integrated fashion for a problem that combines real time and object-oriented aspects.
- Pointed the way to employing use case maps as common denominators for making trade-offs between real time and object-oriented issues.
- Attempted to point the way to general approaches, rather than just develop solutions to one particular problem.

Patterns

This chapter draws together various patterns threads in this book and the literature. It does so by sketching some elements that might go into a patterns handbook that covers a wide range of concerns, including patterns in use case maps (called path patterns), IPC patterns, layering patterns, object interaction patterns, construction patterns for objects to fill slots, and construction patterns for processes and teams. The patterns are illustrated by examples drawn from the MTU and BGETool case studies. We point to code examples in previous chapters and in Appendix B for those who want to follow the ideas right down to implementation.

Patterns are currently the focus of much attention in the object-oriented community. In the patterns literature (for example [14]), they are expressed in terms that we have identified in this book as detailed-design ones, for example, class relationship diagrams that include methods, collaboration graphs, interaction sequence diagrams, visibility graphs, and code fragments. These kinds of descriptions do not express behaviour patterns as first-class abstractions that can be reused independently of the means of implementation, such as messages, methods, and so forth.We think that use case maps represent a different, complementary kind of pattern, in which behaviour is a first-class abstraction. In this chapter, we use the term "path patterns" to distinguish them from patterns of the kind more familiar to the object-oriented community.

The path patterns that have been presented in this book could form the beginning of a catalogue of such patterns: a one-way producer consumer pattern, several variations of a two-way producer-consumer pattern (the MTU case study), a negotiated producer-consumer pattern (the fax example), several examples of timeout-recovery patterns (mouse double-click, MTU, internet email), a dynamic buffering pattern (MTU), and a model-view-controller (MVC) pattern. Some path patterns are extensible into others, for example, a producer-consumer pattern is extensible into a pipeline pattern. We have shown how to use path patterns to guide high-level design and understanding of both real time and object-oriented systems.

Gamma, Johnson, Helm and Vlissides [14] have done pioneering work on patterns in class and object organizations that promote flexibility, reuse, and maintainability. Their patterns make commitments to interfaces of objects and to interactions between them. As is appropriate at a design level where such commitments have been made, their patterns include descriptions of large-grained behaviour in the form of Jacobson-style interaction sequence diagrams.

The allure of patterns is the prospect of handbooks that will capture design knowledge and programming practices in small, easily digestible pieces that can be reused and extended. This allure is the same for both path patterns and the kinds of patterns described by Gamma, Johnson, Helm and Vlissides.

We begin with patterns that are purely operational, proceed to ones that are concerned with elements of operation, manufacturing and assembly, and end with ones that are purely for manufacturing and assembly. The patterns are expressed with notations appropriate for the domains of concern, sometimes with notations from all three of the domains of operation, manufacturing and assembly (illustrating that useful patterns are often multifaceted).

11.1 OPERATIONAL ORGANIZATIONS OF PROCESSES

The patterns we shall be concerned with in this section are purely operational. We show how IPC patterns that express ways in which processes interact with each other follow from a path patterns expressed in a use case map, and from decisions about IPC that have nothing to do with the map. We point out that choosing among the IPC patterns often involves applying rules such as *no polling*, *avoid critical races*, and *wait in one place* at the IPC level.

11.1.1 One-Way IPC Patterns.

Use case paths traversing processes in one direction lead to a need for IPC along the paths. We saw a producer-consumer path pattern in Chapter 5 and examined two IPC patterns for implementing it. These patterns, along with three new IPC patterns, are shown in Figure 11.1. The IPC patterns (a) and (b), both one-way synchronous, were discussed in Chapter 5. An alternate IPC pattern (c), one-way asynchronous, may be used if the implementation technology supports asynchronous messaging with data exchange, and if message acknowledgment to the sender is not required. The remaining IPC patterns use a third process.

The buffer pattern (d) uses a buffer process B to store data for later pickup by the consumer process. This pattern allows a producer process to generate many small pieces of data without interrupting the consumer each time. The consumer can pick up its data when it wants it. The buffer process can be replaced by a passive buffer object or team with mutual exclusion protection, if there is no requirement for the buffer process ever to take any spontaneous actions and if the overhead of an active process is unacceptable.

The transporter pattern (e) uses a transporter process T to deliver the data to the consumer on behalf of the producer. This means that the producer is not affected by possible congestion (caused by many other processes interacting with the consumer) or latency (caused by the consumer doing other things). To choose one of these patterns requires more information about other use case paths through the producer and consumer processes. For example, if a producer is responsible for several path segments, a designer might choose the transporter pattern to decouple the producer from delays at the consumer.

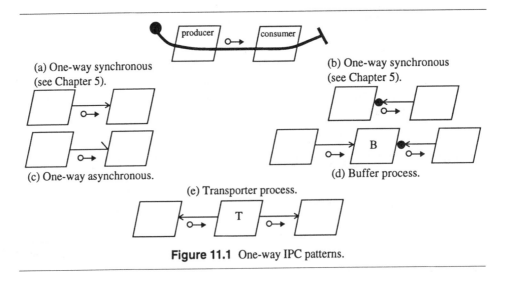

(a) One-way synchronous (see Chapter 5).

(b) One-way synchronous (see Chapter 5).

(c) One-way asynchronous.

(d) Buffer process.

(e) Transporter process.

Figure 11.1 One-way IPC patterns.

11.1.2 Two-Way IPC Patterns

Concurrent use case paths that traverse the same processes in different directions lead to richer IPC patterns (Figure 11.2). The concern when implementing a process organization to achieve this sort of map is avoiding mutual waiting patterns between the processes (possible deadlock). This can be done in a rather rigid way by lock-stepping the interactions between the processes in a fixed order, as in pattern (a), lock-step. Lock-step can be dangerous because it relies on programming conventions to avoid deadlock (making calls in the right order in different places). The remaining approaches avoid deadlock by breaking the mutual waiting between the processes in one direction. The approaches are variations on the one-way producer-consumer patterns presented above, for example, (b), transporter in one direction, (c), asynchronous in one direction, and (d), buffer in one direction. Another approach is to make one of the processes a pure server as in (e), waiting in one direction.

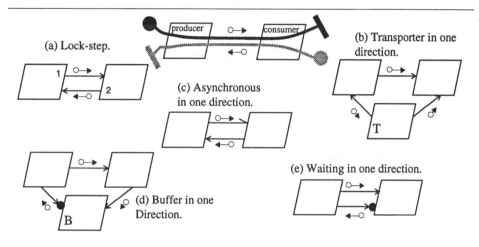

Figure 11.2 Two-way IPC for independent paths.

11.1.3 IPC Patterns for Coupled Paths

The foregoing IPC patterns resulted from a use case path traversing several processes in a way that requires IPC *along* the paths. However, IPC is also required *between* paths when there is explicit or implicit coupling between path segments assigned to different processes. We saw examples of such patterns in Chapter 9. For completeness, Figure 11.3 repeats two of them.

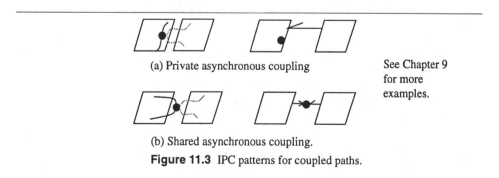

(a) Private asynchronous coupling   See Chapter 9
                                                 for more
                                                 examples.

(b) Shared asynchronous coupling.

Figure 11.3 IPC patterns for coupled paths.

11.1.4 Pipeline IPC Patterns

Figure 11.4 shows three possible IPC patterns for process pipelines, among many others
(see [7]). Patterns (a) and (b) were discussed in Chapter 10. As illustrated by this figure,
pipeline IPC patterns may have macroscopic scope across a system.

Patterns like those in Figure 11.4 may be composed of smaller patterns like the ones
presented in the previous sections. For example, pattern (a) of Figure 11.4 uses the shared
asynchronous coupling pattern of Figure 11.3(b) for coupling in the P team; it also uses
the one-way synchronous interaction pattern of Figure 11.1(a) to link the rxL and rxM
processes.

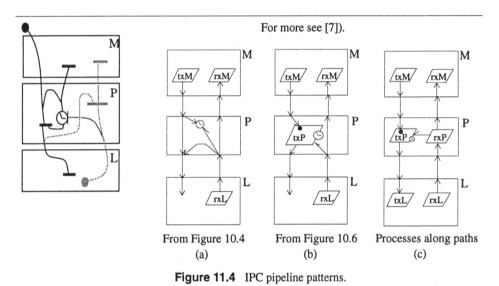

From Figure 10.4   From Figure 10.6   Processes along paths
        (a)   (b)   (c)

Figure 11.4 IPC pipeline patterns.

11.2 LAYERING AND EVENT DISPATCHING

Our aim here is relate the concept of layering as we explained it in relation to paths in
Chapter 3 to the concept as it is implemented in object oriented frameworks, in particular
as it is used to implement the Smalltalk dependency mechanism. Thus we intend to show
that path patterns can imply reuse of patterns in existing class hierarchies, even if they are
developed independently of any knowledge of the class hierarchies Our starting point is
the now familiar Model-View-Controller path pattern, shown again in Figure 11.5, for reference, except we have replaced the notification AND fork with a layer fold (in effect, this
moves the AND fork inside the layer, thereby hiding it). We do this to identify an intent to
use *layering through inheritance* and *dispatcher* patterns, as embodied in the Smalltalk
dependency mechanism, to implement the AND fork (therefore the layer fold symbol is

labeled D, for dependency). The shaded shapes identify the scope of the class patterns in relation to the map.

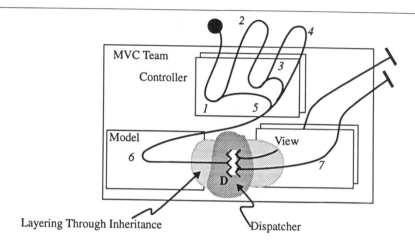

Figure 11.5 MVC path pattern.

11.2.1 Layering Through Inheritance Pattern

Organize class hierarchies such that lower-layer services are provided by base classes (superclasses). Subclasses can access the lower layer services by inheriting from the base classes.

Layering is an operational concept that means the details of lower layers are suppressed when viewing an upper layer (Chapter 3). The lower layers provide services to the upper layer.

The Smalltalk dependency mechanism may be used to maintain consistency between Model and View objects in an MVC team by propagating notifications of Model data changes to Views. For the purposes of understanding the operation of an MVC team, it is not necessary to understand how the dependency mechanism is implemented. For this reason, the dependency mechanism used by an MVC team may be modeled as a lower layer service, as suggested by the use case map of Figure 11.5.

In Smalltalk, the dependency mechanism is a service implemented in the base class Object. Almost all Smalltalk classes inherit from Object, therefore, almost all Smalltalk objects can use the dependency mechanism. Figure 11.6 shows the Object class and the methods it provides related to the dependency mechanism. The Model and View classes both derive from the Object class, therefore, instances of these classes are able to participate in the dependency mechanism.

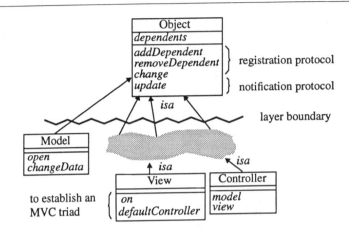

Figure 11.6 The MVC pattern in Smalltalk.

Discussion The layering-through-inheritance pattern is a common one in object-oriented programming that exists each time there is a division between an application framework (like the one provided by Smalltalk) and the application itself. The advantage of the pattern is that subclasses can extend or modify the behaviour of the services that they inherit. The disadvantage is that the subclasses may become dependent on the implementation of those services. Another approach for implementing a layer (not shown) is to use a separate server class that is used by applications that require it.

At the level of Figure 11.5, we are only concerned with the effect of the dependency mechanism: that View objects are notified of changes to Model objects. The next pattern, *Dispatcher*, shows how the effect of the dependency mechanism may be implemented.

11.2.2 Dispatcher Pattern

When several objects are dependent on another object (a source object), provide a registration protocol for establishing a dependency relationship between a source object and a dependent object, and a notification protocol for propagating notifications of updates to dependent objects.

A code snapshot diagram of a Smalltalk implementation of the dispatcher pattern is given in Figure 11.7 (note that we use a code snapshot diagram here not as a design diagram but as a means of explaining the code). The arrows represent messages between objects. The *registration protocol* (grey arrows) begins with dependent objects sending *addDependent* messages to a source object. The dependent objects pass their identifiers as a parameter of the *addDependent* message. When a source object changes some data that it maintains (perhaps as a result of receiving a message like *change* shown in the figure) the *notification protocol* begins (black arrows). The source object sends itself the *changed* message and as a result all previously registered dependents are sent the *update* message to inform them of the change to the source object. Dependent objects may later send a *removeDependent* message to a source object so that they do not receive any further update notifications. The implementation of the dispatcher pattern decouples a source object from the objects that may depend on it, because dependent objects are responsible for registering themselves in the dependency relationships.

In the Smalltalk implementation, the *registration protocol* is implemented in the Object class: the methods *addDependent* and *removeDependent* can be found there (Figure 11.6). The Object class also has an instance variable for holding the identifiers of dependents who have sent *addDependent* messages. The basics of the *notification protocol* are also provided by the Object class of Smalltalk. The *changed* method sends the message *update* to all objects in the dependents list. The *update* method is deferred in the Object class, meaning that subclasses of object must provide an implementation of it.

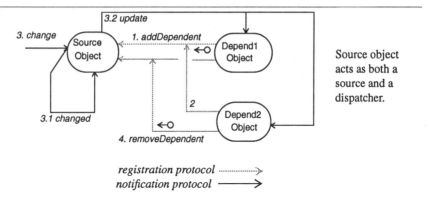

Source object acts as both a source and a dispatcher.

registration protocol ·················⟩
notification protocol ⟶

Figure 11.7 Code snapshot of Smalltalk's implementation of the dispatcher pattern.

The *changed* method implements the effect of the fork in the use case map of the MVC team (highlighted region identified as Dispatcher in Figure 11.5). In use case map terms, the outgoing paths from the layer fold symbol are each taken in some arbitrary order. In the Smalltalk implementation, the *changed* method sends the message *update* to each object in the dependents list in some order. (The actual Smalltalk implementation of the dependency mechanism is much richer than given here for both extensibility and performance, but this is enough to give the essence.)

Discussion An artifact of Smalltalk's class organization is that objects that maintain data (source objects) also dispatch notifications of data changes to dependent objects. In other words, the same object plays the role of source and dispatcher. When a source has its data changed, it sends itself the *changed* message. This changes the role of the object from a source to a dispatcher. There are other approaches for implementing this pattern that are different from that of Smalltalk. For example, a separate event dispatcher object could be used. Dependents would register with the event dispatcher, and source objects would ask the dispatcher to propagate update notifications for them. This approach is appropriate if source objects should be decoupled from the actual delivery of notifications of changes to dependents. Note that the concept of the dependency mechanism in use case map terms as a lower-layer service does not change if the implementation of the service changes.

11.3 MULTIPLE ROLE PLAYING BY OBJECTS IN SLOTS

Here we are concerned with patterns for objects to play roles in slots in use case maps; these patterns span a range that includes paths, slots, classes, and interobject interactions. Of particular interest is multiple role playing, meaning that classes may have to supply objects capable of playing different, related roles in different slots. The roles may be related through constraints or shared data. For example, the transmit buffer slots txmP and txL in the Packet and Link teams of the MTU case study (Figure 11.8) identify roles that are related because they operate on the same data.

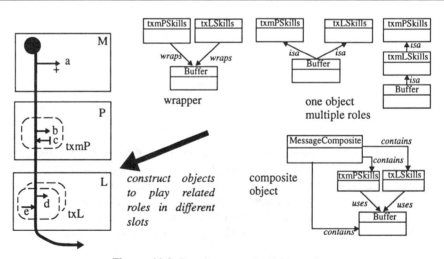

Figure 11.8 Running example of this section.

We will now present some different patterns for constructing objects from classes to fill the txmP and txL slots (symbolized by the arrow pointing from the classes to the use case map in Figure 11.8). Figure 11.8 summarizes (on the right) some of the possible class organizations for constructing the objects that will fill the slots. Each of these class organizations will be explained in detail. Chapter 10 gave a solution for implementing the buffers of the MTU that resulted from considering the subtype/supertype relationships between the types of buffers in that particular problem. The patterns given in this section are more general because they are alternatives that may be considered for any problem that involves multiple role-playing. (Skeletal C++ code for the patterns of this section is presented in Appendix B.)

11.3.1 One Object Multiple Roles

A single object plays multiple roles and the interface of the object is the union of the interfaces of all roles it plays.

This is perhaps the most common pattern because it is the easiest to construct using the building materials of object-oriented programming. The hierarchies are organized such that there is a single concrete class that provides or inherits the interface methods of all the roles its objects will play. The advantage of the pattern is its conceptual simplicity: It is easy to relate the run-time organization of objects to a use case map description in terms of roles. Also, because there is only one object involved, there is no additional programming-level dynamics to worry about beyond the dynamics expressed in a use case map. (We will see that some patterns result in programming dynamics beneath the level of use case maps.)

Figure 11.9 pulls everything down to the detailed design level for the *one object multiple roles* pattern.

While the map of Figure 11.8 reveals the *need* for multiple role playing, the partial collaboration graph in Figure 11.9 enables us to be concrete about the interfaces of slots and objects, and the methods provided by classes, to *implement* multiple role playing.

The collaboration graph shows the data that flows between the teams and some connections to the txmP and txL slots. Because we are using object-oriented implementation techniques, the connections will be implemented as messages between objects. The object that fills the txmP and txL slots must support the connections to the slots with matching methods in its interface.

The slots require three groups of methods to be implemented by classes: txmP methods, txL methods, and methods for manipulating the message data. The latter set of methods do not belong to the interface of any slot and are therefore best regarded as private methods of buffer classes. The slots also require the corresponding classes to have a data attribute, which is a block of storage large enough to hold a message plus the packet and link headers. Two ways of organizing the class hierarchies to build objects to fill these slots are shown in Figure 11.9.

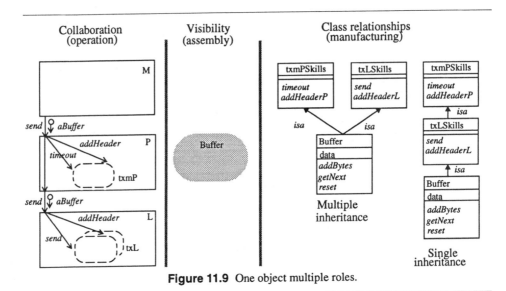

Figure 11.9 One object multiple roles.

If multiple inheritance is available, use an abstract class per slot. An abstract class defines the interface of the slot with which it is associated. A concrete class would then inherit its slot interfaces from each of these abstract classes. The concrete class would provide the methods deferred by the abstract classes. In the MTU example, the concrete class would provide the methods to manipulate and access the message data. The abstract class txmPSkills defines the txmP slot interface, and the class txLSkills defines the txL slot interface.

Multiple inheritance seems like a natural solution to this problem. However, implementations of multiple inheritance suffer from pragmatic problems. For example, which method should be called, if two abstract classes have methods of the same name? Renaming of methods in abstract classes may be required to solve the problem (as is done in the figure for the *addHeader* methods).

Without multiple inheritance, the same run-time object configuration can be achieved with single inheritance. In this case, a concrete class derives the necessary slot interfaces through a single path in an inheritance tree. We have designed the inheritance hierarchy in Figure 11.9 such that there is a single class for each slot. This class organization does not match the MTU problem well because it does not seem logical for a txL-Skills class to be derived from a txmPSkills class. We could create a single abstract class txmPandLSkills that declares the interface methods of both the txmP and txL slots. This has the advantage of putting all of an object's interface methods in one place, but can lead to large classes with complex interfaces.

The visibility graph in Figure 11.9 is not interesting in this case, but is included for comparison with the other patterns. It highlights the fact that there is one dynamic object in this pattern.

Discussion

- The *one object multiple roles* pattern can result in subclasses that are not, from a logical standpoint, subtypes of their superclasses. For example, it does not seem logical to say that a `Buffer` *isa* `txmPSkills`. This can make class hierarchies difficult to understand. This is a significant disadvantage, notwithstanding the fact that, from a purely compilation perspective, this pattern organizes classes into proper supertype-subtype relationships, that is, subclasses inherit their interfaces from superclasses.
- This pattern can cause the interfaces of objects to become large and complex.
- The object is constructed statically, that is, it gains its role interfaces and skills at compile time. Static class-based construction techniques tend to be harder to extend than object-based composition where smallish objects form into collaborating partnerships dynamically. However, object-based composition is more difficult to understand because of the additional objects, interobject messages, and programming-level dynamics involved.
- The context of each role played by the object may become dependent on the organization of the class hierarchies that construct the object. This is a practical concern when delivering and changing software. For example, for the MTU system, it may be desirable to ship the Message, Packet, and Link teams as independent subsystems or to swap old subsystems for new ones. The problem is that the Packet team may be dependent on the `txLSkills` class, and the Link team may be dependent on the `txmPSkills` class, but these teams never make direct use of these classes. This may lead to maintenance headaches when classes are changed.

11.3.2 Composite Object with Internal Role Skills Objects

There is a single composite object with internal skills objects for each role that the composite object plays.

If there are constraints or shared data between the roles, they are maintained as internal properties of the composite. The composite creates the internal role skills objects when needed and provides access to them when the composite moves into a slot. The composite provides *installInXXXSlot* methods that return the appropriate role skills objects.

For the MTU case study this pattern results in a composite object class, called `MessageComposite`, with three classes for internal objects: `Buffer`, `txmPSkills` and `txLSkills` (see Figure 11.10). `Buffer` objects are private to `MessageComposite` objects. `txmPSkills` and `txLSkills` objects operate on `Buffer` objects. `MessageComposite` objects are passed between the M, P and L teams. In the P team, `MessageComposite` objects are sent an *installInPSlot* message, which returns the identifier of a `txmPSkills` object. Connections to the `txmP` slot are directed to the `txmPSkills` object. A similar sequence occurs in the L team.

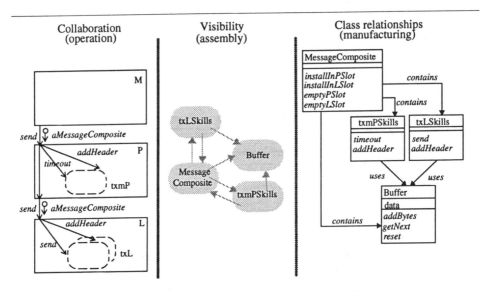

Figure 11.10 Composite object with internal skills objects.

Discussion

- The *composite object* pattern reduces the complexity of the interfaces of the run-time objects over the *one object multiple roles* pattern. However, there are more objects, object interactions and programming-level dynamics to deal with.

- There is one place, the composite object, for controlling the access to and lifetime of the objects that make up the composite. For example, the `MessageComposite` can create the role skills objects as needed when it receives *installInSlot* messages; and if desired, destroy those objects when slots are emptied.

- In contrast to static class-based construction, the composite object pattern is an example of object-based composition. In an object-based approach, associations between objects are established dynamically. This means that the current system state can be used to decide the most appropriate object configuration. For example, different `txmPSkills` objects may use different message timeout algorithms based on the current network load. The `MessageComposite` object could decide upon the most appropriate `txmPSkills` object when it receives the *installInPSlot* message.

- Object-based composition may result in simpler class hierarchies than static class-based construction. With static class-based construction, all possible object configurations must be encoded as *isa* relationships between classes. This can lead to a proliferation of classes. For example, consider extending the class hierarchies of Figure 11.9 with a new `txmPSkillsNew` class that implements message timeout using a new algorithm. In the multiple inheritance case, an additional `BufferNew` class would be needed that would inherit from the `txmPSkillsNew` class.

11.3.3 Wrappers

There is a skills object for each role that wraps a common object with the interface and skill set needed for the role.

The common object is the aspect of the object configuration that is shared between roles. It will typically implement constraints or operations on data that are shared between multiple roles. The common object is hidden by a wrapper object when it is part of a role.

The wrappers pattern as applied to the MTU example is shown in Figure 11.11. We show the object configuration at each team of the MTU collaboration graph. In the P team, the `Buffer` object is wrapped in a `txmPSkills` object. The `txmPSkills` object implements its behaviour using the `Buffer` object. A similar object configuration occurs in the L team. The common aspect of the shared roles, the `Buffer` object, is passed between the M, P and L teams.

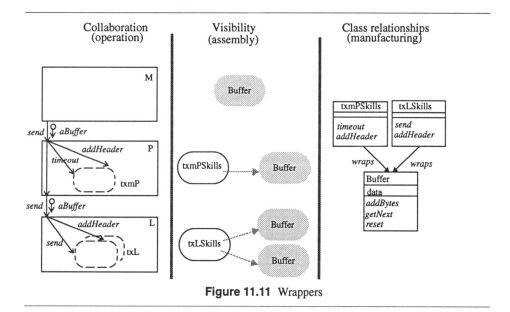

Figure 11.11 Wrappers

Discussion

• The advantage of the *wrappers* pattern is that only the common aspect of the shared roles is passed between the contexts that define the roles. For example, a `Buffer` object flows between the P and L teams. The P team is in no way dependent on classes specific to link buffers. The L team is not dependent on classes specific to the packet buffers. For the MTU case study, this is perhaps the best pattern to apply because it results in the most loosely coupled subsystem teams.

• A disadvantage of this pattern over the composite object pattern is that there is not a centralized place for managing the creation and deletion of the role skills objects and the common object they use. However, use case maps can help to understand the issues if a simple programming technique is followed. The programming technique is to create a role skills wrapper object for each slot during an initialization phase. For example, the L team would create a `txLSkills` object and the P team a `txmPSkills` object. In the L team the `txLSkills` object would switch between two buffer objects to achieve double buffering.

11.3.4 Programming-Level Dynamics of Patterns for Multiple Role Playing

Figure 11.12 uses visibility snapshots over time to compare in detail the programming-level dynamics of the different patterns for multiple role playing. Diagrams at this level of detail are not necessarily recommended for design. However, they are useful as an alternative to discussing code.

To the upper left of Figure 11.12 is a partial use case map showing the dynamics of objects in the txmP and txL slots. The visibility graphs in the figure are snapshots of the objects at points labelled on the use case maps (a, b, c, d, and e). We see that class-based construction approaches do not contribute to any additional programming-level dynamics that cannot be directly inferred from the structural dynamics expressed with use case paths. This simplicity is an advantage of class-based patterns. However, things are more complex with object-based composition approaches, which add structural dynamics not shown in the maps. The object-based approaches can have different visibility snapshots depending on when objects and visibility references are created. The figure shows one possibility for each object-based pattern.

The composite object example of Figure 11.12 creates its skills objects when needed. This approach avoids creating objects unnecessarily, for example, when the composite may not play all its roles and the skills objects are large. In the example shown, the skills objects are retained when a slot is left, for example, the `txLSkills` object remains after the txL slot is emptied (at point e on the use case path). In this way, new skills objects need not be created if a message is resent. The skills objects will be deleted when the message composite is destroyed.

The unique feature of the wrappers pattern shown is that each layer creates its role skills objects during initialization (note the static references from P to `txmPSkills` and L to `txLSkills`). The role skills objects gain visibility of the `Buffer` object as needed.

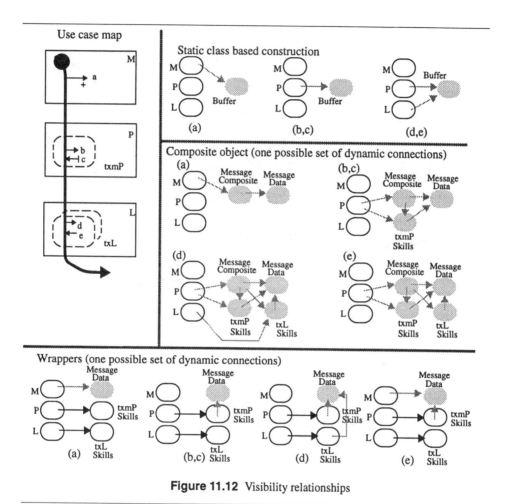

Figure 11.12 Visibility relationships

11.3.5 Putting the Patterns Together for the MTU Case Study

To provide a more complete picture, Figure 11.13 shows the objects that could be used to fill the slots along both the tx and rx paths of the MTU case study. The use case map of Figure 11.13 comes from Chapter 10 (Figure 10.8). We have used the wrappers pattern to fill the slots on the receive side, for symmetry with the transmit side. In Figure 11.13, we give objects that appear in multiple slots the same name, for example, aTxBuffer object appears in both the txmP and txL slots. A partial class hierarchy is shown at the bottom of the figure.

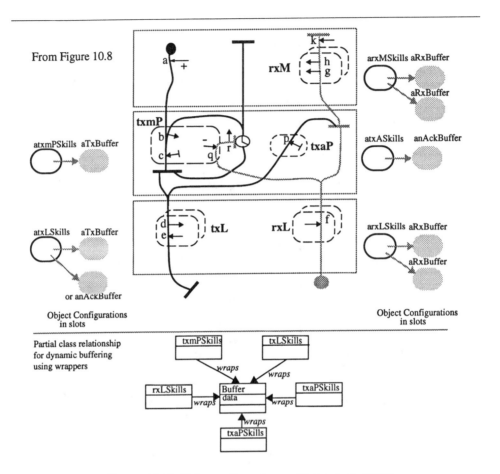

Figure 11.13 Object configurations to fill slots in the MTU.

Several new objects have been introduced for the receive side in Figure 11.13:

- aRxBuffer object is an instance of class Buffer. There are two of these objects: one for each rxL slot in the L team. Instances of this object leave the rxL slot and flow to the P team. If the contents of aRxBuffer object is a message, then this object is deposited into a rxM slot in the M team (at g). Otherwise the object is an ack and aTxBuffer object is destroyed (at q). At points r and k aRxBuffer object is returned to the L team.

- anAckBuffer object is an instance of class Buffer. This is the only object used for transmitting acknowledgements of received data messages. A single copy is created during initialization and gets aliased between the txaP and txL slots.

- arxLSkills object is an instance of class rxLSkills. This object wraps aRxBuffer object while the latter is in the rxL slot. One arxLSkills object will be created during initialization. This object will switch between the two aRxBuffer objects to support double buffering. The skills object does not move but remains in the L team.

- atxASkills object is an instance of class AckSkills. This object wraps anAckBuffer object when it is in the txaP slot. A single copy is created during initialization.

- arxMSkills object is an instance of class rxMSkills. This object wraps aRxBuffer object when the latter fills the rxM slot. There is one instance of arxMSkills object that will switch between the two aRxBuffer objects to support double buffering in the M team.

Note that with the receive side added, the txL slot of the L team may be filled with either an outgoing message or an ack for a received message. This means that aTxL-Skills object may wrap either aTxBuffer object or anAckBuffer object. Both wrapped objects are of the same type (class Buffer) and the skills object is oblivious to whether the data it wraps is part of a message or an acknowledgement.

11.3.6 Final Thoughts

We have devoted a lot of space to the patterns *single object multiple roles* (with multiple and single inheritance), *composite object* and *wrappers* because they bring so many issues together. In general, there are two ways of organizing class hierarchies to build the object organizations: class-based construction and object-based composition. Class-based construction leads to simpler object structures but tends towards large class hierarchies, complex interfaces, and loss of flexibility and extensibility. Object-based composition results in more complex run-time structures with additional programming-level dynamics beyond that implied by use case maps, but the class hierarchies may be easier to extend. The dynamics as expressed on a use case map abstract from such programming-level dynamics and therefore do not change if a class-based or object-based approach is used.

11.4 MANUFACTURING OPERATIONAL COMPONENTS

In this section we are concerned with manufacturing and assembly patterns for processes, slots, and teams. This section has little to do with path patterns directly. However, the fact that path patterns contain such components gives rise to the need for these manufacturing and assembly patterns. We have already seen some specialized patterns relating to slots in the previous section. However, this section gives a more general perspective.

11.4.1 Processes

We discuss two patterns below for implementing processes in languages that do not directly support concurrency. The approaches below are general ones; the details of making them work for a specific language and run-time system are not given. The reader is referred to [1], [33], [5], [21] for more on the topic of adding concurrency to an object-oriented language. Skeletal coding examples in C++ for these patterns are given in Chapter 5 and Appendix B.

Both of the patterns below use a real time executive as a layer to achieve concurrency in programs built using an object-oriented language. The object-oriented language is responsible for dispatching messages to the appropriate objects to resolve polymorphism, for creating new objects, and for destroying old ones (perhaps automatically with garbage collection as in Smalltalk). The real time executive is responsible for creating and destroying processes, scheduling processes to run (context switching), and interprocess communication and synchronization. The most common problem with the layering approach to concurrency are the clashes that can occur between the run-time systems of the object-oriented language and the real time executive. Clashes may occur because the run-time system of the language assumes that it will run in a sequential environment, and the run-time system of the real time executive assumes that the application above it is ready to run concurrently. For example, if the message dispatching code of the object-oriented language is not designed for a concurrent environment, then a context switch by the real time executive during a message dispatch may cause erratic behaviour or even a system crash.

11.4.2 Processes Without Classes

> *Implement processes outside of a class framework using direct calls to a real time executive that is used as a layer.*

In this pattern there is a real time executive (RT-Layer in Figure 11.14) that provides for concurrency. The executive schedules processes and interrupts, and enables interprocess communication. Concurrency is added to an application by making direct calls to RT-Layer. For example to create a process an application would call the *createProcess()* procedure of RT-Layer. To send a message between two processes one process would call the RT-Layer procedure *sendSignal()* with a process identifier, the signal name, and data as parameters.

Many real time executives are implemented in procedural languages and are linked to an application through call-back procedures that the application registers with the executive. For example, to create a process, an application would pass the pointer of a procedure as a parameter to RT-Layer's *createProcess()* procedure. The procedure would represent the main body of the process. To run the process, the real time executive would make a call to the procedure that was registered during the *createProcess()* call.

This pattern clearly separates concerns in the Manufacturing Domain between real time and object-oriented issues. As shown in Figure 11.14, processes are implemented using direct calls to RT-Layer; there are no classes for process objects. Teams, objects, and slots are implemented using class hierarchies in a conventional way.

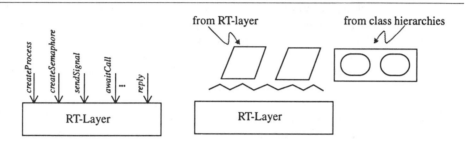

Figure 11.14 Processes from RT-Layer, objects and
teams from class hierarchies.

A source code example of this pattern can be found in Chapter 5 for the producer-consumer problem.

Discussion

• The *processes without classes* pattern limits opportunities for clashes between the run-time system of the object-oriented language and the run-time system of the real time executive. We will see in the next pattern that implementing processes as classes can introduce problems with message passing between process objects and inheritance of process classes.

• Reuse of process code is limited because there is no inheritance between processes. However, see the discussion of processes and inheritance in the next pattern.

11.4.3 Processes as Classes

There is layer above the real time executive that eases its use with an object-oriented language. The layer is implemented as a collection of classes, for example, class Process, class Semaphore. Specific processes are implemented as subclasses of the Process class.

In this pattern, an OO-Wrapper layer is interposed between the real time executive and the application (see Figure 11.15). Operationally, OO-Wrapper translates higher-level interactions between components in the application into calls to RT-layer. OO-Wrapper can hide details such as the initialization of the real time executive and the initialization of processes, thus simplifying the development of an application.

When this pattern is used with a procedure-based real time executive, one job of OO-Wrapper is to map the procedural world of the executive into object-oriented concepts. As mentioned, many real time executives are hooked to the applications that use them through registered call-back procedures. A job of OO-Wrapper would be to register the call-back procedures with the executive, receive calls to the procedures from the executive, and then translate these call-backs into messages to objects.

In the Manufacturing domain, OO-Wrapper is implemented as a collection of classes (a concurrency framework). Users of OO-Wrapper create subclasses from the concurrency framework. For example, the concurrency framework may contain a Process class, a Semaphore class, and a Mailbox class. A specific process would be built by subclassing from the Process class. The Process class would contain the code to create a process with RT-layer. As another example, if a process is to wait on a semaphore, it must first create an instance of a Semaphore class and then send the semaphore object a *wait()* message. The semaphore object would interact with RT-Layer to suspend the process that called it.

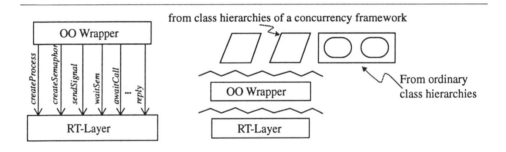

Figure 11.15 Processes from class hierarchies.

A coding example following this pattern can be found in Appendix B for the MTU case study.

Discussion

- The main advantages of the *processes as classes* pattern are a consistent use of the source code language for all types of components, and the use of classes as a packaging mechanism for processes. We used this pattern in Appendix B to make the source code readable. Beyond these advantages, we note below that, without language extensions, interprocess communication and the use of inheritance between Process classes may be cumbersome.

- Without language extensions, direct interprocess communication must be treated differently from interactions between other types of components. In the code examples of Appendix B, we assume that interactions between instances of processes have been mapped (somehow) to interprocess communication primitives of RT-Layer. One approach is to trap interactions between process objects in OO-Wrapper (if possible) and translate them to calls of RT-layer. Another approach is to provide interprocess communication methods in OO-Wrapper that process objects call.

- The degree to which process synchronization code can be reused effectively is a not yet clearly understood. Initialization and finalization code may have standard patterns that can be reused. Synchronization code may also have standard patterns relating to the kinds of IPC patterns we have identified in this book.

- There are two representations of each process: a process object maintained by the run-time system of the programming language, and a process control block in the real time layer. This can complicate the creation of processes because the creation of these two representations must be coordinated; the real time layer cannot schedule the process to receive a message before the process object has been fully created by the language's run-time system. In C++, for example, this can complicate the use of constructors for creating process objects. One would like to put the calls to the real time layer to create a process in the constructor of a base Process class. However, the constructors of base classes execute before the constructors of any subclasses, thus creating the two different process representations in a dangerous order. A solution is to use constructors to create only the programming languages representation of the process followed by a call to RT-Layer to create its representation of the process. Destroying process objects is also complicated because of the existence of two representations of a process in two run time systems.

For an in-depth discussion of the application of this pattern to the C++ programming language the reader is referred to a paper by P. Buhr [5]. Thomas et al [33] give an example, Actra, of adding concurrency to the Smalltalk programming language. A conclusion of the paper by P. Buhr is that language extensions are needed to take full advantage of the integration of concurrency and object-oriented programming. Without language extensions, interprocess communication can be cumbersome and the use of inheritance between process classes limited (see above). However, the processes-as-classes pattern can often be made to work for a specific language and real time executive, and the advantages of the pattern—source code consistency and classes as a packaging mechanism for processes—may outweigh its shortcomings.

11.4.4 Slots as Abstract Classes

Identify an abstract class with a slot when the slot is filled by objects with different behaviour through time.

The abstract class defines the slot interface, but leaves the implementation of some of the interface methods to the subclasses. The subclasses inherit the slot interface from the abstract class, implement the details of the interface methods in different ways, and possibly extend the interface. The advantages of this pattern are the following:

- The common parts of the slot interface are defined in one place: the abstract class.
- If the subclasses are "well behaved" then instances of the subclasses are guaranteed to "fit" into the slot associated with the abstract class. By "well behaved" we mean that the subclasses do not violate the slot interface by changing or removing any of the interface methods it inherits.
- The code of clients that use the slot interface is the same regardless of the occupant of the slot. New subclasses may be added and the client code reused. This is reuse through polymorphism which is the cornerstone of object-oriented programming.

Chapter 6 gave an example application of this pattern in the design of the BGETool.

11.4.5 Teams as Classes

Implement a team as a class.

Teams are identified in the Operation domain as groupings of collaborating objects, slots, and, recursively, other teams (not to mention processes and ISRs). Implementing a team as a class has the following advantages:

- The organization of the system in use case map terms is aligned with its realization as classes. This facilitates understanding system organization from the source code.
- Teams become run-time objects that can act as boundaries for hiding information about their makeup. Other objects can use a team as an object.
- Teams benefit from the full power of the object-oriented paradigm: inheritance, polymorphism, and so on.

The previous chapter gave examples of the application of this pattern for the BGETool and discussed its affect on source code readability. But there were teams in the BGETool case study that were not implemented as classes, for example, the HandlesFigure team. This raises the question, when should a team be a class? Following are some guidelines (see Figure 11.16). Implement teams as classes when:

(a) *Teams model the major functional divisions of a system* (that is, subsystems). This is assuming that the language used does not support a packaging concept larger than a class. If such a construct exists (for example, Ada packages) then it should be used instead of a class.

(b) *Teams act as information hiding units.* Without a boundary to separate the implementation of a team from elements outside the team, it is all too easy for dependencies on that implementation to be introduced. In C++, the implementation of a team can be hidden by making the internal elements private members of the team class.

Ada provides a similar capability. Smalltalk programmers must rely on programming convention.

(c) *There is data that is needed by all members of the team.* A good implementation choice is to encapsulate the shared data in an object that is visible to all members of the team.

(d) *The team itself is an operational entity in some context.* This is true if a team has connections to it or from it in a collaboration graph.

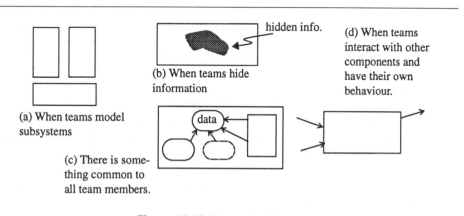

hidden info.

(b) When teams hide information

(d) When teams interact with other components and have their own behaviour.

(a) When teams model subsystems

(c) There is something common to all team members.

Figure 11.16 Teams should be classes.

We suggest having interface methods on a team class for initialization of the team. The input parameters to team initialization methods are the object identifiers or type identifiers of the team members. The initialization methods create the team members if necessary and establish the needed visibility connections. Teams may also have methods for installing objects into internal slots.

Chapter 6 gave an example of the *teams as classes* pattern and showed its effect on code readability.

11.5 RELATIONSHIP TO THE PATTERNS LITERATURE

For readers familiar with Gamma et al [14] , we relate the patterns of this chapter to their patterns.

Gamma et al have documented close to thirty patterns. For the most part, the purpose of their patterns is to reduce the dependencies in a system such that it is easier to change and reuse. The patterns may be seen as templates for designing for change with object-oriented programming languages. The governing principle of designing for change is to determine what is likely to change and then to localize and hide it [24]. Examples of system dependencies that can be lessened through the use of the patterns of Gamma et al include:

Dependence on the name of a particular concrete class when creating classes. Solution: a factory class that creates the specific concrete classes on behalf of others. The factory class hides the names of the concrete classes.

Dependence on the method names a class supports. Solution: an adapter object that translates message calls to the method names of the class in question. The adapter object hides the method names of another object.

Dependence on how objects are connected. Solution: a dispatcher object which knows the location and services offered by several objects and forwards requests to them on behalf of others. The dispatcher hides the objects that implement common services.

The process IPC patterns earlier in this chapter do not have direct counterparts in the object-oriented pattern literature that we know of. The following is a rough correspondence between some of the other patterns we presented and those in the Gamma et al catalogue.

Composite Object with Internal Role Skills Objects This pattern is related to Gamma's *Composite* pattern because both result in a nested object structure. In the Gamma pattern, a composite is an object that encapsulates objects of the same type in a recursive manner. For example, in a parse tree, a node representing a compound language statement may contain simple language statements and recursively other compound language statements. The composite object defines a common interface for accessing the group. However, our pattern nests skills objects that provide the behaviours needed to play roles.

Wrappers This pattern is related to Gamma's *Decorator* pattern. A decorator is an object that adds properties or behaviours to another object by encapsulating it. Decorators themselves may be encapsulated. The wrappers pattern is useful when an object moves between slots, as in the MTU case study. The wrappers pattern is used to add and remove behaviours from an object as needed during normal operation. In contrast, the decorator pattern is more often used during an initialization phase to construct an object of the necessary behaviours by plugging together smaller objects. For example, one may construct a coloured, scrollable window by decorating a window object with a scrolling object and a colourizing object.

Teams as Classes A team may model many things, for example, a group of collaborating objects, a recursive grouping, a subsystem, or an information hiding unit. The modeling abstraction a team represents effects how the team as classes pattern relates to the Gamma et al patterns.

- *As a subsystem or information hiding unit,* the *team as classes* pattern is closely related to Gamma's *Facade* pattern. The Facade pattern localizes the interface of a subsystem in an object. Clients of the subsystem interact only with the facade object. The team object is similar to the facade object.

- *As a recursive grouping,* the *teams as classes* pattern is related to Gamma's *Composite* pattern. The team object is similar to the composite object.
- *As a collaborating group,* the *teams as classes* pattern is related to Gamma's *Mediator* pattern. A mediator object manages the access to the objects and services provided by a collaborating group. The team object is similar to the mediator object

11.6 SUMMARY

This chapter builds a bridge between in our high-level use case maps (path patterns) and patterns for detailed design and coding that are currently the focus of much interest in the object-oriented community. In this chapter we have:

- Brought use case maps into the patterns fold as "path patterns".
- Drawn together pattern threads from this book and the patterns literature.
- Related IPC patterns in concurrent systems to path patterns.
- Related layering patterns in object-oriented frameworks to path patterns.
- Described patterns for multiple role-playing of objects in slots in considerable detail because they illustrate in a very nice way the interplay between different ways of describing patterns (use case maps, collaboration graphs, visibility graphs, class relationship diagrams) and the usefulness of separating concerns between different design levels and different design models.
- Described patterns for manufacturing some special components we find in use case maps, namely processes, slots and teams.
- Reemphasized through examples that designing with use case maps at a high level does not preclude reusing existing design patterns of more detailed types, and in fact provides a framework for doing so.
- Referred the reader to code examples of patterns in previous chapters and an appendix.

CHAPTER 12

Supplementing Familiar
Design Methods

*T*his chapter recaps the design models and the context for design used in this book, summarizes the reasons for including use case maps in any suite of design models, and suggests how use case maps may be used to supplement existing design methods.

As a basis for indicating how use case maps may be used to supplement existing design methods, we give an overview of a few selected methods: Object-Oriented Software Engineering (OOSE), Real Time Object-Oriented Modeling (ROOM), Fusion, Object Modeling Technique (OMT), Object-Oriented Design (OOD), and Responsibility-Driven Design. The purpose is not to judge or compare these methods but only to give just enough information about them that we can see how they can be supplemented. Many of these methods build quite similar models during various stages of design and we propose that all of them may be supplemented in a similar way: with use case maps as a model to bridge the gap between requirements and detailed design.

12.1 A RECAP OF THE DESIGN MODELS AND CONTEXT

The novel aspect of our techniques is the way use case maps bring large-grained behaviour patterns explicitly into the design process as first-class abstractions. There are many issues and design concerns for any complex system and use case maps cannot (and should not) address them all. In this book, we have used a suite of diagram types together with use case maps for understanding and designing object-oriented and real time systems (Figure 12.1). These diagrams span the following range:

Requirements. Use cases are used to specify a system's operation as a black box. The purpose is to express *what* the system must do. Class relationship diagrams are used to gain an understanding of the problem. This is done by modeling problem domain entities and abstractions as classes. The class relationship diagrams are kept light at this point.

High-Level Design. Use case maps are used to express system operation as a precursor to the collaboration graphs of detailed design. The maps express sequences of responsibilities across the components of the system. The maps become first-class design abstractions. Structural dynamics, the creation and movement of components, is modelled with use case maps and slots in the assembly domain. Class relationship diagrams are used much as they were at the requirements level. However, they may contain more "solution" classes discovered in part through use case maps. The class relationship diagrams are still free of details, for example, methods are not shown.

Detailed Design. Collaboration graphs are used to model the interaction sequences among components. Visibility graphs are used to model structural dynamics in terms of the changing visibility references between components. These details follow from the decisions made during high-level design. Class relationship diagrams are now more detailed than in the previous stages: Inheritance hierarchies are typically deeper and methods and attributes may be specified. Class relationships specify the static layout of the source code of a system if an object-oriented language is used for implementation.

Implementation. Implementation proceeds by taking all the previous design diagrams as input. This book has had little to say about this stage of development, except to give a few examples that enable readers to follow examples all the way to implementation, should they so wish.

In previous chapters, we have illustrated the use of the conceptual framework of Figure 12.1 with a number of examples drawn from both real time and conventional object-oriented arenas. In doing so, we have tried to demonstrate how the framework enables object-oriented issues to be combined with real time ones in a straightforward and natural fashion. At the apex of the triangle, the distinctions between object-oriented and real time systems diminish and their common design concerns emerge as the important issues. We have referred to design near the apex of the triangle as *system-level* design. Here the concerns are large-grained components, component relationships (of which there are many types, for example, *containment, visibility, uses, isa*), and large-grained behaviour patterns. As we move down from the apex of the triangle, different design concerns begin to emerge. For real time systems, performance and robustness become important and cannot be completely addressed without an understanding of the physical makeup of the target environment. Processes and interrupt service routines emerge as component types to address performance and robustness issues. The techniques of this book allow processes to be introduced relatively early in the design process (in comparison to some other techniques), without in any way forcing them to be introduced early. For systems implemented with object-oriented programming languages, moving down from the apex introduces reusability and extensibility concerns that are addressed by such languages. Reuse and extensibility are handled through class-based modeling and implementation, and the use of existing frameworks (in the object-oriented sense of the term) and patterns.

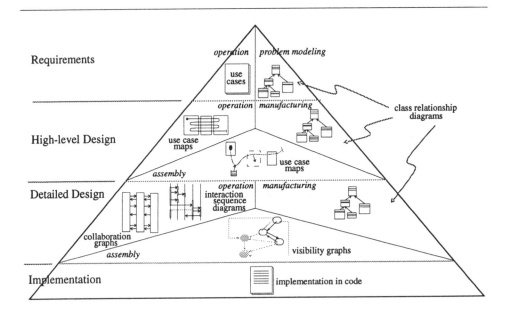

Figure 12.1 Design models used in this book.

None of this constitutes a *method* in the sense of a prescribed set of steps to be followed through the diagram types, levels of abstraction, and domains of concern of this figure. In fact, we have tried to stay away from being prescriptive about sequences of steps. Although the case studies followed specific sequences of steps in relation to the models of Figure 12.1, these steps were only intended to be illustrative, not prescriptive. The book offers a new design model (use case maps), a context for designing with them in relation to other design models (Figure 12.1), some guidelines for design, and some examples and case studies that are intended to provide starting points to enable readers to develop their own methods for particular types of problems. All this is more like a design framework than a method, using the term "framework" in an analogous sense to the way the object-oriented community uses it, namely to identify something that is usable as is in a basic way, but that also may be extended.

We have tried to promote the idea that the design process is an opportunistic one that jumps between diagrams at different levels of abstraction and in different domains of concern in any order that works.

Prescribing sequences of steps in a method covering all possible types of problems and combinations of issues is outside the scope of this book. It would make the book too long even if we wanted to do it and thought we could. We do not want to do it, because it would violate our philosophy that design at this level of abstraction is essentially an opportunistic process in which designers use whatever techniques are helpful whenever they need them. We do not think we can do it at this stage, because the techniques are new and more experience with them is required before trying to be prescriptive about how to use them. For one thing, a prescriptive a book would have to build on a suite of reusable patterns at all levels that covers many problems and issues; such a suite remains to be developed, although this book contains the beginnings of one.

There is another important issue. We have not attempted in this book to cover every-thing that a life-cycle method must cover (for example, software management, design repository organization, testing), so any set of steps that the reader develops from the material of this book will not necessarily cover everything that is needed. We view our techniques as supplementary to others (Figure 12.2) in the sense that others treat details in depth that we have skimmed over or ignored in order to focus on higher-level issues.

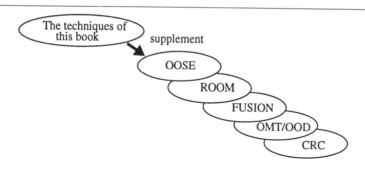

Figure 12.2 Our techniques are supplementary.

The rest of this chapter lays the groundwork to help the reader to develop life-cycle methods that use our techniques to supplement existing published methods. We first sum-marize the unique characteristics of use case maps that make them worth adding to other methods. Then we characterize some specific methods (the ones in the figure above) in terms of the models that their proponents say should be built. Finally we give a general indication of how our techniques may be used to supplement these methods. In most cases, it took a book to describe each of the original methods, and it would not be unrea-sonable to expect that it would take a second edition of the same book with some significant additions to describe in detail how to supplement each method with our techniques. Doing this in detail in this chapter for all the methods is obviously out of our reach; all we try for is a general indication of how to do it. Following the sections on the individual methods, we provide a cross-reference of our diagram types to those of each method to help the reader integrate them.

Missing from this chapter is a treatment of the relationship between use case maps and the patterns approach of Gamma et al [24], because it was covered in Chapter 11.

12.2 ARE USE CASE MAPS FOR YOU?

Our motivation in developing use case maps was to fill a perceived need for a first-class design model of large-grained behaviour patterns of systems. We thought that such a model was missing from popular design models in textbooks. The key features of a first-class design model are that it may be developed independently of related models and cross-referenced to them at any time. Collaboration graphs, visibility graphs, and class relationship diagrams are all examples of first-class design models relative to each other. Use case maps are now added to this list.

We will now try to draw together threads from the book to summarize how use case maps are different from other design models and why they are worth adopting as a supplementary model.

12.2.1 Use Case Maps Versus Stretched Versions of Other Models

The first question a potential adopter of use case maps might ask is: Why not make do with familiar models by stretching them to express the same ideas? While this is possible to a degree, we do not think it is the best use of models that already have other purposes.

We can stretch class relationship diagrams by annotating them to indicate intended patterns of communication among instances (for example, using *communicates with* relationships). This is often a standard part of a design method. However, we suggest that carrying this kind of thing too far overloads a model that already has enough to express, making it more difficult to understand and maintain. Furthermore, it does not solve the problem of making large-grained behaviour patterns into first-class design abstractions.

We can stretch collaboration graphs by adopting a style in which the intercomponent arrows are used to indicate causal transfer of responsibility. If we overlap the arrows on the components they connect, we can form arrow chains like the stylized representation of point-to-point and ripple patterns in Section 2.4. We can then interpret each head-to-tail join as a responsibility point. However, the intent is so different from the usual interpretation of collaboration graphs that calling such arrow-chain diagrams "collaboration graphs" would confusing. They effectively *are* use case paths in a different notation that is both clumsy and easy to misinterpret (because arrows have too many meanings).

In relation to such a stretched version of "collaboration graphs" (we put the term in quotes because they are actually something different), interaction sequence diagrams in

Jacobson style would effectively be a form of use case map in which the responsibility sequences along paths are represented as time sequences. Any use case map can be turned into such a diagram by providing a timeline for each component, representing responsibility points as short segments of these timelines, and joining these segments by arrows that capture the causal sequences in the map.

There is another way of stretching collaboration graphs to make them more abstract: Weinberg's wiggle charts [30]. Wiggle charts are, in essence, collaboration graphs with tentative parts shown by wiggly lines. We think wiggle charts are a good way of stretching collaboration graphs. We think that trying to make collaboration graphs into use case maps is a bad way of stretching them.

An example of a use of conventional interaction sequence diagrams that does not stretch them is provided in the book by Gamma et al [24]. Interaction sequence diagrams are suitable for documenting the patterns of that book because the patterns make a commitment to implementation details like interfaces, interaction sequences, and interaction parameters. Use case maps are helpful before such commitments have been made, or to get a higher-level perspective after they have been made.

In general, stretching a model too far to cover too many issues may not be the best use of a model. There is a difference between *interaction* and *causality* that is worth keeping distinct in different models:

- In general, *interactions* involve messy details like the following: the existence and internal logic of functions, procedures, methods, semaphores, mailboxes, messages, or entries (as in Ada); directions of calls; static versus dynamic binding of calls; unsynchronized, asynchronous, synchronous and timed-out interactions between components; different forms of data transfer during interactions, including parameter passing, and direct sharing; and the changing of visibility relationships by passing pointers.

- Causality is at a different level entirely, unconcerned with any of these details, as has been explained in many places in this book. For example, Section 11.1 provides a number of different interaction patterns among processes for the same produce-consume causal sequence, including some where the interaction arrows go in opposite directions to the path in the map. All of the interaction patterns implement the same producer-consumer causality. Different design issues than causality along paths come into play in choosing one of them for a particular application.

12.2.2 Redundant Models

The reader may observe that use case maps are redundant—and therefore think they are not needed—because the information in them can be derived from details in other models. However, the term "redundant" should not be interpreted to mean "not needed". We need redundant models precisely *because* they are redundant. Think of the relationship between code and design models like collaboration graphs, interaction sequence diagrams, visibility graphs, and class relationship diagrams. These design models are, in a formal sense, redundant relative to code because an expert can infer them from code. However, the redundancy is useful because it provides a separate description of important issues that otherwise tend to get lost when implementing or modifying code.

A similar issue arises with formal models like Petri nets, Statecharts, or Lotos that may be used to specify behaviour. One can use such models to capture the large-grained behaviour patterns expressed by use case maps, but then the patterns become embedded in a lot of other detail in the models and become hard to separate. Yes, once you have the formal models, the use case maps are formally redundant. No, the formal models do not replace use case maps, because the latter have a different purpose, namely helping humans to express and reason about large-grained behaviour patterns above the level of details required by the formal models.

We need redundant software design models to improve the probability that software will be correct when it is finally put into service, to shorten the overall time required to make it correct, and to reduce the chances of introducing errors when changes are made. Few would argue that we should abandon all design models that are formally redundant relative to code. Everyone would surely agree that a balance must be struck between the time and effort needed to learn, use and maintain redundant models and the expected payoff in terms of reduced errors and shortened overall development time. We think that this trade-off is in favour of adopting use case maps as a high-level design model.

12.2.3 Wide Spectrum Model

Use case maps are wide spectrum, meaning they are applicable without modification over a wide range of problem domains, implementation technologies, and scales.

Perhaps the simplest illustration is provided by the maps in the Preface that show different patterns of reading this book. Showing the same patterns with, say, collaboration graphs and interaction sequence diagrams would require making the readers explicit components, with arrows going from readers to other readers to indicate coordination, from readers to chapters to indicate reading, and possibly also from chapters to readers if the book was made into an electronic one with chapters implemented as objects that could guide readers through the book. It would require specifying what the arrows mean in relation to interactions between and among readers and chapters for either the paper book or the electronic book. The meanings would likely be very specific to the implementation technology (paper or electronic). Use case maps convey the patterns as first-class abstractions without committing to these details. Furthermore they encourage a mindset that does not worry about these details, because they provide no means of expressing them.

A number of examples in the book illustrate the application of use case maps to object-oriented programs (for example, Chapter 2, Chapter 6) and real time systems (for example, Chapter 2, Chapter 8, Chapter 10). The map notation and its interpretation is the same in all cases.

The lack of commitment to detail that is an inherent feature of use case maps makes them eminently scalable to apply to large-grained patterns spanning whole systems.

Large-scale maps may be very distant from the details of how the patterns are realized in code, and seen to be distant. This is particularly well illustrated by maps that express structural dynamics. Such maps may be used equally well at scales that are very distant from details of dynamic objects or pointer passing in code, or very close to such details. Section 10.3 gives an example at the scale of dynamic buffer objects in the MTU example, but there is nothing in the structural dynamics model that binds it to this scale.

Use case maps at different scales use the same notation and may be developed independently and related to each other in an easy and natural fashion in map terms. Section 8.4 gives an example of a communications subsystem that is treated as an invisible layer at one scale, as a packet communications system at another scale, and as a character communication system at yet another scale, with all scales related in explicit map terms.

12.2.4 Lightweight Model

The notation is lightweight in the sense that it expresses its main elements (paths) compactly in a way that is free of commitment to the means of realizing them. Therefore, making meaningful, rough sketches for high-level design purposes, and changing them, is relatively painless and quick. This encourages exploration of design alternatives. The importance of having lightweight diagramming notations for this purpose is emphasized by Weinberg [30], who offers wiggle charts. Use case maps are similarly lightweight, but come at the problem from a somewhat different, higher-level angle.

Because paths are so compactly expressed and so close to how experienced designers think anyway (Chapter 2), the essence of the notation is easy to learn and understand.

Such a seemingly trivial feature as the lack of component-like shapes in the notation for unbound maps is important, because it makes the maps easy to superimpose on diagrams containing components, without adding confusing clutter in the form of shapes that could be confused with components.

The existence of interpath coupling is an extremely important property of both requirements and designs that is highlighted in a lightweight fashion in use case maps. It is not hidden in prose as with use cases. It can be expressed in use case maps independently of the details of components that will achieve it.

These are all important elements in achieving the objective expressed early in this book of finding design models that help humans, not machines.

12.2.5 Seamless Bridge Between Requirements and Design

Use case maps may be freely superimposed on each other and on components to construct composite maps. Paths in composite maps may be shaped into patterns that are meaningful to humans, because the only technical information is in the ordering of responsibility points along paths, the coupling of paths, and the positioning of responsibility points on components. Therefore, exactly the same maps may express (in unbound form) overall system requirements, independent of the configuration of the internal components of the system, and (in bound form) the realization of the requirements in relation to some component configuration. This blurs the distinction between requirements and design and enables use case maps to provide a seamless bridge between the two.

An important aspect of maps that enhances the process of transforming requirements seamlessly into designs is the way in which teams may be freely used to give an overview of the operational organization in high-level bound maps, without being concerned about whether or not they will be actual implementation components.

An example is the fax system from Chapter 2. Figure 2.12 shows a use case map that defines a strategy for fax stations to interact over a telephone network. The strategy is a general one that is valid whether or not each fax station is composed of a simple fax machine and a human operator that mediates switching between sending and receiving by making separate telephone calls, or a fully automated fax machine that can perform the mediation itself. Although the map is bound to the fax stations and the telephone network, it is unbound relative to the internal organization of the fax stations that perform this mediation. In other words, it leaves open the issue of whether or not there is a human operator. Binding the map later may be performed by opening up the fax station black box and binding the paths to internal components by superposition. The result would be along the lines of Figure 2.10, which performs a similar binding for Figure 2.8, of which Figure 2.12 is a refinement.

In contrast, going directly from requirements stated in prose to design diagrams at the level of collaboration graphs like Figure 2.13 and interaction sequence diagrams like Figure 2.14 requires committing to internal details of the fax station, specifically to the existence or not of a human operator. Otherwise we cannot draw an interaction sequence diagram.

We might get around this by the artificial and cumbersome approach of developing an abstract interface model of the fax station team to enable the development of collaboration graphs and interaction sequence diagrams in terms of that interface. However, making commitments to interfaces of teams that may not exist as implementation components is unproductive. By the time collaboration graphs and interaction sequence diagrams are to be drawn, decisions should have been made about which teams will be implementation components and which will not. In this example we know that the fax station team is not an implemention component in the case where it is composed of a person and a dumb fax machine, so being forced to define an interface for it just to be able to draw design diagrams is unproductive in that case.

Other examples of maps that seamlessly bridge the gap between requirements and design are the Internet communication map in Figure 7.1 and the MTU map in Figure 8.12.

12.2.6 Coordinated High-Level Design

Because use case maps are first-class models, they enable a coordinated design effort to be made on different models. For example large-grained behaviour patterns and high-level class relationship diagrams may be jointly designed before becoming concerned with the details of classes that will enable the patterns in the maps to be realized. This reduces the chances of having to redo the class design to achieve desired behaviour patterns. The case studies in Chapter 6 (see Section 6.1 through Section 6.3) and Chapter 10 (see Section 10.1 and Section 10.4) provide examples.

12.2.7 Invariant patterns

Use case maps document design intentions that can remain stable relative to details that may change.

For example, Chapter 11 (Section 11.1) shows a map of a producer-consumer pattern that is invariant relative to a number of different implementations of it at the level of collaboration graphs and interaction sequence diagrams.

Other examples of maps that provide invariant patterns are the Internet communication map in Figure 7.1 and the MTU map in Figure 8.12.

12.2.8 Common Denominator for Trade-offs

Use case maps provide a common denominator for making tradeoffs between issues that are otherwise very difficult to relate to each other at a high level. For example Section 10.1 explained how use case maps and class relationship diagrams may be used in a coordinated way to make trade-offs between object-oriented and real time issues, above the level of detail that would be represented in collaboration graphs and interaction sequence diagrams.

12.2.9 Real Time Issues

Use case maps enable concurrency and robustness to be expressed at the path level without making detailed commitments to IPC or associated timer mechanisms.

For example, the Internet timeout-recovery pattern of Figure 7.1 leaves open the question of how the coupling between the timer and the return path will be accomplished. Will a timer be set in the user's email package that, when it runs out, rings a bell on the user's computer console or sends a message to the user? Will the user make a mental note to try again after some elapsed time without a response? All options are left open by the map.

By bringing such issues to the common denominator of paths, a means is provided for trading them off against other issues that are also brought to the same common denominator.

12.2.10 Structural Dynamics

Use case maps show structural dynamics in a uniquely lightweight and expressive fashion. Details of structural dynamics are often so complicated that they obscure the big picture. Implementations do not distinguish between true structural dynamics and initialization boiler plate. Detailed design notations enable structural dynamics to be shown only by sequences of snapshots (of, say visibility graphs, or diagrams of messaging connections at the code level). Expressing structural dynamics in a higher level way, as we do with slots, pools, and create-move arrows in use case maps, gives a simpler, more compact representation of the essence (compare Figure 5.9 and Figure 5.11). Structural dynamics patterns are expressed in maps in a way that is very distant from the details of pointer passing in code, yet that captures the essence of structural dynamics at any scale.

12.2.11 Mental models

The form of the paths in use case maps, namely continuous curves showing causal sequences that traverse sets of components, mirrors a way we have observed that designers in industry often think about large-grained behaviour patterns (see Chapter 2). The notation is a very natural one for designers to use, as evidenced by the fact it has—even before publication of this book—been adopted in some places in industry for design review meetings.

   In our opinion, an important element of the notation is its effect on mindset. The lack in the use case map model of any direct means of expressing details of components, such as interface elements, or connections between components through their interfaces, creates a mindset where these things are naturally deferred as details. The issue is particularly important for novices (students, inexperienced designers). However, experts can also be seduced into filling in details too early just because a notation or tool provides means to do it. Use case maps support high-level thinking in a suitably high-level way.

12.2.12 Architecture

The use case map model gives its own meaning to the term "architecture", while supplementing conventional views of architecture in a way that is consistent with them. Architecture is hard to define in the abstract, but companies that make products with software in them have a view of what it is. The term is typically associated with the kind of information contained in many of the use case maps of this book, such as large-grained components and layering. The fact that the use case maps also represent large-grained behaviour patterns is icing on the cake.

12.3 OBJECT-ORIENTED SOFTWARE ENGINEERING (OOSE)

The OOSE method of Jacobson is a full life-cycle method that covers requirements analysis, design, implementation and testing. This method is mature and parts of it have been used in the telecom industry for over 20 years. The method is documented in the text "Object-Oriented Software Engineering: A Use Case Driven Approach," by Ivar Jacobson et al [18].

The use case concept of OOSE has had an impact on the development of use case maps. The map notation was developed in part to fill the gap between the specification of system behaviour as use cases and the "realization" of that behaviour as interaction sequences among components. Use case maps as a bridging technique has been a running theme throughout this book.

The analysis phase of OOSE is concerned with specifying what a system must do. The models built are ideal because no consideration of the real implementation environment is given. The OOSE models built during analysis are the following (see Figure 12.3):

Use Case Model. A textual description of the scenarios that a user and system will perform. The use case model is the central model of OOSE because it is one of the first models built and it is used to develop subsequent models. The individual named use cases can be related to reduce the amount of effort in describing them, but one must read the details of the use cases to understand the relationships.

System Interfaces. Mock-ups of user interfaces using drawing tools or simulation packages. This is a very useful technique to which many methods give little emphasis. (Chapter 6 of this book used interface mock-ups in the design of the BGETool.)

Problem Domain Model. A class-relationship-style diagram of the important entities appearing in the problem domain. Such diagrams are the central model of many object-oriented design methods, for example, OMT and OOD, but are not positioned quite so centrally in OOSE; they are one of several, equally-important, related models in OOSE.

Analysis Model. An extension to the problem domain model that adds three object types: controller, entity, and interface. It is with the analysis model that the responsibilities or role of each object in each use case is determined. The responsibilities are described using informal text. The responsibilities of the object types are as follows: interface objects are responsible for system input and output; entity objects are normal types of objects found during problem analysis, they encapsulate application information and operations on that information; control objects contain the behaviour that does not naturally belong in interface or entity objects, they sequence interactions. The purpose of the analysis model is to build object structures that are more resilient to change than problem-domain models that do not distinguish object types.

The design phase, called *construction* in OOSE, is based on the analysis models and continues into testing. The design phase considers the implementation and realizes the analysis models as interacting objects. The design (construction) models of OOSE are the following:

Block Model. A translation of the analysis model into components (blocks) which have the semantics of the target implementation environment. The mapping from an analysis model to a block model is often one-to-one. For real time system design, a block model would introduce processes as distinct from other blocks. (This is a late commitment to processes, but understandable if the design abstractions associated with processes bring with them a lot of detailed baggage. We believe that a use case map approach allows processes to be introduced earlier in a more lightweight fashion.)

Interaction Diagrams. Describe message sequences between blocks. (We saw several examples of these expressed with a simplified notation in early chapters of this book.)

Object Behaviour. A description of the internal behaviour of blocks. OOSE recommends state machines or state description language (SDL) diagrams.

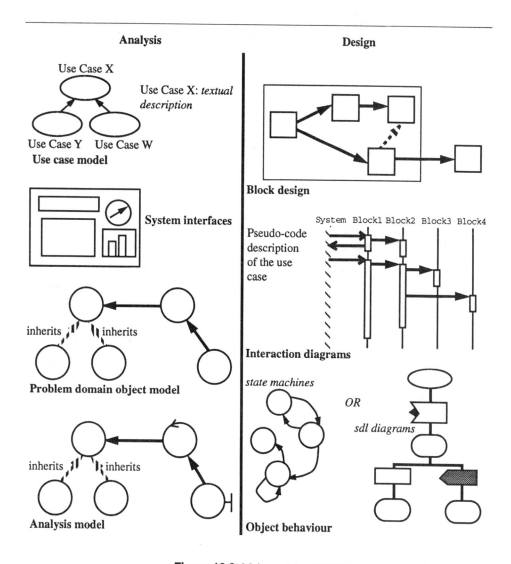

Figure 12.3 Main models of OOSE.

12.3.1 Supplementing OOSE with Use-Case Maps

Use case maps may be used with OOSE as a bridge between textual use cases and interaction diagrams as illustrated in Figure 12.4. In Figure 12.4, a use case map is drawn over a block diagram that has had its association arrows removed. This block diagram is related to our component context diagrams. Use case maps may also be combined with the OOSE analysis model. Because OOSE does not have the slot concept, the integration of use case maps with the existing models of OOSE cannot express structural dynamics at as abstract a level as in this book (although we note an ad hoc way of expressing it in at least one OOSE example by showing that several classes may be related to a single node in an object model diagram).

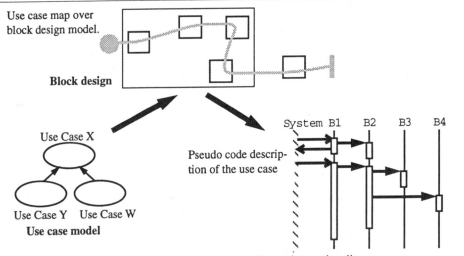

Figure 12.4 Use case maps as a bridge to interaction diagrams.

12.4 REAL TIME OBJECT-ORIENTED MODELING (ROOM)

The Real Time Object-Oriented Modeling (ROOM) method is documented in a text of the same name by Selic, Ward, and Gulekson [27]. The method is unique in the following respects:

- It is targeted specifically for real time and distributed systems,
- It uses executable models throughout development.
- It is supported by a powerful CASE tool that allows models built in the ROOM

modeling language to be executed, incrementally extended and transformed into source code implementations.

The models used in ROOM are as follows (see Figure 12.5):

Scenarios. Text-based descriptions of scenarios applied against a system. Similar to Jacobson's use cases or Rumbaugh's scenarios but more emphasis is given to the internal components of a system.

Message Sequence Charts. Graphical representation of the messages between the components (actors in ROOM terms) of a system and the environment for a given scenario. The Message Sequence Charts used by ROOM are more abstract than the interaction diagrams of Jacobson or the collaboration graphs of this book. This is because diagrams showing communication pathways between actors in ROOM are not committed to the nature of the interactions. This leaves the nature of the interactions open in message sequence charts as well. However, message sequence charts are less abstract than use case maps.

Actor Model. A structural description of the components and connections of the system. The actor model is the central model of the ROOM method. Scenarios and message sequence charts are used for preliminary reasoning about the system requirements. An actor model is built during the early stages and incrementally refined and extended into the final system. An actor is an autonomous black box that communicates with other actors by sending messages over connections (bindings in ROOM terms). Bindings attach to ports on the interface of actors, and ports define the messages that may be sent and received over a binding. The actor model supports many advanced structural properties, including nesting of actors, layering, and dynamic structure. For example, a shaded box indicates a type of component called an imported actor that is very close to our slot concept.

Actor Behaviour Model. A state machine description of the internal behaviour of an actor. Every actor has an internal state machine. The events that drive the state machines are the messages received from other actors. During a state transition an actor may send messages across a binding.

Detailed Behaviour Model. A source code level description of the action sequences performed by an actor's state machine during state transitions and the data variables used by the state machine. Currently, C++ and a Smalltalk-like dialect may be used.

Actor Hierarchy. The supertype/subtype relationships between actor classes. The actor hierarchies express supertype/subtype relationships only.

Port Hierarchy. The supertype/subtype relationships between port classes.

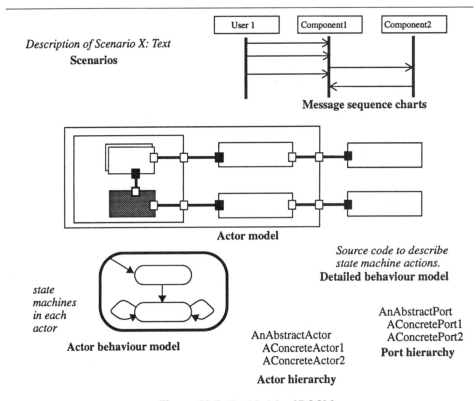

Description of Scenario X: Text
Scenarios

Message sequence charts

Actor model

*Source code to describe
state machine actions.*
Detailed behaviour model

*state
machines
in each
actor*

Actor behaviour model

AnAbstractActor
AConcreteActor1
AConcreteActor2

Actor hierarchy

AnAbstractPort
AConcretePort1
AConcretePort2

Port hierarchy

Figure 12.5 The Models of ROOM.

The ROOM method benefits from an operational approach to development. ROOM designers begin with simple actor models that are incrementally extended, validated through execution and ultimately translated into source code of the target language. Designers can get early feedback of design decisions by executing the models they have built. There are no paradigm shifts between analysis, design, and implementation phases because the same set of models is used throughout.

The ROOM method and the supporting toolset called ObjecTime had an influence on our slot model of structural dynamics. In ROOM, actors in an Actor Model may be characterized as *fixed*, *optional*, or *imported*. Roughly, ROOM's characterization of actors corresponds with our characterization of components in the following way: a fixed actor corresponds to a fixed component, an optional actor corresponds to a dynamic component, and an imported actor corresponds to a slot. An imported actor defines a place in an Actor Model that is to be filled by optional actor instances. The filling of an imported actor "slot" (our term) occurs by passing the identifier of an optional actor in a message to another actor which places the optional actor in the "slot". However, this is all done using language-level statements in the Detailed Behaviour Model; there is no visual representation of structural dynamics analogous to the one provided by use case maps.

Scenarios and Message Sequence Charts are not as central to the ROOM method as are its other models. The other models are central because building a design in terms of them results in an executable system specification. Scenarios and Message Sequence Charts are used informally during the early stages of design to help with the development of the first Actor models. Currently, designers are responsible for making the associations between the Scenarios and Message Sequence Charts and the other ROOM models. However, the ObjecTime tool supporting ROOM does provide record keeping for these two models and generation of Message Sequence Charts from the execution of Actor Models.

12.4.1 Supplementing ROOM with Use Case Maps

Use case maps can be used in two ways to supplement the existing ROOM design method (Figure 12.6). The first way is to express structural dynamics involving optional actors and imported actors with use case maps instead of programming statements. The second way is to employ use case maps as a bridge between textual use cases and the Actor/Message Sequence Charts Models. The closeness of ROOM's Actor Model to our slot model makes the addition of use case maps to ROOM straightforward relative to other methods. Use case maps can be used with ROOM's Actor model to express responsibility sequences and dynamic structure in one diagram.

These ideas suggest the possibility of providing formal links between use case maps and ROOM models to aid in the process of converting high-level design ideas into ROOM models. This is an area of current investigation.

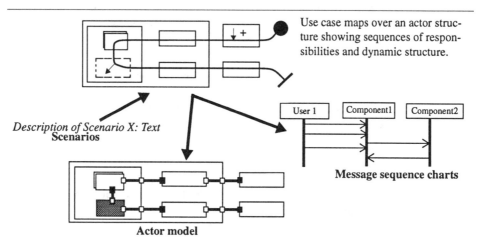

Use case maps over an actor structure showing sequences of responsibilities and dynamic structure.

Description of Scenario X: Text
Scenarios

Message sequence charts

Actor model

Figure 12.6 Using use case maps with ROOM.

12.5 FUSION

The Fusion method is described in the book, "Object-Oriented Development: The Fusion Method," by Coleman et al [13]. The method covers the complete life cycle from requirements analysis to implementation. As its name implies, the method is a synthesis of several other approaches, including: Object Modeling Technique (OMT), Jacobson's Use Case Driven design (from OOSE), Responsibility-Driven Design (CRC), and formal techniques.

Figure 12.7 presents a picture of each of the main models built using the Fusion method. The analysis models are used to specify the behaviour of the system (that is , what the system must do but not how it does it) and the static aspects of the objects that will be part of the system (that is, classes, attributes, and relationships). The models built during analysis are the following:

Object Model. A class relationship diagram similar in semantic depth to the object model of Rumbaugh's OMT. During analysis, methods are not specified. This keeps the specification of system behaviour declarative at the early stages. Fusion has added aggregation to their object model notation. An aggregation is a grouping of classes; it allows a relationship to be treated as an object. This simplifies the specification of higher-order relationships, for example, many three-way relationships can be reduced to a binary relationship between an aggregation and another object. An aggregation is similar to our team concept, because both are groupings. However, the perspectives of the two concepts are different because a team groups operational components and an aggregation groups classes.

System Scenarios. Textual description of use cases in the style of Jacobson supplemented with interaction diagrams involving the system and the environment. The internals of the system are not expressed on these interaction diagrams.

Operation Schema. Textual specification of the effect of use cases (system operations) on the system's object model. Preconditions and postconditions of operations are described in terms of the object model (objects, attributes, and relationships). How the operation turns a precondition into a postcondition is not described.

Lifecycle Model. Regular expressions are used to describe the allowable sequences of use cases against a system.

During the design phase, the behaviour specified during analysis is realized as a collection of interacting objects. The models built during the design phase are the following:

Object Interaction Graphs. These describe message sequences between objects in a similar fashion to our collaboration graphs. However, interaction graphs show the creation and destruction of objects.

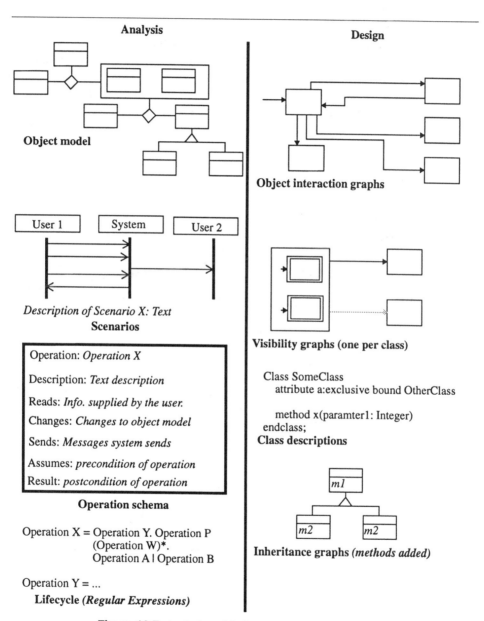

Figure 12.7 Analysis and design models of the Fusion method.

Visibility Graphs. Show the visibility relationships between a client class and server objects. There is a visibility graph for each important class. These graphs can express object lifetime binding, reference mutability, reference lifetime, and the visibility of objects. Unlike Fusion's visibility graphs which are at the level of individual classes, our visibility graphs are more globally scoped. This leads to a difference in semantics. For example, in Fusion, a reference is dynamic relative to the lifetime of the object that holds it; in our approach, a reference is dynamic relative to the lifetime of the use case maps in which the dynamic object appears (indirectly in slots).

Class Interface Description. A syntactic textual description of the interface of a class.

Inheritance Graphs. More detailed class relationship diagrams. These graphs are said to be prescriptive and the ones developed during analysis descriptive. This is another way of saying that class hierarchies are subject to change once detailed design considerations like reusability and extensibility are considered.

12.5.1 Supplementing FUSION with Use Case Maps

Use case maps may be used in two ways to supplement the existing models of the Fusion method. The first approach is shown in Figure 12.8. Use case maps are used to express how an operation performed by the system translates the object model at the beginning of an operation to the object model at the end of the operation. The beginning state of the object model is expressed in the Assumes clause of the operation schema (the precondition). The ending state of the object model is expressed in the Results clause of the operation schema (the postconditions). The bottom of Figure 12.8 gives a generic example of the application of use case maps. Following the path, an object is created at 1, a relation is created at 2 and an object is deleted at 3. Use case maps are used to express the structural dynamics (that is, the creation of objects and relations) that transform an object model from a precondition to a postcondition.

The Fusion method warns against specifying how a precondition of an operation is translated into a postcondition. This is true during analysis, but during design one must commit to a sequence of actions. In Fusion, the sequence is specified in object interaction diagrams that combine normal operation with structural dynamics. This may result in a large semantic gap between the declarative Operation Schemas and the detailed and prescriptive object interaction diagrams that combine operation and dynamics. Use case maps as used in Figure 12.8 may be used as a bridge.

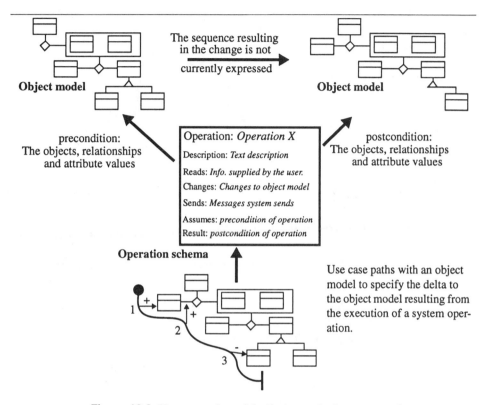

Figure 12.8 Use case paths and the Fusion method: one approach.

Another approach would be to use use case maps to express sequences of responsibilities prior to the development of object interaction graphs. As shown in Figure 12.9, use case maps would be a bridge between the system use cases (expressed as textual scenarios and interaction diagrams) and object interaction diagrams. The use case paths would be drawn over the same objects that appear in an object interaction diagram.

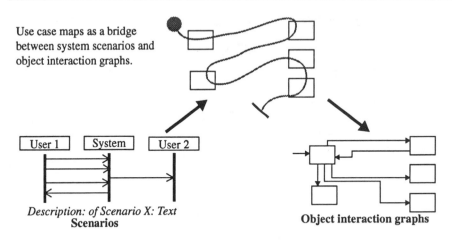

Use case maps as a bridge between system scenarios and object interaction graphs.

Description: of Scenario X: Text
Scenarios

Object interaction graphs

Figure 12.9 Another way of using use case paths with Fusion.

It is possible that both of the above approaches could be used with the Fusion method. Use case maps with an object model as in Figure 12.8 expresses the structural dynamics resulting from the application of a use case. Use case maps with an object diagram as in Figure 12.9 expresses sequences of responsibilities prior to developing object interaction graphs. However, this results in two new models: one that expresses structural dynamics and another that expresses responsibility sequences. A simpler approach may be to extend the object diagram in Figure 12.9 with the slot concept proposed in this book. In this way, structural dynamics and responsibility sequences could be easily expressed on a single diagram, reducing the need for two models.

12.6 OTHER METHODS

The above examples should give the reader a sense of how to supplement existing methods with use case maps. We cannot repeat this exercise for every object-oriented method (there are just too many!). Below we discuss three more popular methods, OMT, OOD and CRC, and describe briefly, without pictures, how use case maps may be used with them. OMT and OOD are described together because these methods are in the process of being merged as this book is being written.

12.6.1 Object Modeling Technique (OMT) and Booch's Object-Oriented Design (OOD)

We group OMT and OOD together because their techniques are similar. In fact, the authors of the methods are now working together to find a common set of notations and concepts. In both techniques, class relationship models are central; however, recent extensions to the methods are adding use cases and interaction diagrams, as in Jacobson.

We see the power of these methods as providing:

Well-developed models and heuristics for class relationship diagrams.

Implementation guidelines for translating the class relationship diagrams into code. The OOD method in particular has a rich set of notations for expressing programming-level issues, such as scoping and packaging, that can be translated almost directly into source code.

We believe that both methods could benefit from the addition of use case maps. As with Jacobson, maps would be used to bridge the gap between use cases and models of object collaboration.

12.6.2 Responsibility Driven Design (or Class Responsibilities and Collaborations (CRC))

Like OOSE and the approach of this book, responsibility driven design approaches use scenarios as a driver of the design process. The approaches have been documented by Wirfs-Brock in the text, "Designing Object-Oriented Software" [32] and by Beck and Cummingham in [2]. The techniques use CRC cards as a tool for design thinking. On each card is written the name of a class, the responsibilities of instances of the class, and the names of other classes that are collaborated with to perform the responsibilities. Scenarios are played through the card set by lifting a card, reading a responsibility, lifting another card, reading its responsibility, and so on until the scenario is complete. The understanding gained from the design exercises with the cards are used to develop class relationship models and collaboration-graph-style diagrams. The diagrams are not exactly collaboration graphs because the arrows between objects represent client-server contracts. A single arrow may represent several messages from a client to a server; the server must provide the methods of the contract to fulfil its obligation to a client. Classes are grouped into subsystems during design.

Use case maps provide a visual representation of the scenarios that designers play through decks of CRC cards. CRC cards is a useful technique because it is physical and works well with groups. A problem is recording the information of design exercises using CRC cards. Use case maps provide a means of doing so.

12.7 CROSS-REFERENCE OF DIAGRAM TYPES

A summary comparison of all the methods discussed in this chapter is presented in Table 12.1. On the left of the table are the six diagram types used in this book. An entry in the table means that two models roughly correspond.

Table 12.1 Relating Design Models

Use Case Map Design	OOSE	ROOM	FUSION	OMT and OOD	CRC
Use case	Use case	Use case	System Scenarios	Scenario	Scenario
Use case map	N/A	N/A	N/A	N/A	Scenarios through CRC cards
Class relationship diagram (High-level design)	Problem Domain Object Model and Analysis model	Actor Hierarchy	Object Model	Object Model (OMT), Class Diagram (OOD)	Class Hierarchies and Cards
Collaboration graph	Interaction Diagram	(Actor Model + Message Sequence Charts)	Object Interaction Diagrams	Interaction Diagrams (both)	Collaboration graphs
Class relationship diagrams (Detailed Design)	Block Model	Actor Hierarchy + Port Hierarchy	Hierarchy Graphs	Object Model (OMT), Class Diagram (OOD)	Class Hierarchies, Class Specifications and Contract Specifications
Visibility graphs	N/A	Actor Model (the bindings of actors imply visibility)	Visibility graphs	Object Diagrams (unique to OOD)	N/A
Models Not Explicitly Discussed in this Book.					
Models of internal component behaviour. N/A	State machines or SDL	ROOMCharts	Operation model and Life-cycle model (But these are used at the level of the entire system).	Behavioural Model (State machines, both.)	N/A
Diagrams of code packaging N/A	N/A	N/A	N/A	Module Diagrams show allocation of classes to modules. Process Diagram shows allocation of processes to processors (unique to OOD)	N/A

Below is an explanation of some of the nuances of our models that result from their use in the conceptual framework for design given at the beginning of this chapter (Figure 12.1):

Use cases. Jacobson describes use cases with textual prose and we see this as an appropriate technique, especially when supplemented by unbound use case maps. Fusion and ROOM supplement use cases with high-level interaction diagrams that describe sequences of stimuli to a system and responses from a system for each use case.

Use case maps. Use case maps as first-class design abstractions appear to be new relative to the current popular design methods. Playing scenarios through decks of CRC cards comes closest in philosophy to the use case map approach. However, the CRC method does not have an explicit notation for the paths, and the method does not address real time design concerns.

There are overlaps between Fusion's Lifecycle and Operation models and our use case maps. Fusion's Lifecycle model describes allowable sequences of use cases through a system using regular expressions. Fusion's Operation model describes changes to a system's object organization as a result of a use case. Use case maps can show the sequencing of use cases with direct couplings between paths. The maps are also good at expressing the relationships between concurrent use cases, as was illustrated in the MTU case study. Changes to a system's organization are described using annotations for structural dynamics as it occurs along use case paths. The models of Fusion overlap somewhat with use case maps, but the important point is that use case maps provide a visual medium for exploring design alternatives and act as bridge between abstract models (like Fusion's Lifecycle and Operation models) and models during detailed design (for example, collaboration graphs). Use case maps are techniques for thinking and transitioning between levels of abstraction.

Class relationship diagram (high-level design). During high-level design, class relationship diagrams are uncommitted to details, such as how methods are assigned to classes. This is in anticipation of later design decisions that will effect the class relationship diagrams. The OOSE design method takes the same approach with their Problem Domain object model. The Analysis model of OOSE assigns generic roles to instances of classes in the Problem Domain object model; we rely on naming of classes to express the same information. Fusion also ignores methods of classes in their Object Model. However, Fusion's Object Model is more central to their method than class relationship diagrams are to the approach of this book. For example, Fusion models many Operational concerns as relationships between classes in an Object Model. In OMT and OOD class relationship-like diagrams are the central model. Our approach is to emphasize manufacturing concerns in class relationship diagrams and address operational concerns using use case maps and collaboration graphs. The CRC design method uses a very simple Class Hierarchy notation that shows only the inheritance relationships between classes; relationships other than inheritance are not shown.

Collaboration graphs. Collaboration graphs show interaction sequences between teams, processes, objects, and slots. They do not show how slots are filled or how objects are created to fill slots. This information is described using annotations for structural dynamics along use case paths. Almost all methods have some form of collaboration graph and most show interactions related to structural dynamics on them. The use of maps allows our collaboration graphs to be simpler because issues of structural dynamics are not expressed on them.

Class relationship diagrams (detailed design). During detailed design we may extend the earlier class relationship diagrams by adding methods, solution domain classes, and deeper inheritance hierarchies. Detailed class relationship diagrams describe how source code will be organized. Fusion's Inheritance graphs serve a similar purpose. The Actor and Port hierarchies in the ROOM method are also at this level of detail.

Visibility graphs. We use visibility graphs to describe how the organization of run-time components in a system have access to each other through visibility references. Our visibility graphs show the layout of groups of objects. Fusion also has a Visibility Graph diagram but the scope of these diagrams is at the level of individual classes.

Models not developed in this book. We have not described in this book models of internal component behaviour, nor models of source code packaging. State machines are the most common and often the best approach for models of internal component behaviour. They describe the allowable messages a component may receive and the actions the component performs upon receiving a particular message. OOSE, ROOM, and OMT all take this approach. We are in agreement with using state machines this way provided they are not introduced too early in the design process, because they can easily lead to an over-commitment to detail. We believe that a use case map analysis should precede the development of internal state machines for components. The OOD method provides the most complete set of models of source packaging. We have not discussed issues of source code packaging in this book.

12.8 SUMMARY

In this chapter we have:

- Summarized the design levels (requirements, high-level design, detailed design) and models (use case maps, class relationship diagrams, collaboration graphs, interaction sequence diagrams, visibility graphs) that provide a context for designing with use case maps.
- Summarized the roles of use case maps: to supplement existing techniques by providing a bridge between requirements (*what* a system must do), and high-level design (the first phase of determining *how* a system will be built to do it); to provide an abstract view of structural dynamics allowing this important design concern to addressed above the often-messy details of implementation.
- Given reasons for adopting use case maps as a design model to provide first-class descriptions of large-grained behaviour patterns to supplement other techniques.
- Wrapped up the book by giving an overview of how use case maps relate to and supplement selected, well-known existing methods.

Notation Summary

A.1: USE CASE MAPS

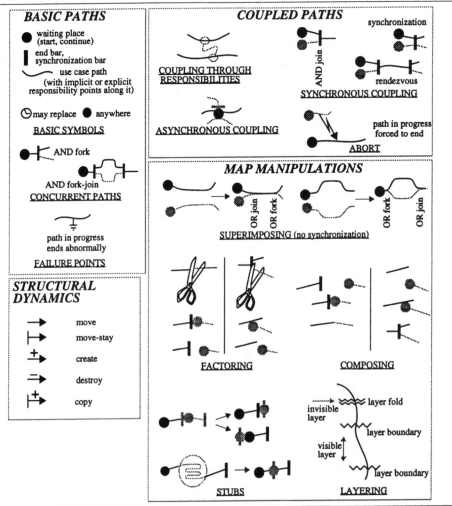

A.2: NOTATIONAL NUANCES FOR USE CASE MAPS

Here we point out some notational nuances that are not used in the body of the book.

Metering Multiple main paths *intersecting* the same waiting place indicates metering. Metering is, in a loose sense, opposite to AND joining. Where AND-joining

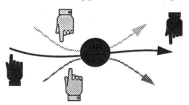

forces different scenarios to follow the same path together, metering prevents too many scenarios from following the same path together. The general idea is that there is some limit set by the waiting place on the number that may proceed past it (in the case where the limit is one, metering is precisely the opposite of AND joining). When this limit is reached, the waiting place is closed (it is assumed to be initially open). It may be opened again by a separate triggering path, or by the intersecting paths looping back to touch it. The details are not specified by the notation.

Standard Coupling Configuration and Compound Coupling Compound coupling occurs when we combine asynchronous and synchronous modes of coupling, for example, to indicate a timeout of *one* of the paths in an AND join. Compound coupling is best understood by viewing synchronization bars as shorthand for mutually coupled waiting places. Then all forms of compound coupling are just variations of coupling through

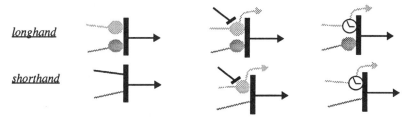

waiting places. The waiting places are redundant when there is no separate triggering other than through the synchronization bars, and are therefore omitted in that case (yielding the shorthand notation). With this in mind, the configurations above the following meanings (the reader should be able to construct variations).

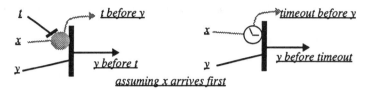

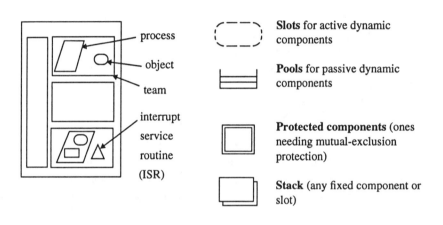

A.3: COMPONENTS

A.4: COLLABORATION-GRAPHS

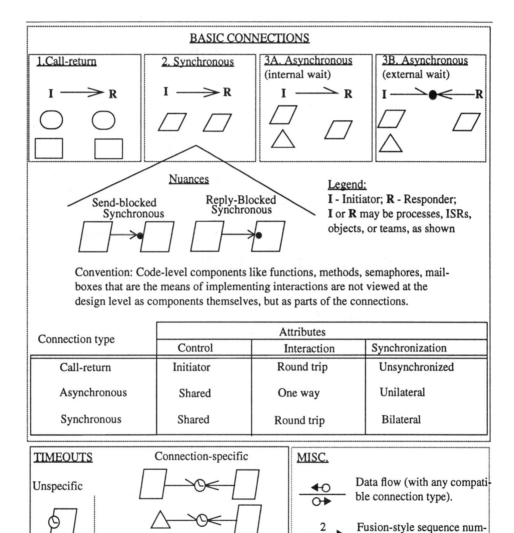

BASIC CONNECTIONS

1. Call-return

2. Synchronous

3A. Asynchronous (internal wait)

3B. Asynchronous (external wait)

I ⟶ R

I ⟶ R

I ⟶ R

I ⟶●⟵ R

Nuances

Send-blocked Synchronous

Reply-Blocked Synchronous

Legend:
I - Initiator; R - Responder;
I or R may be processes, ISRs, objects, or teams, as shown

Convention: Code-level components like functions, methods, semaphores, mailboxes that are the means of implementing interactions are not viewed at the design level as components themselves, but as parts of the connections.

Connection type	Attributes		
	Control	Interaction	Synchronization
Call-return	Initiator	Round trip	Unsynchronized
Asynchronous	Shared	One way	Unilateral
Synchronous	Shared	Round trip	Bilateral

TIMEOUTS — Connection-specific

Unspecific

MISC.

Data flow (with any compatible connection type).

Fusion-style sequence numbers (context distinguishes connection names from sequence numbers)

2

2.3

A.5: VISIBILITY GRAPHS

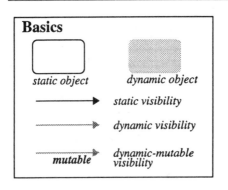

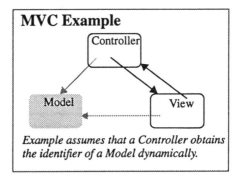

A.6: CLASS RELATIONSHIP DIAGRAMS

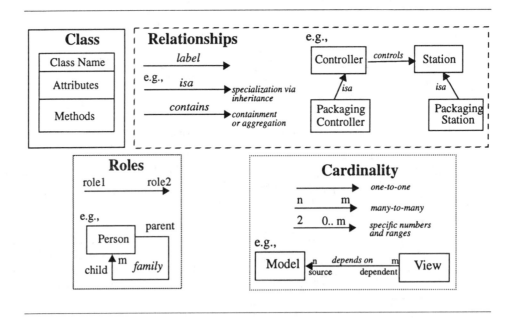

Some Coding Examples

*T*his Appendix contains some skeletal coding examples for the MTU case study (Chapter 10) and the multiple-role-playing patterns (Chapter 11). The coding examples are written in C++. We chose C++ because the packaging facilities lead to code which is relatively easy to read, given an understanding of the design descriptions from earlier chapters from which this code was generated. The concepts of this text are in no way tied to any particular programming language.

B.1: BACKGROUND ON C++

The following is a brief survey of some the C++ language features used in the coding examples of this appendix. The purpose of this section is to help one to *read* the programming examples, not to teach one how to *write* C++ code. C++ is a large and complex programming language and the description here is in no way complete. Readers requiring or wanting more information should consult a text on the C++ programming language, such as [29].

The text below refers to the code of Figure B.1 (MTU case study example).

- A *constructor* is a method for creating an instance of a class. The constructor for a class has the same name as the class and is called automatically when needed. For example, a constructor is invoked when an object is created dynamically using the *new* operator. In Figure B.1, the following code creates an instance of class MessageBuffer invoking the constructor of that class. The aMessageBuffer variable is set to reference the newly created MessageBuffer object.

```
aMessageBuffer = new  MessageBuffer;
```

- A constructor is also invoked when the scope of a statically defined object becomes active. For example, the following declaration in the definition of the LinkTeam class:

```
RxLProcess    aRxLProcess;
```

results in the creation of a RxLProcess object each time a LinkTeam class is created. The constructor of the RxLProcess class is invoked automatically.
- A *destructor* is a method for destroying an instance of a class. The destructor for a class has the same name as the class but is preceded with a tilde character (~). As for constructors, destructors are called automatically when needed, for example, when a dynamically created object is destroyed using the *delete* operator, and when the scope of a statically declared object becomes inactive. There are no example uses of destructors in this appendix.
- Classes in C++ have *public*, *private*, and *protected* parts. The *public* part defines methods and attributes that may be referenced by clients of a class. The *private* part of a class is local to it. Subclasses cannot see the private parts of their superclasses. The *protected* part of a class is visible to the class and its subclasses. However, clients of the class cannot use its protected parts. For example, the Buffer class has a public *print()* method that anyone with visibility of a Buffer instance can call; a private data[max_len] array that is visible only to the methods of this class (and so called *friends* of this class); and a protected method called *addBytes()* that only subclasses of this class may call.
- Methods which may be called in a polymorphic way must be labeled as *virtual*. Virtual methods may be overridden in subclasses. For example, the *addHeaderL()* method of the TxBuffer class is virtual and may be overridden by subclasses MessageBuffer and AckBuffer. A pure virtual method has no method body in the class where it is defined. A class with a pure virtual method is an *abstract class* because the class is incomplete. The subclasses of an abstract class must implement the bodies of the pure virtual methods they inherit. A pure virtual method is set equal to zero in its definition. For example, the *send()* method of class MTUTeam is a pure virtual method.

- C++ supports different forms of inheritance. We use only the simplest form: *public inheritance*. Public inheritance means that the subclass does not change the public, private, and protected designations of its superclass. For example, class `TxBuffer` inherits publicly from class `Buffer`.
- A reference (pointer) to an object is declared using an asterisk. For example, the statement `MessageBuffer* txmP` defines `txmP` as a reference to an object of type `MessageBuffer`. References to objects must have their values (the identifiers of objects) assigned dynamically. A message is sent to an object identified by a reference using the arrow operator, for example, *txmP->addHeaderP()*, would send the message *addHeaderP()* to the object referenced by `txmP`. An object may also be referenced directly, for example, `TxProcess aTxProcess` in class `MessageTeam`, defines an object called `aTxProcess` of type `TxProcess`. Messages are sent to an object using the dot operator. For example, *aTxProcess.send()*, would send the message *send()* to the object `aTxProcess`. Note also that the declaration, `TxProcess aTxProcess`, would automatically create a `TxProcess` object when the scope of the declaration becomes active, in this case, whenever a `MessageTeam` object is created.

Coding Conventions There is one coding convention that we use throughout the examples to relate source code to the models of structural dynamics we build in the Operation domain. The convention is to provide special interface methods on objects that will fill slots. If an object is to fill a slot called *XXX*, the object will have two interface methods: *installInXXXSlot()* and *emptyXXXSlot()*. The *installInXXXSlot()* method allows the object to ready itself to play the role associated with the slot. This may involve establishing necessary visibility relationships and creating any support objects to help in playing the role. The install method returns a pointer to the object that will fill the slot. Subsequent interaction with the slot occupant occurs through the returned pointer reference. The *emptyXXXSlot()* method informs the object that it is to be removed from the *XXX* slot. The object can perform any necessary cleanup actions. There are several examples of this coding convention in the source code that follows.

We assume the existence of a framework for real time programming that has classes in it for things like processes and semaphores. We do this to make the code more structured and readable. For more information on the issues associated with adding concurrency to an object-oriented programming language, the reader is referred to the discussion of the patterns for manufacturing processes in Chapter 11 and the paper by [5].

B.2: MTU CASE STUDY CODING EXAMPLES (see Chapter 10)

The source code that follows can be derived in a straight-forward way from earlier design diagrams developed for the MTU case study. The figures are repeated here for easy reference.

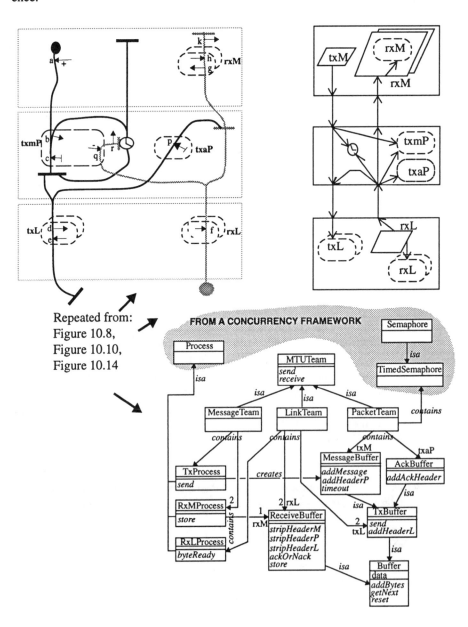

Repeated from:
Figure 10.8,
Figure 10.10,
Figure 10.14

```
// Classes for Buffers

class Buffer
{
public:
    Buffer();                   // Constructor
    virtual ~Buffer(){};        // Destructor

    void print();

private:                        // for this class only
    // Data attributes
    char data[max_len];
    int index;

protected:                      // for this class and subclasses
    // Methods to access bytes
    void addBytes(String &str);
    char getNext();
    void reset();
};

class TxBuffer: public Buffer
{
public:
    TxBuffer();
    virtual ~TxBuffer();

    // Methods for the Link Team
    virtual void addHeaderL();
    virtual bool send ();

    // Methods to install TxBuffer objects in slots
    virtual TxBuffer* installInLSlot();
    virtual void emptyLSlot();
}

class MessageBuffer: public TxBuffer
{
public:
    MessageBuffer();
    ~MessageBuffer();

    // Methods for the Message Team
    bool addMessage(String& str);

    // Methods for the Packet Team
    void addHeaderP();
    double timeout();
```

```
        // Methods to install MessageBuffer objects in slots
        MessageBuffer* installInPSlot();
        void emptyPSlot();
}

class AckBuffer: public TxBuffer
{
public:
        AckBuffer();
        ~AckBuffer();

        // Methods for the Packet Team
        void addAckHeader();

        //Methods to install AckBuffer objects in slots
        AckBuffer* installInAckSlot();
        void emptyAckSlot();
}

class ReceiveBuffer: public Buffer
{
public:
        ReceiveBuffer();
        ~ReceiveBuffer();

        // Methods for M Team
        void stripHeaderM();
        bool store(File& file);

        // Methods for Packet Team
        void stripHeaderP();
        AckOrNack ackOrNack();

        // Methods for Link Team
        void stripHeaderL();

        // Methods to install ReceiveBuffer objects into slots
        ReceiveBuffer* installInRxMSlot();
        ReceiveBuffer* installInRxLSlot();
        void emptyRxMSlot();
        void emptyRxLSlot();
}

// Classes for Teams
class MTUTeam
{
public:
        MTUTeam();
        virtual ~MTUTeam();
```

```
    // Objects of type Buffer flow between the teams.
    // These methods must be provided by subclasses.
    virtual void send(Buffer* aBuffer) = 0;
    virtual void receive(Buffer* aBuffer) = 0;
}

class MessageTeam: public MTUTeam
{
public:
    MessageTeam(PacketTeam* aPacketTeam);
    ~MessageTeam();

    // Inter-team connections
    PacketTeam* packetTeam;

    void send(Buffer *aBuffer);
    void send(String& str);
    void receive(Buffer *aBuffer);

private:
    // Internal Processes
    TxProcess   aTxProcess;
    RxMProcess aRxMProcess1;
    RxMProcess aRxMProcess2
}

class PacketTeam: public Team
{
public:
    PacketTeam(MessageTeam* aMessageTeam, LinkTeam* aLinkTeam);
    ~PacketTeam();

    // Inter-team connections
    MessageTeam* messageTeam;
    LinkTeam* linkTeam;

    // Sent by Message team
    void send(MessageBuffer* aBuffer);

    // Sent by Link team
    void receive(ReceiveBuffer* aBuffer);

private:
    // Internal Process Machinery
    // Semaphore waited on for messages.
    TimedSemaphore aTimedSemaphore;

    // Internal Slots
    MessageBuffer* txmP;
    AckBuffer* txAP;
}
```

```
class LinkTeam: public MTUTeam
{
public:
    LinkTeam(PacketTeam* aPacketTeam);
    ~LinkTeam();

    // Inter-team connections
    PacketTeam* packetTeam;

    // Sent by Packet team
    void send(TxBuffer* aBuffer);
    // Null method never called
    void receive(Buffer* aBuffer) {};
private:
    // Processes
    RxLProcess rxLProcess;
    // Internal Slots
    TxBuffer* txL; // current slot
    TxBuffer* txL1;
    TxBuffer* txL2;
    ReceiveBuffer* rxL; // current slot
    ReceiveBuffer* rxL1;
    ReceiveBuffer* rxL2;
}

// Classes for Processes
class RxMProcess: public Process
{
public:
    RxMProcess();
    ~RxMProcess();
    void init();

    void store(File* file);
private:
    // Outer Team
    MessageTeam* messageTeam;
    // Internal Slots
    ReceiveBuffer* rxM;
}

class RxLProcess: public Process
{
public:
    RxLProcess();
    ~RxLProcess();

    void init(LinkTeam* aLinkTeam){
        linkTeam = aLinkTeam;
    }
```

```
class TxProcess: public Process
{
public:
    TxProcess();
    ~TxProcess();

    void init(MessageTeam* aMessageTeam){
        messageTeam = aMessageTeam;
    }
    void send(String& str){
        // release caller, create Message Buffer, send to Packet
        // Team;
    }
    void byteReady(); // Called by an Interrupt Service Routine
                      // (ISR)
private:
    // Outer Team
    LinkTeam* linkTeam;
}
```

B.3: ROLE PLAYING EXAMPLES (See Chapter 11)

B.3.1 One Object Multiple Roles - Multiple Inheritance

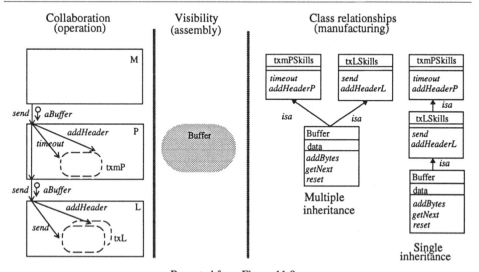

Repeated from Figure 11.9.

```
// Declaration of teams
MessageTeam mTeam;
PacketTeam  pTeam;
LinkTeam    lTeam;

class txmPSkills {
public:
    ...;
    // Packet Team Methods
    virtual double timeout();
    virtual void addHeaderP()
            {String str;
            // Form a packet header
            ....;
            addBytes(str);}
protected:
    virtual void addBytes(String& str) = 0;
    virtual char getNext() = 0;
    virtual void reset() = 0;
};
class txLSkills {
public:
    ...;
    //Link team Methods
    virtual bool send();
    virtual void addHeaderL(){
            String str;
            // Form a link header
            ....;
            addBytes(str);}
protected:
    virtual void addBytes(String &str) = 0;
    virtual char getNext() = 0;
    virtual void reset() = 0;
};

// Syntax for multiple inheritance follows
class Buffer: public txmPSkills, public txLSkills {
    // A friend class has special access priveleges to
    // the class it is a friend of.
    friend class MessageTeam;
public:
    ...;
private:
    // Methods to access bytes
    void addBytes(String &str);
    char getNext();
    void reset();
    // Data attributes
    char dataArray[max_len]; int index;
};
```

```
// The double colon is a scope operator.
bool MessageTeam::send(String& str)
{
    Buffer *aMessage;
    aMessage = new Buffer();
    aMessage->addBytes(str);
    return pTeam.send(aMessage);
}
// aMessage is passed by reference.
bool PacketTeam::send(Buffer& aMessage)
{
    bool ReturnCode;
    aMessage.addHeaderP(); aMessage->timeout();
    ReturnCode = lTeam.send(Buffer& aMessage);
    // Wait on timeout. Retransmit if necessary.
    ...
    return ReturnCode;
}

bool LinkTeam::send(Buffer& aPacket)
{
    aMessage.addHeaderL();
    return aMessage.send();
}
```

B.3.2 One Object Multiple Roles - Single Inheritance

```
// Delaration of teams
MessageTeam mTeam;
PacketTeam  pTeam;
LinkTeam    lTeam;

class txmPSkills {
public:
    ...;
    // Packet Team Methods
    virtual double timeout();
    virtual void addHeaderP()
            {String str;
            // Form a packet header
            ....;
            addBytes(str);}
protected:
    virtual void addBytes(String& str) = 0;
    virtual char getNext() = 0;
    virtual void reset() = 0;
};
```

```
class txLSkills: public txmPSkills{
public:
    ...;
    //Link team Methods
    virtual bool send();
    virtual void addHeaderL(){
            String str;
            // Form a link header
            ....;
            addBytes(str);};
protected:
    virtual void addBytes(String &str) = 0;
    virtual char getNext() = 0;
    virtual void reset() = 0;
};

class Buffer: public txLSkills
{
    friend class MessageTeam;
public:
    ...;
private:
    // Methods to access bytes
    void addBytes(String &str);
    char getNext();
    void reset();
    // Data attributes
    char dataArray[max_len]; int index;
};

bool MessageTeam::send(String& str)
{
    Buffer *aMessage;
    aMessage = new Buffer();
    aMessage->addBytes(str);
    return pTeam.send(aMessage);
}
bool PacketTeam::send(Buffer& aMessage)
{
    bool ReturnCode;
    aMessage.addHeaderP(); aMessage->timeout();
    ReturnCode = lTeam.send(Buffer& aMessage);
    // Wait on timeout. Retransmit if necessary.
    ...
    return ReturnCode;
}

bool LinkTeam::send(Buffer& aPacket)
{
    aMessage.addHeaderL();
    return aMessage.send();
}
```

B.3.3 Composite Object

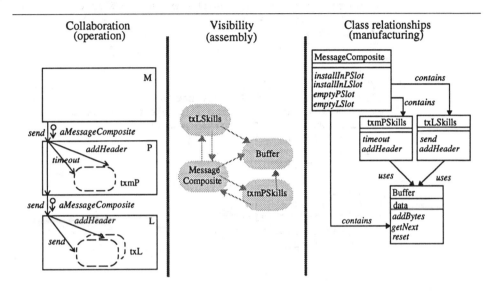

Repeated from Figure 11.10.

```
// Declaration of teams
MessageTeam mTeam;
PacketTeam  pTeam;
LinkTeam    lTeam;

class Buffer {
public:
    ...;
    // Methods to access bytes
    void addBytes(String &str);
    char getNext();
    void reset();
private:
    // Data attributes
    char dataArray[max_len]; int index;
};

class txmPSkills;
class txLSkills;
```

```
class MessageComposite {
    // The skills objects are friends of a MessageComposite
    // so that they may access the private Buffer object
    // of MessageComposite.
    friend class txmPSkills;
    friend class txLSkills;
public:
    ...;
    //Message Team Methods
    virtual void message(String& str);
    // Methods to install composite objects in slots.
    virtual txmPSkills *installInPSlot();
    virtual txLSkills *installInLSlot();
    virtual void emptyPSlot();
    virtual void emptyLSlot();
private:
    //Role Skills objects
    txmPSkills *aTxmPSkills;
    txLSkills *aTxLSkills;
    // Shared data of the composite
    Buffer aBuffer;
};

class txmPSkills {
public:
    // Constructor and destructor
    txmPSkills(MessageComposite *composite);
    virtual ~txmPSkills();
    // Packet Team Methods
    virtual double timeout();
    virtual void addHeader();
private:
    MessageComposite *aMessageComposite;
};

class txLSkills {
public:
    // Constructor and Destructor
    txLSkills(MessageComposite *composite);
    virtual ~txLSkills();
    //Link team Methods
    virtual bool send();
    virtual void addHeader();
private:
    MessageComposite *aMessageComposite;
};
```

```
//Methods of class MessageComposite
void MessageComposite::message(String& str) {
    aBuffer.addBytes(str);
}

txmPSkills* MessageComposite::installInPSlot() {
    aTxmPSkills = new txmPSkills(this);
    return aTxmPSkills;
}

txLSkills* MessageComposite::installInLSlot(){
    aTxLSkills = new txLSkills(this);
    return aTxLSkills;
}

// Methods of class txmPSkills
txmPSkills::txmPSkills(MessageComposite *composite) {
    aMessageComposite = composite;
}

void txmPSkills::addHeader() {
    String str;
    // Construct a packet header
    ...;
    aMessageComposite->aBuffer.addBytes(str);
}

// Methods of class txLSkills
txLSkills::txLSkills(MessageComposite *composite) {
    aMessageComposite = composite;
}

void txLSkills::addHeaderL() {
    String str;
    // Construct a link header
    ...;
    aMessageComposite->aBuffer.addBytes(str);
}

// Methods of the Teams
bool MessageTeam::send(String& str) {
    MessageComposite *aMessageComposite;
    aMessageComposite = new MessageComposite();
    aMessageComposite->message(str);
    return pTeam.send(aMessageComposite);
}
bool PacketTeam::send(MessageComposite& aMessage){
    bool ReturnCode;
    // aTxmPSkills is a private instance variable of the Packet
    // team.
    aTxmPSkills = aMessage.installInPSlot();
```

```
    aTxmPSkills->addHeader(); aTxmPSkills->timeout();
    ReturnCode = lTeam.send(MessageComposite& aMessage);
    // Wait on timeout. Retransmit if necessary.
    ...
    return ReturnCode;
}

bool LinkTeam::send(MessageComposite& aPacket) {
    // aTxLSkills is a private instance variable of the Packet
    // team.
    aTxLSkills = aMessage.installInPSlot();
    aTxLSkills->addHeader();
    return aTxLSkills->send();
}
```

B.3.4 Wrappers

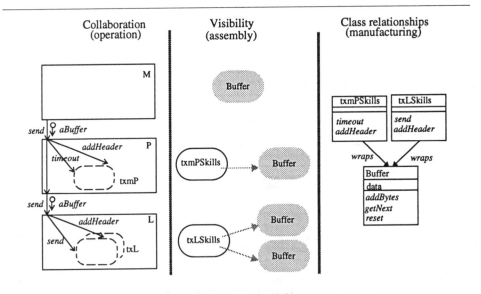

Repeated from Figure 11.11.

```
// Declaration of the teams
MessageTeam mTeam;
PacketTeam  pTeam;
LinkTeam    lTeam;

class Buffer {
public:
```

```
        ...;
        // Methods to access bytes
        void addBytes(String &str);
        char getNext();
        void reset();
    private:
        // Data attributes
        char dataArray[max_len];
        int index;
    };

    class txmPSkills {
    public:
        ...;
        // Packet Team Methods
        virtual double timeout();
        virtual void addHeader();
        // Role playing methods
        txmPSkills* installInPSlot(Buffer *Buffer);
        void emptyPSlot();
    private:
        Buffer *aBuffer;
    };

    class txLSkills {
    public:
        ...;
        //Link team Methods
        virtual bool send();
        virtual void addHeader();
        // Role playing methods
        txLSkills* installInLSlot(Buffer *Buffer);
        void emptyLSlot();
    private:
        Buffer *aBuffer;
    };

    class PacketTeam {
        ...;
    private:
        txmPSkills aTxmPSkills;
    };

    class LinkTeam {
        ...;
    private:
        txLSkills aTxLSkills;
    };
```

```
// Methods of class txmPSkills
void txmPSkills::addHeader() {
    String str;
    // Construct a Packet header
    ...;
    aBuffer->addBytes(str);
}

txmPSkills* txmPSkills::installInPSlot(Buffer *Buffer)
{
    aBuffer = Buffer;
    return this;
}

// Methods of class txLSkills
void txLSkills::addHeader(){
    String str;
    // Construct a Link header
    ...;
    aBuffer->addBytes(str);
}

txLSkills* txLSkills::installInLSlot(Buffer *Buffer) {
    aBuffer = Buffer;
    return this;
}

//Message Team
bool MessageTeam::send(String& str) {
    Buffer *aBuffer;
    aBuffer = new Buffer();
    aBuffer->addBytes(str);
    return pTeam.send(aBuffer);
}
bool PacketTeam::send(Buffer& aMessage){
    bool ReturnCode;
    // aTxmPSkills is a private instance variable of the Packet
    // team.
    (void) aTxmPSkills.installInPSlot(aMessage);
    aTxmPSkills.addHeader(); aTxmPSkills.timeout();
    ReturnCode = lTeam.send(aMessage);
    // Wait on timeout. Retransmit if necessary.
    ...
    return ReturnCode;
}

bool LinkTeam::send(Buffer& aPacket) {
    // aTxLSkills is a private instance variable of the Packet
    // team
    (void) aTxLSkills.installInPSlot(aPacket);
    aTxLSkills.addHeader();
    return aTxLSkills.send();
}
```

References

1 C. Atkinson, *Object-Oriented Reuse, Concurrency and Distribution.* Addison-Wesley, 1991.

2 K. Beck and W. Cunningham, "A Laboratory for Teaching Object-Oriented Thinking." In *Proceedings of OOPSLA '89*, ACM/SIGPLAN, New Orleans, Louisiana, October 1989.

3 G. Booch, *Object-Oriented Design.* Benjamin/Cummings, Second Edition, 1994.

4 G.Booch, "Coming of Age in an Object-Oriented World." IEEE Software, Vol. 11, No. 6, 1994.

5 P. A. Buhr and G. Ditchfield, "Adding Concurrency to a Programming Language." In *Proceedings of the Usenix C++ Technical Conference*, 1992.

6 R.J.A. Buhr, *System Design with Ada.* Prentice Hall, 1984.

7 R.J.A. Buhr, *Practical Visual Techniques in System Design (with Applications to Ada).* Prentice-Hall, 1990.

8 R.J.A. Buhr, "Pictures that Play: Design Notations for Real-Time and Distributed Systems." *Software Practice and Experience*, Vol. 23, No. 8, August 1993.

9 R.J.A. Buhr and R.S. Casselman, "Architectures with Pictures." In *Proceedings*

of OOPSLA'92, ACM/SIGPLAN, Vancouver, Canada, October 1992.

10   R.J.A. Buhr and R.S. Casselman, "Timethread-Role Maps for Object-Oriented Design of Real-time and Distributed Systems." In *Proceedings of OOPSLA'94*, ACM/SIGPLAN, Portland, Oregon, October 1994.

11   D. de Champeaux, D. Lea, and P. Faure, *Object-Oriented System Development*. Addison-Wesley, 1993.

12   P. Coad and E. Yourdan, *Object-Oriented Analysis*. Yourdan Press, Prentice Hall, 1990.

13   D. Coleman et al *Object-Oriented Development: The Fusion Method*. Prentice Hall Object-Oriented Series, 1993.

14   E. Gamma, R. Helm, R. Johnson and J. Vlissides, *Design Patterns: Elements of Reusable Object-Oriented Software*. Addison-Wesley, 1995.

15   D. Garlan and M. Shaw, "An Introduction to Software Architecture." In Advances in Software Engineering and Knowledge Engineering, Vol. 1, World Scientific Publishing Company, 1993.

16   A. Goldberg and D. Robson, *Smalltalk-80: The Language and Its Implementation*. Addison-Wesley, 1985.

17   D. Harel, "Statecharts: A Visual Formalism for Complex Systems." *Science of Computer Programming*, Vol. 8, 1987.

18   I. Jacobson, M. Christeron, and G. Overgaard, *Object-Oriented Software Engineering: A Use Case Driven Approach*. Addison-Wesley, 1992.

19   R. E. Johnson, "Documenting Frameworks using Patterns." In *Proceedings of OOPSLA'92*, ACM/SIGPLAN, Vancouver, Canada, October 1992.

20   R. E. Johnson and B. Foote, "Designing Reusable Classes." *Journal of Object Oriented Programming (JOOP)*, Vol. 1, No. 2, June/July 1988.

21   M. Karaorman and J. Bruno, "Introducing Concurrency to a Sequential Language." *Communications of the ACM*, Vol. 36, No. 9, September 1993.

22   G. E. Krasner and S. T. Pope, "A Cookbook for Using the Model-View-Controller User Interface Paradigm in Smalltalk-80." *Journal of Object Oriented Programming (JOOP)*, Vol. 1, No. 3, September 1988.

23   M. Mulhauser, W. Gerteis, and L. Heusr, "DoCase: A Methodic Approach to Distributed Programming." *Communications of the ACM*, Vol. 36, No. 9, September 1993.

24   D.L. Parnas, "On the Criteria to be used in Decomposing Systems into Modules."- *Communications of the ACM*, Vol. 15, No. 2, 1972.

25   T. Reenskaug, et al, "OORASS: Seamless Support for the Creation and Mainte-
        nance of Object Oriented Systems." *Journal of Object Oriented Programming
        (JOOP)*, October 1992.

26   J. Rumbaugh, M. Blaha, W. Premerlani, F. Eddy, and W. Lorensen, *Object-Ori-
        ented Modeling and Design*. Prentice Hall, 1991.

27   B. Selic, G. Gulekson, and P. Ward, *Real-Time Object-Oriented Modeling*. Wiley,
        1994.

28   S. Shlaer and S.J. Mellor, *Object Lifecycles Modeling the World in States*. Your-
        don Press Computing Series, Prentice Hall, 1992.

29   B. Stroustrup, *The C++ Programming Language*, Second Edition, Addison-Wes-
        ley, 1992.

30   G.M. Weinberg, *Rethinking Systems Analysis and Design*. Dorset House Publish-
        ing, 1988.

31   R. Wirfs-Brock and R. Johnson, "Surveying Current Research in Object-Oriented
        Design." *Communications of the ACM*, Vol. 33, No. 9, 1990.

32   R. Wirfs-Brock, B. Wilkerson, and L. Wiener, *Designing Object-Oriented Soft-
        ware*. Prentice Hall, 1990.

33   D.A. Thomas, W.R. LaLonde, and R. Pugh, "Actors in a Smalltalk Multiproces-
        sor: A Case for Limited Parallelism." SCS-TR-91, School of Computer Science,
        Carleton University, Ottawa, Canada, May 1986.

34   U.S. Department of Defense, *Reference Manual for the Ada Programming Lan-
        guage*. MI-STD-1815a, 1983.

Index